MariaDB
Crash Course

Ben Forta

Addison-Wesley

Upper Saddle River, NJ • Boston • Indianapolis • San Francisco
New York • Toronto • Montreal • London • Munich • Paris • Madrid
Cape Town • Sydney • Tokyo • Singapore • Mexico City

Many of the designations used by manufacturers and sellers to distinguish their products are claimed as trademarks. Where those designations appear in this book, and the publisher was aware of a trademark claim, the designations have been printed with initial capital letters or in all capitals.

The author and publisher have taken care in the preparation of this book, but make no expressed or implied warranty of any kind and assume no responsibility for errors or omissions. No liability is assumed for incidental or consequential damages in connection with or arising out of the use of the information or programs contained herein.

The publisher offers excellent discounts on this book when ordered in quantity for bulk purchases or special sales, which may include electronic versions and/or custom covers and content particular to your business, training goals, marketing focus, and branding interests. For more information, please contact:

U.S. Corporate and Government Sales
(800) 382-3419
corpsales@pearsontechgroup.com

For sales outside the United States, please contact:

International Sales
international@pearson.com

Visit us on the Web: informit.com/aw

Library of Congress Cataloging-in-Publication Data

Forta, Ben.
  MariaDB crash course / Ben Forta.
      p. cm.
  Includes index.
  ISBN 978-0-321-79994-4 (pbk.)
  1. MariaDB. 2. Database management. 3. Client/server computing. I. Title.

  QA76.9.D3F663 2012
  004'.36–dc23
                                    2011023506

ISBN-13: 978-0-321-79994-4
ISBN-10: 0-321-79994-1

Text printed in the United States on recycled paper at R.R. Donnelley in Crawfordsville, Indiana.

First printing September 2011

Editor-in-Chief
Mark Taub

Acquisitions Editor
Mark Taber

Managing Editor
Kristy Hart

Project Editors
Elaine Wiley

Jovana San Nicolas-Shirley

Copy Editor
Geneil Breeze

Indexer
Erika Millen

Proofreader
Leslie Joseph

Publishing Coordinator
Vanessa Evans

Book Designer
Gary Adair

Compositor
Gloria Schurick

Table of Contents

Introduction   1
What Is MariaDB Crash Course?   1
Who Is This Book For?   2
Companion Web Site   3
Conventions Used in This Book   3

1: Understanding SQL   5
Database Basics   5
    What Is a Database?   6
    Tables   6
    Columns and Datatypes   7
    Rows   8
    NULL   8
    Primary Keys   9
What Is SQL?   10
Try It Yourself   11
Summary   11

2: Introducing MariaDB   13
What Is MariaDB?   13
    Client-Server Software   14
    MySQL Compatibility   15
MariaDB Tools   16
    mysql Command Line   16
    MySQL Workbench   17
Summary   19

3: Working with MariaDB   21
Making the Connection   21
Selecting a Database   22
Learning About Databases and Tables   23
Summary   26

4: Retrieving Data   27
The SELECT Statement   27
Retrieving Individual Columns   27
Retrieving Multiple Columns   29
Retrieving All Columns   30

Retrieving Distinct Rows   31
Limiting Results   32
Using Fully Qualified Table Names   34
Using Comments   35
Summary   36

5: **Sorting Retrieved Data   37**
Sorting Data   37
Sorting by Multiple Columns   39
Specifying Sort Direction   40
Summary   43

6: **Filtering Data   45**
Using the WHERE Clause   45
The WHERE Clause Operators   46
Checking Against a Single Value   47
Checking for Nonmatches   48
Checking for a Range of Values   49
Checking for No Value   50
Summary   51

7: **Advanced Data Filtering   53**
Combining WHERE Clauses   53
Using the AND Operator   53
Using the OR Operator   54
Understanding Order of Evaluation   55
Using the IN Operator   57
Using the NOT Operator   58
Summary   59

8: **Using Wildcard Filtering   61**
Using the LIKE Operator   61
The Percent Sign (%) Wildcard   62
The Underscore (_) Wildcard   64
Tips for Using Wildcards   65
Summary   65

9: **Searching Using Regular Expressions   67**
Understanding Regular Expressions   67
Using Regular Expressions   68

Basic Character Matching   68

Performing OR Matches   70

Matching One of Several Characters   71

Matching Ranges   72

Matching Special Characters   73

Matching Character Classes   75

Matching Multiple Instances   75

Anchors   77

Summary   79

10: Creating Calculated Fields   81

Understanding Calculated Fields   81

Concatenating Fields   82

Using Aliases   84

Performing Mathematical Calculations   85

Summary   87

11: Using Data Manipulation Functions   89

Understanding Functions   89

Using Functions   90

Text Manipulation Functions   90

Date and Time Manipulation Functions   92

Numeric Manipulation Functions   96

Summary   96

12: Summarizing Data   97

Using Aggregate Functions   97

The AVG() Function   98

The COUNT() Function   99

The MAX() Function   100

The MIN() Function   101

The SUM() Function   102

Aggregates on Distinct Values   103

Combining Aggregate Functions   104

Summary   105

13: Grouping Data   107

Understanding Data Grouping   107

Creating Groups   108

Filtering Groups   109

Grouping and Sorting   112

SELECT Clause Ordering   113

Summary   114

14: Working with Subqueries   115

Understanding Subqueries   115

Filtering by Subquery   115

Using Subqueries as Calculated Fields   119

Summary   122

15: Joining Tables   123

Understanding Joins   123

Understanding Relational Tables   123

Why Use Joins?   125

Creating a Join   125

The Importance of the WHERE Clause   127

Inner Joins   129

Joining Multiple Tables   130

Summary   132

16: Creating Advanced Joins   133

Using Table Aliases   133

Using Different Join Types   134

Self Joins   134

Natural Joins   136

Outer Joins   137

Using Joins with Aggregate Functions   139

Using Joins and Join Conditions   140

Summary   140

17: Combining Queries   141

Understanding Combined Queries   141

Creating Combined Queries   141

Using UNION   142

UNION Rules   144

Including or Eliminating Duplicate Rows   144

Sorting Combined Query Results   145

Summary   146

18: Full-Text Searching   147

Understanding Full-Text Searching   147

Using Full-Text Searching   148

  Enabling Full-Text Searching Support   148

  Performing Full-Text Searches   149

  Using Query Expansion   152

  Boolean Text Searches   154

  Full-Text Search Usage Notes   158

Summary   159

19: Inserting Data   161

Understanding Data Insertion   161

Inserting Complete Rows   161

Inserting Multiple Rows   165

Inserting Retrieved Data   166

Summary   168

20: Updating and Deleting Data   169

Updating Data   169

Deleting Data   171

Guidelines for Updating and Deleting Data   172

Summary   173

21: Creating and Manipulating Tables   175

Creating Tables   175

  Basic Table Creation   176

  Working with NULL Values   177

  Primary Keys Revisited   179

  Using AUTO_INCREMENT   180

  Specifying Default Values   181

  Engine Types   182

Updating Tables   183

Deleting Tables   185

Renaming Tables   185

Summary   186

22: Using Views   187

Understanding Views   187

   Why Use Views   188

   View Rules and Restrictions   188

Using Views   189

   Using Views to Simplify Complex Joins   189

   Using Views to Reformat Retrieved Data   191

   Using Views to Filter Unwanted Data   192

   Using Views with Calculated Fields   193

   Updating Views   194

Summary   195

23: Working with Stored Procedures   197

Understanding Stored Procedures   197

Why Use Stored Procedures   198

Using Stored Procedures   199

   Executing Stored Procedures   199

   Creating Stored Procedures   200

   Dropping Stored Procedures   201

   Working with Parameters   202

   Building Intelligent Stored Procedures   205

   Inspecting Stored Procedures   208

Summary   208

24: Using Cursors   209

Understanding Cursors   209

Working with Cursors   209

   Creating Cursors   210

   Opening and Closing Cursors   210

   Using Cursor Data   212

Summary   216

25: Using Triggers   217

Understanding Triggers   217

Creating Triggers   218

Dropping Triggers   219

x   Contents

Using Triggers 219
   INSERT Triggers 219
   DELETE Triggers 221
   UPDATE Triggers 223
   More on Triggers 223
Summary 224

26: **Managing Transaction Processing 225**
Understanding Transaction Processing 225
Controlling Transactions 227
   Using ROLLBACK 227
   Using COMMIT 228
   Using Savepoints 229
   Changing the Default Commit Behavior 230
Summary 230

27: **Globalization and Localization 231**
Understanding Character Sets and Collation Sequences 231
Working with Character Set and Collation Sequences 232
Summary 234

28: **Managing Security 235**
Understanding Access Control 235
Managing Users 236
   Creating User Accounts 237
   Deleting User Accounts 238
   Setting Access Rights 238
   Changing Passwords 241
Summary 242

29: **Database Maintenance 243**
Backing Up Data 243
Performing Database Maintenance 243
Diagnosing Startup Problems 245
Review Log Files 245
Summary 246

30: **Improving Performance 247**
Improving Performance 247
Summary 249

A: Getting Started with MariaDB 251
What You Need 251
Obtaining the Software 252
Installing the Software 252
Preparing to Try It Yourself 253

B: The Example Tables 255
Understanding the Sample Tables 255
    Table Descriptions 256
Creating the Sample Tables 259
    Using `mysql` 260
    Using MySQL Workbench 261

C: MariaDB Datatypes 263
String Datatypes 263
Numeric Datatypes 265
Date and Time Datatypes 266
Binary Datatypes 266

D: MariaDB Reserved Words 269

Index 275

Foreword

As the creator of MariaDB (and MySQL), I am thrilled to see the first MariaDB book in print. I am equally thrilled that Ben Forta wrote it. Ben has a gift for presenting complex topics (and really understanding SQL can be complex) in an easy-to-understand way. *MariaDB Crash Course* is an easy read and goes from explaining the basics to the very complex (including joins, regular expressions, and triggers) simply and without painful effort. I recommend this book to anyone new to SQL who wants to quickly learn how to get the best out of MariaDB.

Michael "Monty" Widenius
Creator of MariaDB and MySQL

Acknowledgments

I'd like to thank the folks at Addison-Wesley for once again granting me the flexibility and freedom to build this book as I saw fit. Special thanks to Mark Taber for helping turn this one around in record time, and for his guidance into what this series is evolving into.

Thanks to project editor Elaine Wiley for keeping the project moving and me on schedule, no easy task.

Thanks to Monty Widenius, (creator of MariaDB and MySQL), Daniel Bartholomew, and Colin Charles for their thorough technical review and feedback.

And finally, this book was written in response to an unsolicited request by Monty Widenius. Monty is the driving force behind some of the most successful database projects in history, and yet he still took the time to review the manuscript, provide feedback, and write a much-appreciated foreword and recommendation. Thank you for your time and support, Monty. I hope this title lives up to your expectations.

About the Author

Ben Forta is Adobe Systems' Director of Developer Relations and has more than 20 years experience in the computer industry in product development, support, training, and product marketing. Ben is the author of the best-selling *Sams Teach Yourself SQL in 10 Minutes* (now in its third edition, and translated into more than a dozen languages), spinoff titles on MySQL and SQL Server T-SQL, *ColdFusion Web Application Construction Kit* and *Advanced ColdFusion Application Development* (both published by Adobe Press), *Sams Teach Yourself Regular Expressions in 10 Minutes*, as well as books on Flash, Java, Windows, and other subjects. He has extensive experience in database design and development, has implemented databases for several highly successful commercial software programs and Web sites, and is a frequent lecturer and columnist on Internet and database technologies. Ben lives in Oak Park, Michigan, with his wife, Marcy, and their seven children. Ben welcomes your e-mail at ben@forta.com and invites you to visit his Web site at http://forta.com/.

Introduction

MariaDB is an offshoot of MySQL, one of the most popular database management systems in the world. From small development projects to some of the best-known and most prestigious sites on the Web, MySQL has proven itself to be a solid, reliable, fast, and trusted solution to all sorts of data storage needs.

In 2008, MySQL was acquired by Sun Microsystems, which was in turn acquired by Oracle Corporation in 2010. While the initial acquisition by Sun was hailed by many in the MySQL community as exactly what the project needed, that sentiment did not last, and the subsequent acquisition by Oracle was unfortunately met with far lower expectations. Many of MySQL's developers left Sun and Oracle to work on new projects. Among them was Michael "Monty" Widenius, creator of MySQL and one of the project's longtime technical leads.

Monty and his team created a fork (offshoot) of the MySQL codebase and named his new DBMS MariaDB. The stated goals for the new MariaDB DBMS include

- Create a DBMS that is so compatible with MySQL that it could be used as a drop-in replacement (you could uninstall MySQL, install MariaDB, and your programs should continue to run as is). This is accomplished by building MariaDB on the MySQL codebase.

- Improve the source code to make MariaDB far more reliable and stable.

- Add features (and community contributions) at a faster rate.

- Develop a new underlying database engine (don't worry if that sounds obscure for now) named Aria to improve performance and reliability.

What Is MariaDB Crash Course?

This book is based on my best-selling *Sams Teach Yourself SQL in 10 Minutes*. That book has become one of the most-used SQL tutorials in the world, with an emphasis on teaching what you really need to know—methodically, systematically, and simply. But as popular and as successful as that book is, it does have some limitations:

- In covering all the major DBMSs, coverage of DBMS-specific features and functionality had to be kept to a minimum.

- To simplify the SQL taught, the lowest common denominator had to be found—SQL statements that would (as much as possible) work with all major DBMSs. This requirement necessitated that better DBMS-specific solutions not be covered.

- Although basic SQL tends to be rather portable between DBMSs, more advanced SQL most definitely is not. As such, that book could not cover advanced topics, such as triggers, cursors, stored procedures, access control, transactions, and more, in any real detail.

And that is where this book comes in. *MariaDB Crash Course* builds on the proven tutorials and structure of *Sams Teach Yourself SQL in Ten Minutes*, without getting bogged down with anything but MariaDB. Starting with simple data retrieval and working on to more complex topics, including the use of joins, subqueries, regular expression and full text-based searches, stored procedures, cursors, triggers, table constraints, and much more. You learn what you need to know methodically, systematically, and simply—in highly focused chapters designed to make you immediately and effortlessly productive.

Who Is This Book For?

This book is for you if

- You are new to SQL.

- You are just getting started with MariaDB and want to hit the ground running.

- You want to quickly learn how to get the most out of MariaDB.

- You want to learn how to use MariaDB in your own application development.

- You want to be productive quickly and easily using MariaDB without having to call someone for help.

It is worth noting that this book is not intended for all readers. If you are an experienced SQL user, you may find the content in this book too elementary. Similarly, if you have existing MySQL experience, you'll likely find this book to be less useful (as noted, MariaDB is based on MySQL). If you own my *MySQL Crash Course*, I do not recommend that you buy this book, as much of the content is similar, and your existing MySQL knowledge will easily transfer as is to MariaDB.

But, if the preceding list describes you and your needs relative to MariaDB, you'll find this *MariaDB Crash Course* to be the fastest and easiest way to get up to speed with MariaDB.

This book is also useful if you are new to MySQL, as most of the content also applies to that DBMS. For you, this book has an extra benefit in that it helps demonstrate some reasons to consider switching to MariaDB.

Companion Web Site

This book has a companion Web site online at http://forta.com/books/0321799941/. Visit the site to access

- Table creation and population scripts used to create the example tables used throughout this book

- The online support forum

- Online errata (should one be required)

- Other books that may be of interest to you

Conventions Used in This Book

This book uses different typefaces to differentiate between code and regular English, and also to help you identify important concepts.

Text that you type and text that should appear on your screen is presented in `monospace` type. `It looks like this to mimic the way text looks on your screen.`

Placeholders for variables and expressions appear in `monospace italic` font. You should replace the placeholder with the specific value it represents.

This arrow (➥) at the beginning of a line of code means that a single line of code is too long to fit on the printed page. Continue typing all the characters after the ➥ as though they were part of the preceding line.

Note

A Note presents interesting pieces of information related to the surrounding discussion.

Tip

A Tip offers advice or teaches an easier way to do something.

Caution

A Caution advises you about potential problems and helps you steer clear of disaster.

New Term

Provides clear definitions of new, essential terms.

▼ Input

The Input icon identifies code that you can type in yourself. It usually appears next to a listing.

▼ Output

The Output icon highlights the output produced by running MariaDB code. It usually appears after a listing.

▼ Analysis

The Analysis icon alerts you to the author's line-by-line analysis of input or output.

1

Understanding SQL

In this chapter, you learn about databases and SQL, prerequisites to learning MariaDB.

Database Basics

The fact that you are reading this book indicates that you, somehow, need to interact with databases. And so before diving into MariaDB and its implementation of the SQL language, it is important that you understand some basic concepts about databases and database technologies.

Whether you are aware of it or not, you use databases all the time. Each time you select a name from your e-mail address book, you are using a database. If you conduct a search on an Internet search site, you are using a database. When you log in to your network at work, you are validating your name and password against a database. Even when you use your ATM card at a cash machine, you are using databases for PIN verification and balance checking.

But even though we all use databases all the time, there remains much confusion over what exactly a database is. This is especially true because different people use the same database terms to mean different things. Therefore, a good place to start our study is with a list and explanation of the most important database terms.

> **Tip**
>
> **Reviewing Basic Concepts**   What follows is a brief overview of some basic database concepts. It is intended to either jolt your memory if you already have some database experience, or to provide you with the absolute basics, if you are new to databases. Understanding databases is an important part of mastering MariaDB, and you might want to find a good book on database fundamentals to brush up on the subject if needed.

What Is a Database?

The term *database* is used in many different ways, but for our purposes a database is a collection of data stored in some organized fashion. The simplest way to think of it is to imagine a database as a filing cabinet. The filing cabinet is simply a physical location to store data, regardless of what that data is or how it is organized.

> **New Term**
>
> **Database**   A container (usually a file or set of files) to store organized data.

> **Caution**
>
> **Misuse Causes Confusion**   People often use the term *database* to refer to the database software they are running. This is incorrect, and it is a source of much confusion. Database software is actually called the *Database Management System* (or DBMS). The database is the container created and manipulated via the DBMS. A database might be a file stored on a hard drive, but it might not. And for the most part this is not even significant as you never access a database directly anyway; you always use the DBMS, and it accesses the database for you.

Tables

When you store information in your filing cabinet you don't just toss it in a drawer. Rather, you create files within the filing cabinet, and then you file related data in specific files.

In the database world, that file is called a table. A table is a structured file that can store data of a specific type. A table might contain a list of customers, a product catalog, or any other list of information.

> **New Term**
>
> **Table**   A structured list of data of a specific type.

The key here is that the data stored in the table is one type of data or one list. You would never store a list of customers and a list of orders in the same database table. Doing so would make subsequent retrieval and access difficult. Rather, you'd create two tables, one for each list.

Every table in a database has a name that identifies it. That name is always unique—meaning no other table in that database can have the same name.

> **Note**
>
> **Table Names** What makes a table name unique is actually a combination of several things, including the database name and table name. This means that while you cannot use the same table name twice in the same database, you definitely can reuse table names in different databases.

Tables have characteristics and properties that define how data is stored in them. These include information about what data may be stored, how it is broken up, how individual pieces of information are named, and much more. This set of information that describes a table is known as a *schema*, and schema are used to describe specific tables within a database, as well as entire databases (and the relationship between tables in them, if any).

> **New Term**
>
> **Schema** Information about database and table layout and properties.

> **Note**
>
> **Schema or Database?** Occasionally *schema* is used as a synonym for database (and *schemata* as a synonym for databases). While unfortunate, it is usually clear from the context which meaning of schema is intended. In this book, schema will refer to the definition given previously.

Columns and Datatypes

Tables are made up of columns. A column contains a particular piece of information within a table.

> **New Term**
>
> **Column** A single field in a table. All tables are made up of one or more columns.

The best way to understand this is to envision database tables as grids, somewhat like spreadsheets. Each column in the grid contains a particular piece of information. In a customer table, for example, one column contains the customer number, another contains the customer name, and the address, city, state, and Zip Code are all stored in their own columns.

> **Tip**
>
> **Breaking Up Data** It is important to break data into multiple columns correctly. For example, city, state, and Zip Code should always be separate columns. By breaking these out, it becomes possible to sort or filter data by specific columns (for example, to find all customers in a particular state or in a particular city). If city and state are combined into one column, it would be difficult to sort or filter by state.

Each column in a database has an associated datatype. A datatype defines what type of data the column can contain. For example, if the column is to contain a number (perhaps the number of items in an order), the datatype would be a numeric datatype. If the column were to contain dates, text, notes, currency amounts, and so on, the appropriate datatype would be used to specify this.

> **New Term**
> **Datatype**   A type of allowed data. Every table column has an associated datatype that restricts (or allows) specific data in that column.

Datatypes restrict the type of data that can be stored in a column (for example, preventing the entry of alphabetical characters into a numeric field). Datatypes also help sort data correctly, and play an important role in optimizing disk usage. As such, special attention must be given to picking the right datatype when tables are created.

Rows

Data in a table is stored in rows; each record saved is stored in its own row. Again, envisioning a table as a spreadsheet style grid, the vertical columns in the grid are the table columns, and the horizontal rows are the table rows.

For example, a customers table might store one customer per row. The number of rows in the table is the number of records in it.

> **New Term**
> **Row**   A record in a table.

> **Note**
> **Records or Rows?**   You might hear users refer to database *records* when referring to *rows*. For the most part, the two terms are used interchangeably, but *row* is technically the correct term.

NULL

Data is stored in rows and columns, and the exact data that may be stored is based on the defined datatype. Columns may also be defined to accept no value, meaning no data at all. In SQL, the term NULL is used to mean *no value*. If a column is defined to allow NULL, then data can be omitted from that column when a row is inserted or updated. You will be seeing lots more of NULL as you work through the lessons in this book.

Primary Keys

Every row in a table should have some column (or set of columns) that uniquely identifies it. A table containing customers might use a customer number column for this purpose, whereas a table containing orders might use the order ID. An employee list table might use an employee ID or the employee Social Security number column.

> **New Term**
>
> **Primary key**   A column (or set of columns) whose values uniquely identify every row in a table.

This column (or set of columns) that uniquely identifies each row in a table is called a *primary key*. The primary key is used to refer to a specific row. Without a primary key, updating or deleting specific rows in a table becomes difficult because there is no guaranteed safe way to refer to just the rows to be affected.

> **Tip**
>
> **Always Define Primary Keys**   Although primary keys are not actually required, most database designers ensure that every table they create has a primary key so future data manipulation is possible and manageable. In fact, if you omit the primary key, some database engines create one automatically for you, and the odds of it being what you'd have wanted are pretty slim. Bottom line, always define primary keys!

Any column in a table can be established as the primary key, as long as it meets the following conditions:

- No two rows can have the same primary key value.

- Every row must have a primary key value (primary key columns may not contain NULL values).

> **Tip**
>
> **Primary Key Rules**   The rules listed here are enforced by MariaDB itself.

Primary keys are usually defined on a single column within a table. But this is not required, and multiple columns may be used together as a primary key. When multiple columns are used, the rules previously listed must apply to all columns that make up the primary key, and the values of all columns together must be unique (individual columns need not have unique values).

> **Tip**
>
> **Primary Key Best Practices**   In addition to the rules that MariaDB enforces, several universally accepted best practices should also be adhered to
>
> - Don't update values in primary key columns.
> - Don't reuse values in primary key columns.
> - Don't use values that might change in primary key columns. (For example, when you use a name as a primary key to identify a supplier, you would have to change the primary key when the supplier merges and changes its name.)

There is another important type of key called a foreign key, but we discuss that later on in Chapter 15, "Joining Tables."

What Is SQL?

SQL (pronounced as the letters *S-Q-L* or as *sequel*) is an abbreviation for Structured Query Language. SQL is a language designed specifically for communicating with databases.

Unlike other languages (spoken languages such as English, or programming languages such as Java or Visual Basic), SQL is made up of very few words. This is deliberate. SQL is designed to do one thing and do it well—provide a simple and efficient way to read and write data from a database.

What are the advantages of SQL?

- SQL is not a proprietary language used by specific database vendors. Almost every major DBMS supports SQL, so learning this one language enables you to interact with just about every database you run into.

- SQL is easy to learn. The statements are all made up of descriptive English words, and there aren't that many of them.

- Despite its apparent simplicity, SQL is actually a powerful language, and by cleverly using its language elements you can perform complex and sophisticated database operations.

> **Note**
>
> **DBMS-Specific SQL**   Although SQL is not a proprietary language and there is a standards committee that tries to define SQL syntax that can be used by all DBMSs, the reality is that no two DBMSs implement SQL identically. The SQL taught in this book is specific to MariaDB (and MySQL), and while much of the language taught will be usable with other DBMSs, do not assume complete SQL syntax portability.

Try It Yourself

All the chapters in this book use working examples, showing you the SQL syntax, showing what it does, and explaining why it does it. I strongly suggest that you try each and every example for yourself so as to learn MariaDB firsthand.

Appendix B, "The Example Tables," describes the example tables used throughout this book, and explains how to obtain and install them. If you have not done so, refer to this appendix before proceeding.

> **Note**
>
> **You Need MariaDB** Obviously, you need access to a copy of MariaDB to follow along. Appendix A, "Getting Started with MariaDB," explains where to get a copy of MariaDB and provides some pointers for getting started. If you do not have access to a copy of MariaDB, refer to that appendix before proceeding.

Summary

In this first chapter, you learned what SQL is and why it is useful. Because SQL is used to interact with databases, you also reviewed some basic database terminology.

2

Introducing MariaDB

In this chapter, you learn what MariaDB is, and the tools you can use when working with it.

What Is MariaDB?

In Chapter 1, "Understanding SQL," you learned about databases and SQL. As explained, it is the database software (*DBMS* or *Database Management System*) that actually does all the work of storing, retrieving, managing, and manipulating data. MariaDB is a DBMS, that is, it is database software.

MariaDB is based on MySQL, which has been around for a long time, and is now in use at millions of installations worldwide. Why do so many organizations and developers use MySQL? Here are some of the reasons:

- **Cost**—MySQL is open-source, and free to use (and even modify) without paying for it.

- **Performance**—MySQL is fast (make that very fast).

- **Trusted**—MySQL is used by some of the most important and prestigious organizations and sites, all of whom entrust it with their critical data.

- **Simplicity**—MySQL is easy to install and get up and running.

The biggest technical criticism of MySQL is that it has not always supported the functionality and features offered by other DBMSs. There have also been criticisms leveled at how MySQL software is licensed. And more recently, MySQL has been criticized for a slowdown in updates and innovation.

In 2008, MySQL was acquired by Sun Microsystems, which was in turn acquired by Oracle Corporation in 2010. While the initial acquisition by Sun was hailed by many in the MySQL community as exactly what the project needed, that sentiment did not last, and the subsequent acquisition by Oracle was unfortunately met with far lower expectations. Many of MySQL's developers left Sun and Oracle to work on new projects. Among them was Michael

"Monty" Widenius, creator of MySQL and one of the project's longtime technical leads.

Monty and his team created a fork of the MySQL codebase, and named his new DBMS MariaDB. As MariaDB is based on MySQL, it shares the MySQL benefits listed previously. And as for those criticisms? Those are exactly what the MariaDB team set out to resolve.

> **Note**
>
> **What's in a Name?**   Does MariaDB strike you as a strange name for a DBMS? Actually, the name makes perfect sense once its origin has been explained. MySQL was named after Monty Widenius' daughter, My (and not for the possessive case of the word "I," as often assumed). Monty named the MaxDB database engine after his son, Max. And now, his new MariaDB project is named for his younger daughter, Maria.

Client-Server Software

DBMSs fall into two categories: shared file based and client-server. The former (which include products such as Microsoft Access and File Maker) are designed for desktop use and are generally not intended for use on higher-end or more critical applications (including Web sites and Web-based applications).

Databases such as MariaDB, MySQL, Oracle, and Microsoft SQL Server are client-server based databases. Client-server applications are split into two distinct parts. The *server* portion is a piece of software responsible for all data access and manipulation. This software runs on a computer called the *database server*.

Only the server software interacts with the data files. All requests for data, data additions and deletions, and data updates are funneled through the server software. These requests or changes come from computers running client software. The *client* is the piece of software with which the user interacts. If you request an alphabetical list of products, for example, the client software submits that request over the network to the server software. The server software processes the request; filters, discards, and sorts data as necessary; and sends the results back to your client software.

> **Note**
>
> **How Many Computers?**   The client and server software may be installed on two computers or on one computer. Regardless, the client software communicates with the server software for all database interaction, be it on the same machine or not.

All this action occurs transparently to you, the user. The fact that data is stored elsewhere or that a database server is even performing all this processing for you is hidden. You never need to access the data files directly. In fact, most networks are set up so that users have no access to the data, or even the drives on which it is stored.

Why is this significant? Because to work with MariaDB you need access to both a computer running the MariaDB server software and client software with which to issue commands to MariaDB.

- The server software is the MariaDB DBMS. You can run a locally installed copy, or you can connect to a copy running on a remote server to which you have access.

- The client can be MariaDB-provided tools, MySQL tools, scripting languages (such as Perl), Web application development languages (such as ASP, ColdFusion, JSP, and PHP), programming languages (such as C, C++, and Java), and more.

MySQL Compatibility

MariaDB was designed to be a drop-in replacement for MySQL. And while MariaDB is already evolving to include features and innovation not in the core MySQL DBMS, the MariaDB team has been careful to maintain true backwards compatibility.

For all intents and purposes, MariaDB is MySQL with new functionality added. In fact, MariaDB's MySQL legacy is readily apparent in everything from tooling (the command line client is still named `mysql`), to documentation, and more.

What does this mean in practice? Simply, it means that MySQL knowledge and know-how translates easily to MariaDB. It also means that any tools and clients designed for use with MySQL will work with MariaDB as well.

> **Tip**
>
> **MySQL 5** MariaDB is based on the MySQL 5 codebase. If you are using tools or languages that do not list MariaDB as an option, you should be able to select MySQL 5 and everything should just work.

> **Note**
>
> **Converting From MySQL To MariaDB** MariaDB can read all MySQL data formats and use the MySQL protocol to communicate with the server. If you are planning on upgrading from MySQL to MariaDB, you don't have to convert your data or change the tools you use.

MariaDB Tools

As just explained, MariaDB is a client-server DBMS, and so to use MariaDB you need a client, an application that you use to interact with MariaDB (giving it commands to be executed).

There are many client application options, but when learning MariaDB (and indeed, when writing and testing MariaDB scripts) you are best off using a utility designed for just that purpose. Two tools in particular warrant specific mention.

mysql **Command Line**

Every MariaDB installation comes with a simple command line utility called mysql. This utility does not have any drop-down menus, fancy user interfaces, mouse support, or anything like that.

Typing mysql at your operating system command prompt displays a welcome message followed by a simple prompt that looks like this:

```
Welcome to the MariaDB monitor.  Commands end with ; or \g.

Your MariaDB connection id is 1
Server version: 5.2.4-MariaDB Source distribution

This software comes with ABSOLUTELY NO WARRANTY. This is free software,
and you are welcome to modify and redistribute it under the GPL v2
license

Type 'help;' or '\h' for help. Type '\c' to clear the current input
statement.

MariaDB [(none)]>
```

> **Note**
>
> **MySQL Options and Parameters** If you just type mysql by itself, you might receive an error message. This will likely be because security credentials are needed or because MySQL is not running locally or on the default port. mysql accepts an array of command line parameters you can (and might need to) use. For example, to specify a user login name of ben, you'd use mysql -u ben. To specify a username, host name, port, and be prompted for a password, you'd use mysql -u ben -p -h myserver -P 9999.
>
> A complete list of command line options and parameters can be obtained using mysql --help.

Of course, your version and connection information might differ, but you'll be able to use this utility regardless. Note that:

- Commands are typed after the `MariaDB >` prompt. (`MariaDB >` indicates that you are connected to a MariaDB server, the prompt would be `MySQL >` if you were connected to a MySQL server.)

- Commands end with `;` or `\g`; in other words, just pressing Enter will not execute the command.

- You can use the up and down arrow keys to scroll through previously entered commands.

- You can type `help` or `\h` to obtain help. You can also provide additional text to obtain help on specific commands (for example, `help select` to obtain help on using the `SELECT` statement).

- You can type `quit` or `exit` to quit the command line utility.

> **Note**
>
> **Execute Saved Scripts** You can use `mysql` to execute saved scripts—the scripts used to create and populate the tables used throughout this book, for example. To do this, enter `\. filename` (specifying the full path to the file) and press Enter. Appendix B, "The Example Tables," walks you through this process for the chapters in this book.

The `mysql` command line utility is one of the most used, and is invaluable for quick testing and executing scripts (such as the sample table creation and population scripts mentioned in the previous chapter and in Appendix B). In fact, all the output examples used in this book are captured from `mysql` command line output.

> **Tip**
>
> **Familiarize Yourself with the `mysql` Command Line** Even if you opt to use a graphical tool like the one described next, you should make sure to familiarize yourself with the `mysql` command line utility, as this is the one client you can safely rely on to always be present (as it is part of the core MariaDB installation).

MySQL Workbench

MySQL Workbench is a graphical interactive client designed to simplify the administration of MySQL servers. And, as you'd expect, it works really well with MariaDB, as well.

> **Note**
>
> **Obtaining MySQL Workbench**   MySQL Workbench is not installed as part of the MariaDB installation (nor MySQL installations, actually). Instead, it must be downloaded from http://wb.mysql.com/ (versions are available for Linux, Mac OS X, and Windows, and source code is downloadable, too).

When MySQL Workbench is launched, you see a screen organized in three columns. From left to right these are:

- **SQL Development**—Used to connect and actually perform database and table operations, including executing SQL statements. If you opt to use MySQL Workbench with this book, the Open Connection To Start Querying option is what you use.

- **Data Modeling**—Used to create and manage database and table structures. This is not covered in this book.

- **Server Administration**—Used to manage the MariaDB server, including stopping and starting the services, importing and exporting data, and more.

> **Tip**
>
> **Saving Connections**   MySQL Workbench needs to know information about your MariaDB server before it can open a connection to the server for you to use. At a minimum, this information includes the server address (hostname or IP address) and login information. Rather than having to enter this every time you use MySQL Workbench, you can save the details for future use (next time you just double-click on the saved settings to connect).

The SQL Editor screen is accessed via Open Connection To Start Querying in the SQL Development options. This is where you can type and execute SQL statements. Note the following:

- SQL statements are typed into the window at the top of the screen. When the statement has been entered, click the Execute button (the one with the yellow lightning bolt on it) to submit it to MySQL for processing.

- Generated results (if there are any) are displayed in a grid at the bottom of the screen, in a tab named Output.

- The leftmost tab in the bottom section of the screen, named Overview, lists all available databases (called *schema* here) and the tables within them. Click on any database to see its tables.

- You can right-click on tables to have MySQL Workbench write SELECT and other statements for you.

- The rightmost tab is a History tab that maintains a history of executed SQL statements. This is useful when you need to test different versions of SQL statements.

- You can have multiple SQL Editor windows open at the same time, each in its own tab, allowing you to work with multiple databases or SQL statements at once.

> **Note**
>
> **Execute Saved Scripts**   You can use MySQL Workbench to execute saved scripts—the scripts used to create and populate the tables used throughout this book, for example. To do this, select File, Open Script; select the script (which will be displayed in a new tab); and click the Execute button. Appendix B walks you through this process for the chapters in this book.

Summary

In this chapter, you learned exactly what MariaDB is. You were also introduced to two client utilities (one included command line utility, and one optional but highly recommended graphical utility).

3

Working with MariaDB

In this chapter, you learn how to connect and log in to MariaDB, how to issue MariaDB SQL statements, and how to obtain information about databases and tables.

Making the Connection

> **Note**
>
> **Example Tables Required** From this point on, all chapters will use the example databases and tables. If you have yet to install these, see Appendix B, "The Example Tables," before proceeding.

Now that you have a MariaDB DBMS and client software to use with it, it would be worthwhile to briefly discuss connecting to the database.

MariaDB, like all client-server DBMSs, requires that you log in to the DBMS before being able to issue commands. Login names might not be the same as your network login name (assuming that you are using a network); MariaDB maintains its own list of users internally and associates rights with each.

When you first installed MariaDB, you may have been prompted for an administrative login (usually named root) and a password (if you weren't, then the root user account was created with no password). If you are using your own local server and are simply experimenting with MariaDB, using this login is fine. In the real world, however, the administrative login is closely protected (as access to it grants full rights to create tables, drop entire databases, change logins and passwords, and more).

To connect to MariaDB you need the following pieces of information:

- The hostname (the name of the computer)—this is localhost if connecting to a local MariaDB server
- The port (if a port other than the default 3306 is used)
- A valid user name
- The user password (if required)

As explained in Chapter 2, "Introducing MariaDB," all this information can be passed to the `mysql` command line utility, or entered into the server connection screen in MySQL Workbench.

> **Note**
>
> **Using Other Clients**   If you are using a client other than the ones mentioned here, you still need to provide this information to connect to MariaDB.

After you are connected, you have access to whatever databases and tables your login name has access to. (Logins, access control, and security are revisited in Chapter 28, "Managing Security.")

Selecting a Database

When you first connect to MariaDB, you do not have any databases open for use. Before you can perform any database operations, you need to select a database. To do this you use the USE keyword.

> **New Term**
>
> **Keyword**   A reserved word that is part of the MariaDB SQL language. Never name a table or column using a keyword. Appendix D, "MariaDB Reserved Words," lists the MariaDB keywords.

For example, to use the `crashcourse` database you would enter the following:

▼ Input

```
USE crashcourse;
```

▼ Output

```
Database changed
```

▼ Analysis

The USE statement does not return any results. Depending on the client used, some form of notification might be displayed. For example, the `Database changed` message shown here is displayed by the `mysql` command line utility upon successful database selection.

> **Tip**
>
> **Preselecting a Database**   If you are using the `mysql` command line tool, you can pre-select a database by typing its name after `mysql` when running the tool.

Remember, you must always USE a database before you can access any data in it.

Learning About Databases and Tables

But what if you don't know the names of the available databases? And for that matter, how are clients like MySQL Workbench able to display a list of available databases?

Information about databases, tables, columns, users, privileges, and more is stored within databases and tables themselves (yes, MariaDB uses MariaDB to store this information). But these internal tables are generally not accessed directly. Instead, the MariaDB SHOW command can be used to display this information (information that MariaDB then extracts from those internal tables). Look at the following example:

▼ **Input**

```
SHOW DATABASES;
```

▼ **Output**

```
+--------------------+
| Database           |
+--------------------+
| information_schema |
| crashcourse        |
| mysql              |
| forta              |
| coldfusion         |
| flex               |
| test               |
+--------------------+
```

▼ **Analysis**

SHOW DATABASES; returns a list of available databases. Included in this list might be databases used by MariaDB internally (such as mysql and information_schema in this example). Of course, your own list of databases might not look like those shown here.

To obtain a list of tables within a database, use SHOW TABLES;, as seen here:

▼ **Input**

```
SHOW TABLES;
```

▼ Output

```
+-----------------------+
| Tables_in_crashcourse |
+-----------------------+
| customers             |
| orderitems            |
| orders                |
| products              |
| productnotes          |
| vendors               |
+-----------------------+
```

▼ Analysis

SHOW TABLES; returns a list of available tables in the currently selected database.

To show a table's columns, you can use DESCRIBE:

▼ Input

```
DESCRIBE customers;
```

▼ Output

```
+--------------+-----------+------+-----+---------+----------------+
| Field        | Type      | Null | Key | Default | Extra          |
+--------------+-----------+------+-----+---------+----------------+
| cust_id      | int(11)   | NO   | PRI | NULL    | auto_increment |
| cust_name    | char(50)  | NO   |     |         |                |
| cust_address | char(50)  | YES  |     | NULL    |                |
| cust_city    | char(50)  | YES  |     | NULL    |                |
| cust_state   | char(5)   | YES  |     | NULL    |                |
| cust_zip     | char(10)  | YES  |     | NULL    |                |
| cust_country | char(50)  | YES  |     | NULL    |                |
| cust_contact | char(50)  | YES  |     | NULL    |                |
| cust_email   | char(255) | YES  |     | NULL    |                |
+--------------+-----------+------+-----+---------+----------------+
```

▼ Analysis

DESCRIBE requires that a table name be specified (customers in this example), and returns a row for each field containing the field name, its datatype, whether NULL is allowed, key information, default value, and extra information (such as auto_increment for field cust_id).

> **Note**
>
> **What Is Auto Increment?**   Some table columns need unique values. For example, order numbers, employee IDs, or (as in the example just seen) customer IDs. Rather than have to assign unique values manually each time a row is added (and having to keep track of what value was last used), MariaDB can automatically assign the next available number for you each time a row is added to a table. This functionality is known as *auto increment*. If it is needed, it must be part of the table definition used when the table is created using the CREATE statement. We look at CREATE in Chapter 21, "Creating and Manipulating Tables."

> **Tip**
>
> **The SHOW COLUMNS FROM Statement**   DESCRIBE is actually a shortcut for SHOW COLUMNS FROM. In other words, the statement DESCRIBE customers; is functionally identical to the statement SHOW COLUMNS FROM customers;.

Other SHOW statements are supported too, including

- **SHOW STATUS**—Used to display extensive server status information

- **SHOW CREATE DATABASE and SHOW CREATE TABLE**—Used to display the MariaDB statements used to create specified databases or tables respectively

- **SHOW GRANTS**—Used to display security rights granted to users (all users or a specific user)

- **SHOW ERRORS and SHOW WARNINGS**—Used to display server error or warning messages

It is worthwhile to note that client applications use these same MariaDB SQL commands as you've seen here. Applications that display interactive lists of databases and tables, that allow for the interactive creation and editing of tables, that facilitate data entry and editing, or that allow for user account and rights management, and more, all accomplish what they do using the same MariaDB SQL commands that you can execute directly yourself.

> **Tip**
>
> **Learning More About SHOW**   In the mysql command line utility, execute command HELP SHOW; to display a list of allowed SHOW statements.

> **Note**
>
> **Want Even More Information?**   MariaDB supports the use of INFORMATION_ SCHEMA to obtain and filter even more schema details. Coverage of INFORMATION_ SCHEMA is beyond the scope of this book. But, if you should need it, know that it's there for you.

Summary

In this chapter, you learned how to connect and log in to MariaDB; how to select databases using USE; and how to introspect MariaDB databases, tables, and internals using SHOW and DESCRIBE. Armed with this knowledge, you can now dig into the all-important SELECT statement.

4

Retrieving Data

In this chapter, you learn how to use the SELECT statement to retrieve one or more columns of data from a table.

The SELECT Statement

As explained in Chapter 1, "Understanding SQL," SQL statements are made up of plain English terms called *keywords*. Every SQL statement is made up of one or more keywords. The SQL statement you'll probably use most frequently is the SELECT statement. Its purpose is to retrieve information from one or more tables.

To use SELECT to retrieve table data you must, at a minimum, specify two pieces of information—what you want to select, and from where you want to select it.

Retrieving Individual Columns

We start with a simple SQL SELECT statement, as follows:

▼ **Input**
```
SELECT prod_name
FROM products;
```

▼ **Analysis**

The previous statement uses the SELECT statement to retrieve a single column called prod_name from the products table. The desired column name is specified right after the SELECT keyword, and the FROM keyword specifies the name of the table from which to retrieve the data. The output from this statement is shown in the following:

▼ Output

```
+----------------+
| prod_name      |
+----------------+
| .5 ton anvil   |
| 1 ton anvil    |
| 2 ton anvil    |
| Oil can        |
| Fuses          |
| Sling          |
| TNT (1 stick)  |
| TNT (5 sticks) |
| Bird seed      |
| Carrots        |
| Safe           |
| Detonator      |
| JetPack 1000   |
| JetPack 2000   |
+----------------+
```

> **Note**
>
> **Unsorted Data** If you tried this query yourself, you might have discovered that the data was displayed in a different order than shown here. If this is the case, don't worry—it is working exactly as it is supposed to. If query results are not explicitly sorted (we get to that in the next chapter), data will be returned in no order of any significance. It might be the order in which the data was added to the table, but it might not. As long as your query returned the same number of rows, then it is working.

A simple SELECT statement like the one just shown returns all the rows in a table. Data is not filtered (so as to retrieve a subset of the results), nor is it sorted. We discuss these topics in the next few chapters.

> **Note**
>
> **Terminating Statements** Multiple SQL statements must be separated by semicolons (the ; character). MariaDB (like most DBMSs) does not require that a semicolon be specified after single statements. Of course, you can always add a semicolon if you want. It'll do no harm, even if it isn't needed.
>
> If you are using the mysql command line client, the semicolon is always needed (as was explained in Chapter 2, "Introducing MariaDB").

> **Note**
>
> **SQL Statements and Case** It is important to note that SQL statements are not case sensitive, so SELECT is the same as select, which is the same as Select. Many SQL developers find that using uppercase for all SQL keywords and lowercase for column and table names makes code easier to read and debug.

> However, be aware that while the SQL language is not case sensitive, identifiers (the names of databases, tables, and columns) might be. As a best practice, pick a case convention, and use it consistently.

> **Tip**
>
> **Use of White Space**   All extra white space within a SQL statement is ignored when that statement is processed. SQL statements can be specified on one long line or broken up over many lines. Most SQL developers find that breaking up statements over multiple lines makes them easier to read and debug.

Retrieving Multiple Columns

To retrieve multiple columns from a table, the same SELECT statement is used. The only difference is that multiple column names must be specified after the SELECT keyword, and each column must be separated by a comma.

> **Tip**
>
> **Take Care with Commas**   When selecting multiple columns, be sure to specify a comma between each column name, but not after the last column name. Doing so generates an error.

The following SELECT statement retrieves three columns from the products table:

▼ Input

```
SELECT prod_id, prod_name, prod_price
FROM products;
```

▼ Analysis

Just as in the prior example, this statement uses the SELECT statement to retrieve data from the products table. In this example, three column names are specified, each separated by a comma. The output from this statement is as follows:

▼ Output

```
+---------+----------------+------------+
| prod_id | prod_name      | prod_price |
+---------+----------------+------------+
| ANV01   | .5 ton anvil   |       5.99 |
| ANV02   | 1 ton anvil    |       9.99 |
| ANV03   | 2 ton anvil    |      14.99 |
| OL1     | Oil can        |       8.99 |
```

```
| FU1    | Fuses          |     3.42 |
| SLING  | Sling          |     4.49 |
| TNT1   | TNT (1 stick)  |     2.50 |
| TNT2   | TNT (5 sticks) |    10.00 |
| FB     | Bird seed      |    10.00 |
| FC     | Carrots        |     2.50 |
| SAFE   | Safe           |    50.00 |
| DTNTR  | Detonator      |    13.00 |
| JP1000 | JetPack 1000   |    35.00 |
| JP2000 | JetPack 2000   |    55.00 |
+--------+----------------+----------+
```

> **Note**
>
> **Presentation of Data**   SQL statements typically return raw, unformatted data. Data formatting is a presentation issue, not a retrieval issue. Therefore, presentation (for example, alignment and displaying the price values as currency amounts with the currency symbol and commas) is typically specified in the application that displays the data. Actual raw retrieved data (without application-provided formatting) is rarely displayed as is.

Retrieving All Columns

In addition to being able to specify desired columns (one or more, as seen previously), SELECT statements can also request all columns without having to list them individually. This is done using the asterisk (*) wildcard character in lieu of actual column names, as follows:

▼ Input

```
SELECT *
FROM products;
```

▼ Analysis

When a wildcard (*) is specified, all the columns in the table are returned. The columns are in the order in which the columns appear in the table definition. However, this cannot be relied on because changes to table schemas (adding and removing columns, for example) could cause ordering changes.

> **Caution**
>
> **Using Wildcards**   As a rule, you are better off not using the * wildcard unless you really do need every column in the table. Even though use of wildcards might save you the time and effort needed to list the desired columns explicitly, retrieving unnecessary columns usually slows down the performance of your retrieval and your application.

> **Tip**
>
> **Retrieving Unknown Columns**   There is one big advantage to using wildcards. As you do not explicitly specify column names (because the asterisk retrieves every column), it is possible to retrieve columns whose names are unknown.

Retrieving Distinct Rows

As you have seen, SELECT returns all matched rows. But what if you do not want every occurrence of every value? For example, suppose you want the vendor ID of all vendors with products in your products table:

▼ Input

```
SELECT vesnd_id
FROM products;
```

▼ Output

```
+---------+
| vend_id |
+---------+
|    1001 |
|    1001 |
|    1001 |
|    1002 |
|    1002 |
|    1003 |
|    1003 |
|    1003 |
|    1003 |
|    1003 |
|    1003 |
|    1003 |
|    1005 |
|    1005 |
+---------+
```

The SELECT statement returned 14 rows (even though only four vendors are in that list) because 14 products are listed in the products table. So how could you retrieve a list of distinct values?

The solution is to use the DISTINCT keyword, which, as its name implies, instructs MariaDB to return only distinct values.

▼ Input

```
SELECT DISTINCT vend_id
FROM products;
```

▼ Analysis

SELECT DISTINCT vend_id tells MariaDB to return only distinct (unique) vend_id rows, and so only four rows are returned, as seen in the following output. If used, the DISTINCT keyword must be placed directly in front of the column names.

▼ Output

```
+---------+
| vend_id |
+---------+
|    1001 |
|    1002 |
|    1003 |
|    1005 |
+---------+
```

> **Caution**
>
> **Can't Be Partially DISTINCT**   The DISTINCT keyword applies to all columns, not just the one it precedes. If you were to specify SELECT DISTINCT vend_id, prod_price, all rows would be retrieved unless *both* of the specified columns were distinct.

Limiting Results

SELECT statements return all matched rows, possibly every row in the specified table. To return just the first row or rows, use the LIMIT clause. Here is an example:

▼ Input

```
SELECT prod_name
FROM products
LIMIT 5;
```

▼ Analysis

The previous statement uses the SELECT statement to retrieve a single column. LIMIT 5 instructs MariaDB to return no more than five rows. The output from this statement is shown in the following:

▼ Output

```
+----------------+
| prod_name      |
+----------------+
```

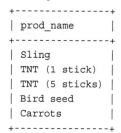

```
|  .5 ton anvil   |
|  1 ton anvil    |
|  2 ton anvil    |
|  Oil can        |
|  Fuses          |
+-----------------+
```

To get the next five rows, specify both where to start and the number of rows to retrieve, like this:

▼ Input

```
SELECT prod_name
FROM products
LIMIT 5,5;
```

▼ Analysis

LIMIT 5,5 instructs MariaDB to return five rows starting from row 5. The first number is where to start, and the second is the number of rows to retrieve. The output from this statement is shown in the following:

▼ Output

```
+-----------------+
| prod_name       |
+-----------------+
| Sling           |
| TNT (1 stick)   |
| TNT (5 sticks)  |
| Bird seed       |
| Carrots         |
+-----------------+
```

So, LIMIT with one value specified always starts from the first row, and the specified number is the number of rows to return. LIMIT with two values specified can start from wherever that first value tells it to.

> **Caution**
>
> **Row 0**   The first row retrieved is row 0, not row 1. As such, LIMIT 1,1 retrieves the second row, not the first one.

Let's review. Does LIMIT 3,4 mean 3 rows starting from row 4, or 4 rows starting from row 3? As you just learned, it means 4 rows starting from row 3, but it is a bit ambiguous. For this reason, MariaDB supports an alternative syntax for LIMIT. LIMIT 4 OFFSET 3 means get 4 rows starting from row 3, just like LIMIT 3,4. So, the following two statements are functionally identical, and you can use whichever you are more comfortable with:

▼ **Input**

```
SELECT prod_name
FROM products
LIMIT 10,2;
```

▼ **Input**

```
SELECT prod_name
FROM products
LIMIT 2 OFFSET 10;
```

> **Note**
>
> **When There Aren't Enough Rows** The number of rows to retrieve specified in LIMIT is the *maximum* number to retrieve. If there aren't enough rows (for example, you specified LIMIT 10,5, but there were only 13 rows), MariaDB returns as many as it can.

Using Fully Qualified Table Names

The SQL examples used thus far have referred to columns by just the column names. It is also possible to refer to columns using fully qualified names (using both the table and column names). Look at this example:

▼ **Input**

```
SELECT products.prod_name
FROM products;
```

This SQL statement is functionally identical to the first one used in this chapter, but here a fully qualified column name is specified.

Table names, too, may be fully qualified, as seen here:

▼ **Input**

```
SELECT products.prod_name
FROM crashcourse.products;
```

Once again, this statement is functionally identical to the one just used (assuming, of course, that the products table is indeed in the crashcourse database).

There are situations where fully qualified names are required, as we see in later chapters. For now, it is worth noting this syntax so you know what it is if you run across it.

Using Comments

As you have seen, SQL statements are instructions processed by MariaDB. But what if you wanted to include text that you do not want processed and executed? Why would you ever want to do this? Here are a few reasons:

■ The SQL statements we've been using here are all short and simple. But, as your SQL statements grow (in length and complexity), you'll want to include descriptive comments (for your own future reference or for whoever has to work on the project next). These comments need to be embedded in the SQL scripts, but they are obviously not intended for MariaDB processing. (For an example of this, see the `create.sql` and `populate.sql` files used in Appendix B, "The Example Tables.")

■ The same is true for headers at the top of SQL files, perhaps containing the programmer contact information and a description and notes. (This use case is also seen in the Appendix B `.sql` files.)

■ Another important use for comments is to temporarily stop SQL code from being executed. If you were working with a long SQL statement, and wanted to test just part of it, you could *comment out* some of the code so that MariaDB saw it as comments and ignored it.

MariaDB supports several forms of comment syntax. We start with inline comments:

▼ Input

```
SELECT prod_name    -- this is a comment
FROM products;
```

▼ Analysis

Comments may be embedded inline using -- (two hyphens). Anything after the -- is considered comment text, making this a good option for describing columns in a CREATE TABLE statement, for example.

Here is another form of inline comment:

▼ Input

```
# This is a comment
SELECT prod_name
FROM products;
```

▼ Analysis

A # at the start of a line makes the entire line a comment. You can see this format comment used in the accompanying `create.sql` and `populate.sql` scripts.

You can also create multiline comments, and comments that stop and start anywhere within the script:

▼ Input

```
/* SELECT prod_name, vend_id
FROM products; */
SELECT prod_name
FROM products;
```

▼ Analysis

`/*` starts a comment, and `*/` ends it. Anything between `/*` and `*/` is comment text. This type of comment is often used to *comment out* code, as seen in this example. Here, two SELECT statements are defined, but the first won't execute because it has been commented out.

Summary

In this chapter, you learned how to use the SQL SELECT statement to retrieve a single table column, multiple table columns, and all table columns. You also learned about commenting and saw various ways that comments can be used. Next you learn how to sort the retrieved data.

5

Sorting Retrieved Data

In this chapter, you learn how to use the SELECT statement's ORDER BY clause to sort retrieved data as needed.

Sorting Data

As you learned in Chapter 4, "Retrieving Data," the following SQL statement returns a single column from a database table. But look at the output. The data appears to be displayed in no particular order at all.

▼ Input

```
SELECT prod_name
FROM products;
```

▼ Output

```
+-----------------+
| prod_name       |
+-----------------+
| .5 ton anvil    |
| 1 ton anvil     |
| 2 ton anvil     |
| Oil can         |
| Fuses           |
| Sling           |
| TNT (1 stick)   |
| TNT (5 sticks)  |
| Bird seed       |
| Carrots         |
| Safe            |
| Detonator       |
| JetPack 1000    |
| JetPack 2000    |
+-----------------+
```

Actually, the retrieved data is not displayed in a mere random order. If unsorted, data is typically displayed in the order in which it appears in the underlying tables. This could be the order in which the data was added to the tables initially. However, if data was subsequently updated or deleted, the order is affected by how MariaDB reuses reclaimed storage space. The end result is that you cannot (and should not) rely on the sort order if you do not explicitly control it. Relational database design theory states that the sequence of retrieved data cannot be assumed to have significance if ordering was not explicitly specified.

> **New Term**
>
> **Clause** SQL statements are made up of clauses, some required and some optional. A clause usually consists of a keyword and supplied data. An example of this is the SELECT statement's FROM clause, which you saw in the last chapter.

To explicitly sort data retrieved using a SELECT statement, the ORDER BY clause is used. ORDER BY takes the name of one or more columns by which to sort the output. Look at the following example:

▼ Input

```
SELECT prod_name
FROM products
ORDER BY prod_name;
```

▼ Analysis

This statement is identical to the earlier statement, except it also specifies an ORDER BY clause instructing MariaDB to sort the data alphabetically by the prod_name column. The results are as follows:

▼ Output

```
+-----------------+
| prod_name       |
+-----------------+
| .5 ton anvil    |
| 1 ton anvil     |
| 2 ton anvil     |
| Bird seed       |
| Carrots         |
| Detonator       |
| Fuses           |
| JetPack 1000    |
| JetPack 2000    |
| Oil can         |
| Safe            |
| Sling           |
```

```
| TNT (1 stick)  |
| TNT (5 sticks) |
+----------------+
```

> **Tip**
>
> **Sorting by Nonselected Columns**   More often than not, the columns used in an ORDER BY clause are ones that were selected for display. However, this is actually not required, and it is perfectly legal to sort data by a column that is not retrieved.

Sorting by Multiple Columns

It is often necessary to sort data by more than one column. For example, if you are displaying an employee list, you might want to display it sorted by last name and first name (first sort by last name, and then within each last name sort by first name). This would be useful if there are multiple employees with the same last name.

To sort by multiple columns, simply specify the column names separated by commas (just as you do when you are selecting multiple columns).

The following code retrieves three columns and sorts the results by two of them—first by price and then by name.

▼ **Input**

```sql
SELECT prod_id, prod_price, prod_name
FROM products
ORDER BY prod_price, prod_name;
```

▼ **Output**

```
+---------+------------+----------------+
| prod_id | prod_price | prod_name      |
+---------+------------+----------------+
| FC      |       2.50 | Carrots        |
| TNT1    |       2.50 | TNT (1 stick)  |
| FU1     |       3.42 | Fuses          |
| SLING   |       4.49 | Sling          |
| ANV01   |       5.99 | .5 ton anvil   |
| OL1     |       8.99 | Oil can        |
| ANV02   |       9.99 | 1 ton anvil    |
| FB      |      10.00 | Bird seed      |
| TNT2    |      10.00 | TNT (5 sticks) |
| DTNTR   |      13.00 | Detonator      |
| ANV03   |      14.99 | 2 ton anvil    |
```

```
| JP1000 |     35.00 | JetPack 1000 |
| SAFE   |     50.00 | Safe         |
| JP2000 |     55.00 | JetPack 2000 |
+--------+-----------+--------------+
```

It is important to understand that when you are sorting by multiple columns, the sort sequence is exactly as specified. In other words, using the output in the previous example, the products are sorted by the prod_name column only when multiple rows have the same prod_price value. If all the values in the prod_price column had been unique, no data would have been sorted by prod_name.

> **Tip**
>
> **An ORDER BY Shortcut**   Instead of type the column names in ORDER BY, you can also type the column number specifying its sequence in the SELECT statement. This statement:
>
> ```
> SELECT prod_id, prod_price, prod_name
> FROM products
> ORDER BY prod_price, prod_name;
> ```
>
> is functionally identical to this statement:
>
> ```
> SELECT prod_id, prod_price, prod_name
> FROM products
> ORDER BY 2, 3;
> ```
>
> Obviously, this syntax can save you some typing. But, keep in mind that if you do use this shortcut, then your ORDER BY statement will essentially break if you ever make changes to the SELECT columns.

Specifying Sort Direction

Data sorting is not limited to ascending sort orders (from A to Z). Although this is the default sort order, the ORDER BY clause can also be used to sort in descending order (from Z to A). To sort by descending order, the keyword DESC must be specified.

The following example sorts the products by price in descending order (most expensive first):

▼ Input

```
SELECT prod_id, prod_price, prod_name
FROM products
ORDER BY prod_price DESC;
```

▼ **Output**

```
+----------+-------------+-----------------+
| prod_id  | prod_price  | prod_name       |
+----------+-------------+-----------------+
| JP2000   |      55.00  | JetPack 2000    |
| SAFE     |      50.00  | Safe            |
| JP1000   |      35.00  | JetPack 1000    |
| ANV03    |      14.99  | 2 ton anvil     |
| DTNTR    |      13.00  | Detonator       |
| TNT2     |      10.00  | TNT (5 sticks)  |
| FB       |      10.00  | Bird seed       |
| ANV02    |       9.99  | 1 ton anvil     |
| OL1      |       8.99  | Oil can         |
| ANV01    |       5.99  | .5 ton anvil    |
| SLING    |       4.49  | Sling           |
| FU1      |       3.42  | Fuses           |
| FC       |       2.50  | Carrots         |
| TNT1     |       2.50  | TNT (1 stick)   |
+----------+-------------+-----------------+
```

But what if you were to sort by multiple columns? The following example sorts the products in descending order (most expensive first), plus product name:

▼ **Input**

```
SELECT prod_id, prod_price, prod_name
FROM products
ORDER BY prod_price DESC, prod_name;
```

▼ **Output**

```
+----------+-------------+-----------------+
| prod_id  | prod_price  | prod_name       |
+----------+-------------+-----------------+
| JP2000   |      55.00  | JetPack 2000    |
| SAFE     |      50.00  | Safe            |
| JP1000   |      35.00  | JetPack 1000    |
| ANV03    |      14.99  | 2 ton anvil     |
| DTNTR    |      13.00  | Detonator       |
| FB       |      10.00  | Bird seed       |
| TNT2     |      10.00  | TNT (5 sticks)  |
| ANV02    |       9.99  | 1 ton anvil     |
| OL1      |       8.99  | Oil can         |
| ANV01    |       5.99  | .5 ton anvil    |
| SLING    |       4.49  | Sling           |
| FU1      |       3.42  | Fuses           |
| FC       |       2.50  | Carrots         |
| TNT1     |       2.50  | TNT (1 stick)   |
+----------+-------------+-----------------+
```

▼ Analysis

The DESC keyword applies only to the column name that directly precedes it. In the previous example, DESC was specified for the prod_price column, but not for the prod_name column. Therefore, the prod_price column is sorted in descending order, but the prod_name column (within each price) is still sorted in standard ascending order.

> **Tip**
>
> **Sorting Descending on Multiple Columns**   If you want to sort descending on multiple columns, be sure each column has its own DESC keyword.

The opposite of DESC is ASC (for *ascending*), which may be specified to sort in ascending order. In practice, however, ASC is not usually used because ascending order is the default sequence (and is assumed if neither ASC nor DESC are specified).

> **Tip**
>
> **Case Sensitivity and Sort Orders**   When you are sorting textual data, is A the same as a? And does a come before B or after Z? These are not theoretical questions, and the answers depend on how the database is set up.
>
> In *dictionary* sort order, A is treated the same as a, and that is the default behavior in MariaDB (and indeed most DBMSs). However, administrators can change this behavior if needed. (If your database contains many foreign language characters, this might become necessary.)
>
> The key here is that, if you do need an alternate sort order, you cannot accomplish it with a simple ORDER BY clause. You need to use the CONVERT() function (functions are introduced in Chapter 11, "Using Data Manipulation Functions") or contact your database administrator if you need the column character set changed.

Using a combination of ORDER BY and LIMIT, it is possible to find the highest or lowest value in a column. The following example demonstrates how to find the value of the most expensive item:

▼ Input

```
SELECT prod_price
FROM products
ORDER BY prod_price DESC
LIMIT 1;
```

▼ Output

```
+------------+
| prod_price |
+------------+
|      55.00 |
+------------+
```

▼ Analysis

prod_price DESC ensures that rows are retrieved from most to least expensive, and LIMIT 1 tells MariaDB to just return one row.

> **Caution**
>
> **Position of ORDER BY Clause**   When specifying an ORDER BY clause, be sure that it is after the FROM clause. If LIMIT is used, it must come *after* ORDER BY. Using clauses out of order generates an error message.

Summary

In this chapter, you learned how to sort retrieved data using the SELECT statement's ORDER BY clause. This clause, which must be the last in the SELECT statement, can be used to sort data on one or more columns as needed.

6

Filtering Data

In this chapter, you learn how to use the SELECT statement's WHERE clause to specify search conditions.

Using the WHERE Clause

Database tables usually contain large amounts of data, and you seldom need to retrieve all the rows in a table. More often than not, you want to extract a subset of the table's data as needed for specific operations or reports. Retrieving just the data you want involves specifying *search criteria*, also known as a *filter condition*.

Within a SELECT statement, data is filtered by specifying search criteria in the WHERE clause. The WHERE clause is specified right after the table name (the FROM clause) as follows:

▼ **Input**
```
SELECT prod_name, prod_price
FROM products
WHERE prod_price = 2.50;
```

▼ **Analysis**

This statement retrieves two columns from the products table, but instead of returning all rows, only rows with a prod_price value of 2.50 are returned, as follows:

▼ **Output**
```
+----------------+------------+
| prod_name      | prod_price |
+----------------+------------+
| Carrots        |       2.50 |
| TNT (1 stick)  |       2.50 |
+----------------+------------+
```

This example uses a simple equality test: It checks to see whether a column has a specified value, and it filters the data accordingly. But SQL enables you to do more than just test for equality.

> **Tip**
>
> **SQL Versus Application Filtering**   Data can also be filtered at the application level. To do this, the SQL SELECT statement retrieves more data than is actually required for the client application, and the client code loops through the returned data to extract just the needed rows.
>
> As a rule, this practice is strongly discouraged. Databases are optimized to perform filtering quickly and efficiently. Making the client application (or development language) do the database's job dramatically impacts application performance and creates applications that cannot scale properly. In addition, if data is filtered at the client, the server has to send unneeded data across the network connections, resulting in a waste of network bandwidth resources.

> **Caution**
>
> **WHERE Clause Position**   When using both ORDER BY and WHERE clauses, make sure ORDER BY comes after the WHERE; otherwise, an error will be generated. (See Chapter 5, "Sorting Retrieved Data," for more information on using ORDER BY.)

The WHERE Clause Operators

The first WHERE clause we looked at tests for equality—determining whether a column contains a specific value. MariaDB supports a whole range of conditional operators, some of which are listed in Table 6.1.

Table 6.1   WHERE Clause Operators

Operator	Description
=	Equality
< >	Nonequality
! =	Nonequality
<	Less than
< =	Less than or equal to
>	Greater than
>=	Greater than or equal to
BETWEEN	Between two specified values

Checking Against a Single Value

We have already seen an example of testing for equality. Here's one more:

▼ Input

```
SELECT prod_name, prod_price
FROM products
WHERE prod_name = 'fuses';
```

▼ Output

```
+-----------+------------+
| prod_name | prod_price |
+-----------+------------+
| Fuses     |       3.42 |
+-----------+------------+
```

▼ Analysis

Checking for WHERE prod_name = 'fuses' returned a single row with a value of Fuses. By default, MariaDB is not case sensitive when performing matches, and so fuses and Fuses match.

Now look at a few examples to demonstrate the use of other operators.

This first example lists all products that cost less than 10:

▼ Input

```
SELECT prod_name, prod_price
FROM products
WHERE prod_price < 10;
```

▼ Output

```
+---------------+------------+
| prod_name     | prod_price |
+---------------+------------+
| .5 ton anvil  |       5.99 |
| 1 ton anvil   |       9.99 |
| Carrots       |       2.50 |
| Fuses         |       3.42 |
| Oil can       |       8.99 |
| Sling         |       4.49 |
| TNT (1 stick) |       2.50 |
+---------------+------------+
```

This next statement retrieves all products costing 10 or less (resulting in two additional matches):

▼ **Input**
```
SELECT prod_name, prod_price
FROM products
WHERE prod_price <= 10;
```

▼ **Output**
```
+-----------------+-------------+
| prod_name       | prod_price  |
+-----------------+-------------+
| .5 ton anvil    |       5.99  |
| 1 ton anvil     |       9.99  |
| Bird seed       |      10.00  |
| Carrots         |       2.50  |
| Fuses           |       3.42  |
| Oil can         |       8.99  |
| Sling           |       4.49  |
| TNT (1 stick)   |       2.50  |
| TNT (5 sticks)  |      10.00  |
+-----------------+-------------+
```

Checking for Nonmatches

This next example lists all products not made by vendor 1003:

▼ **Input**
```
SELECT vend_id, prod_name
FROM products
WHERE vend_id <> 1003;
```

▼ **Output**
```
+---------+---------------+
| vend_id | prod_name     |
+---------+---------------+
|    1001 | .5 ton anvil  |
|    1001 | 1 ton anvil   |
|    1001 | 2 ton anvil   |
|    1002 | Fuses         |
|    1005 | JetPack 1000  |
|    1005 | JetPack 2000  |
|    1002 | Oil can       |
+---------+---------------+
```

> **Tip**
>
> **When to Use Quotes**   If you look closely at the conditions used in the examples'
> WHERE clauses, you will notice that some values are enclosed within single quotes
> (such as 'fuses' used previously), and others are not. The single quotes are used to
> delimit strings. If you are comparing a value against a column that is a string *datatype*,
> the delimiting quotes are required. Quotes are not used to delimit values used with
> numeric columns.

The following is the same example, except this one uses the != operator
instead of <>:

▼ Input

```
SELECT vend_id, prod_name
FROM products
WHERE vend_id != 1003;
```

> **Note**
>
> **!= Versus <>**   Yes, both <> and != look for nonmatches. != means *not equal to*, and
> <> means *less than or greater than* (in other words, *not equal to*). Use whichever you
> prefer.

Checking for a Range of Values

To check for a range of values, you can use the BETWEEN operator. Its syntax is
a little different from other WHERE clause operators because it requires two values: the beginning and end of the range. The BETWEEN operator can be used,
for example, to check for all products that cost between 5 and 10 or for all
dates that fall between specified start and end dates.

The following example demonstrates the use of the BETWEEN operator by
retrieving all products with a price between 5 and 10:

▼ Input

```
SELECT prod_name, prod_price
FROM products
WHERE prod_price BETWEEN 5 AND 10;
```

▼ Output

```
+----------------+------------+
| prod_name      | prod_price |
+----------------+------------+
| .5 ton anvil   |       5.99 |
| 1 ton anvil    |       9.99 |
| Bird seed      |      10.00 |
| Oil can        |       8.99 |
| TNT (5 sticks) |      10.00 |
+----------------+------------+
```

▼ Analysis

As seen in this example, when BETWEEN is used, two values must be specified—the low end and high end of the desired range. The two values must also be separated by the AND keyword. BETWEEN matches all the values in the range, including the specified range start and end values.

Checking for No Value

When a table is created, the table designer can specify whether individual columns can contain no value. When a column contains no value, it is said to contain a NULL value.

> **New Term**
>
> **NULL**   *No value*, as opposed to a field containing 0, or an empty string, or just spaces.

To determine if a value is NULL, you cannot simply check to see if = NULL. Instead, the SELECT statement has a special WHERE clause that can be used to check for columns with NULL values—the IS NULL clause. The syntax looks like this:

▼ Input

```
SELECT prod_name
FROM products
WHERE prod_price IS NULL;
```

This statement returns a list of all products that have no price (an empty prod_price field, not a price of 0), and because there are none, no data is returned. The customers table, however, does contain columns with NULL values—the cust_email column contains NULL if a customer has no e-mail address on file:

▼ Input

```
SELECT cust_id
FROM customers
WHERE cust_email IS NULL;
```

▼ Output

```
+---------+
| cust_id |
+---------+
|   10002 |
|   10005 |
+---------+
```

> **Caution**
>
> **NULL and Nonmatches**   You might expect that when you filter to select all rows that do not have a particular value, rows with a NULL will be returned. But they will not. Because of the special meaning of *unknown*, the database does not know whether they match, and so they are not returned when filtering for matches or when filtering for non-matches.
>
> When filtering data, make sure to verify that the rows with a NULL in the filtered column are really present in the returned data.

Summary

In this chapter, you learned how to filter returned data using the SELECT statement's WHERE clause. You learned how to test for equality, nonequality, greater than and less than, value ranges, and NULL values.

7

Advanced Data Filtering

In this chapter, you learn how to combine WHERE clauses to create powerful and sophisticated search conditions. You also learn how to use the NOT and IN operators.

Combining WHERE Clauses

All the WHERE clauses introduced in Chapter 6, "Filtering Data," filter data using a single criterion. For a greater degree of filter control, MariaDB allows you to specify multiple WHERE clauses. These clauses may be used in two ways: as AND clauses or as OR clauses.

> **New Term**
>
> **Operator** A special keyword used to join or change clauses within a WHERE clause. Also known as *logical operators*.

Using the AND Operator

To filter by more than one column, you use the AND operator to append conditions to your WHERE clause. The following code demonstrates this:

▼ **Input**
```
SELECT prod_id, prod_price, prod_name
FROM products
WHERE vend_id = 1003 AND prod_price <= 10;
```

▼ **Analysis**

The preceding SQL statement retrieves the product name and price for all products made by vendor 1003 as long as the price is 10 or less. The WHERE clause in this SELECT statement is made up of two conditions, and the keyword AND is used to join them. AND instructs the DBMS to return only rows that meet all the conditions specified. If a product is made by vendor 1003 but it costs more than 10, it is not retrieved. Similarly, products that cost less than 10 that are made by a vendor other than the one specified are not retrieved.

The output generated by this SQL statement is as follows:

▼ Output

```
+---------+------------+----------------+
| prod_id | prod_price | prod_name      |
+---------+------------+----------------+
| FB      |      10.00 | Bird seed      |
| FC      |       2.50 | Carrots        |
| SLING   |       4.49 | Sling          |
| TNT1    |       2.50 | TNT (1 stick)  |
| TNT2    |      10.00 | TNT (5 sticks) |
+---------+------------+----------------+
```

> **New Term**
>
> **AND**   A keyword used in a WHERE clause to specify that only rows matching all the specified conditions should be retrieved.

The example just used contained a single AND clause and was thus made up of two filter conditions. Additional filter conditions could be used as well, each separated by an AND keyword.

> **Note**
>
> **No ORDER BY Clause Specified**   In the interests of saving space (and your typing) I omitted the ORDER BY clause in many of these examples. As such, it is entirely possible that your output won't exactly match the output in the book. While the number of returned rows should always match, their order may not. Of course, feel free to add an ORDER BY clause if you want; it needs to go after the WHERE clause.

Using the OR Operator

The OR operator is exactly the opposite of AND. The OR operator instructs MariaDB to retrieve rows that match either condition.

Look at the following SELECT statement:

▼ Input

```
SELECT prod_name, prod_price
FROM products
WHERE vend_id = 1002 OR vend_id = 1003;
```

▼ Analysis

The preceding SQL statement retrieves the product name and price for any products made by either of the two specified vendors. The OR operator tells the DBMS to match either condition, not both. If an AND operator had been used here, no data would be returned (it would have created a WHERE clause that could never be matched). The output generated by this SQL statement is as follows:

▼ Output

```
+----------------+------------+
| prod_name      | prod_price |
+----------------+------------+
| Detonator      |      13.00 |
| Bird seed      |      10.00 |
| Carrots        |       2.50 |
| Fuses          |       3.42 |
| Oil can        |       8.99 |
| Safe           |      50.00 |
| Sling          |       4.49 |
| TNT (1 stick)  |       2.50 |
| TNT (5 sticks) |      10.00 |
+----------------+------------+
```

> **New Term**
>
> **OR** A keyword used in a WHERE clause to specify that any rows matching either of the specified conditions should be retrieved.

Understanding Order of Evaluation

WHERE clauses can contain any number of AND and OR operators. Combining the two enables you to perform sophisticated and complex filtering.

But combining AND and OR operators presents an interesting problem. To demonstrate this, look at an example. You need a list of all products costing 10 or more made by vendors 1002 and 1003. The following SELECT statement uses a combination of AND and OR operators to build a WHERE clause:

▼ Input

```
SELECT prod_name, prod_price
FROM products
WHERE vend_id = 1002 OR vend_id = 1003 AND prod_price >= 10;
```

▼ Output

```
+----------------+------------+
| prod_name      | prod_price |
+----------------+------------+
| Detonator      |      13.00 |
| Bird seed      |      10.00 |
| Fuses          |       3.42 |
| Oil can        |       8.99 |
| Safe           |      50.00 |
| TNT (5 sticks) |      10.00 |
+----------------+------------+
```

▼ Analysis

Look at the previously listed results. Two of the rows returned have prices less than 10—so, obviously, the rows were not filtered as intended. Why did this happen? The answer is the order of evaluation. SQL (like most languages) processes AND operators before OR operators. When SQL sees the previous WHERE clause, it reads *products made by vendor 1002 regardless of price, and any products costing 10 or more made by vendor 1003.* In other words, because AND ranks higher in the order of evaluation, the wrong operators were joined together.

The solution to this problem is to use parentheses to explicitly group related operators. Take a look at the following SELECT statement and output:

▼ Input

```
SELECT prod_name, prod_price
FROM products
WHERE (vend_id = 1002 OR vend_id = 1003) AND prod_price >= 10;
```

▼ Output

```
+-----------------+------------+
| prod_name       | prod_price |
+-----------------+------------+
| Detonator       |      13.00 |
| Bird seed       |      10.00 |
| Safe            |      50.00 |
| TNT (5 sticks)  |      10.00 |
+-----------------+------------+
```

▼ Analysis

The only difference between this SELECT statement and the earlier one is that, in this statement, the first two WHERE clause conditions are enclosed within parentheses. As parentheses have a higher order of evaluation than either AND or OR operators, the DBMS first filters the OR condition within those parentheses. The SQL statement then becomes *any products made by either vendor 1002 or vendor 1003 costing 10 or greater,* which is exactly what you want.

> **Tip**
>
> **Using Parentheses in WHERE Clauses**   Whenever you write WHERE clauses that use both AND and OR operators, use parentheses to explicitly group operators. Don't ever rely on the default evaluation order, even if it is exactly what you want. There is no downside to using parentheses, and you are always better off eliminating any ambiguity.

Using the IN Operator

Parentheses have another different use in WHERE clauses. The IN operator is used to specify a range of conditions, any of which can be matched. IN takes a comma-delimited list of valid values, all enclosed within parentheses. The following example demonstrates this:

▼ Input

```
SELECT prod_name, prod_price
FROM products
WHERE vend_id IN (1002,1003)
ORDER BY prod_name;
```

▼ Output

```
+----------------+------------+
| prod_name      | prod_price |
+----------------+------------+
| Bird seed      |      10.00 |
| Carrots        |       2.50 |
| Detonator      |      13.00 |
| Fuses          |       3.42 |
| Oil can        |       8.99 |
| Safe           |      50.00 |
| Sling          |       4.49 |
| TNT (1 stick)  |       2.50 |
| TNT (5 sticks) |      10.00 |
+----------------+------------+
```

▼ Analysis

The SELECT statement retrieves all products made by vendor 1002 and vendor 1003. The IN operator is followed by a comma-delimited list of valid values, and the entire list must be enclosed within parentheses.

If you are thinking that the IN operator accomplishes the same goal as OR, you are right. The following SQL statement accomplishes the exact same thing as the previous example:

▼ Input

```
SELECT prod_name, prod_price
FROM products
WHERE vend_id  = 1002 OR vend_id = 1003
ORDER BY prod_name;
```

▼ Output

```
+--------------------------+-------------+
| prod_name                | prod_price  |
+--------------------------+-------------+
| 12 inch teddy bear       |      8.9900 |
| 18 inch teddy bear       |     11.9900 |
| 8 inch teddy bear        |      5.9900 |
| Bird bean bag toy        |      3.4900 |
| Fish bean bag toy        |      3.4900 |
| Rabbit bean bag toy      |      3.4900 |
| Raggedy Ann              |     4.99000 |
+--------------------------+-------------+
```

Why use the IN operator? The advantages are

- When you are working with long lists of valid options, the IN operator syntax is far cleaner and easier to read.

- The order of evaluation is easier to manage when IN is used (as there are fewer operators used).

- IN operators almost always execute more quickly than lists of OR operators (although you'll not see any performance difference with very short lists like the ones used here).

- The biggest advantage of IN is that the IN operator can contain another SELECT statement, enabling you to build highly dynamic WHERE clauses. We look at this in detail in Chapter 14, "Working with Subqueries."

New Term

IN   A keyword used in a WHERE clause to specify a list of values to be matched using an OR comparison.

Using the NOT Operator

The WHERE clause's NOT operator has one function and one function only— NOT negates whatever condition comes next.

New Term

NOT   A keyword used in a WHERE clause to negate a condition.

The following example demonstrates the use of NOT. To list the products made by all vendors except vendors 1002 and 1003, you can use the following:

▼ Input

```
SELECT prod_name, prod_price
FROM products
WHERE vend_id NOT IN (1002,1003)
ORDER BY prod_name;
```

▼ Output

```
+--------------+------------+
| prod_name    | prod_price |
+--------------+------------+
| .5 ton anvil |       5.99 |
| 1 ton anvil  |       9.99 |
| 2 ton anvil  |      14.99 |
| JetPack 1000 |      35.00 |
| JetPack 2000 |      55.00 |
+--------------+------------+
```

▼ Analysis

The NOT here negates the condition that follows it; so instead of matching vend_id to 1002 or 1003, MariaDB matches vend_id to anything that is not 1002 or 1003.

So why use NOT? Well, for simple WHERE clauses, there really is no advantage to using NOT. NOT is useful in more complex clauses. For example, using NOT in conjunction with an IN operator makes it simple to find all rows that do not match a list of criteria.

> **Note**
>
> **NOT in MariaDB**   MariaDB supports the use of NOT to negate IN, BETWEEN, and EXISTS clauses. This is different from most other DBMSs that allow NOT to be used to negate any conditions.

Summary

This chapter picked up where the last chapter left off and taught you how to combine WHERE clauses with the AND and OR operators. You also learned how to explicitly manage the order of evaluation, and how to use the IN and NOT operators.

8

Using Wildcard Filtering

In this chapter, you learn what wildcards are, how they are used, and how to perform wildcard searches using the LIKE operator for sophisticated filtering of retrieved data.

Using the LIKE Operator

All the previous operators we studied filter against known values. Be it matching one or more values, testing for greater-than or less-than known values, or checking a range of values, the common denominator is that the values used in the filtering are known. But filtering data that way does not always work. For example, how could you search for all products that contained the text *anvil* within the product name? That cannot be done with simple comparison operators; that's a job for wildcard searching. Using wildcards, you can create search patterns that can be compared against your data. In this example, if you want to find all products that contain the word *anvil*, you could construct a wildcard search pattern enabling you to find that *anvil* text anywhere within a product name.

> **New Term**
> **Wildcards** Special characters used to match parts of a value.

> **New Term**
> **Search pattern** A search condition made up of literal text, wildcard characters, or any combination of the two.

The wildcards themselves are actually characters that have special meanings within SQL WHERE clauses, and SQL supports several wildcard types.

To use wildcards in search clauses, the LIKE operator must be used. LIKE instructs MariaDB that the following search pattern is to be compared using a wildcard match rather than a straight equality match.

> **Note**
>
> **Predicates** When is an operator not an operator? When it is a *predicate*. Technically, LIKE is a predicate, not an operator. The end result is the same; just be aware of this term in case you run across it in the MariaDB documentation.

The Percent Sign (%) Wildcard

The most frequently used wildcard is the percent sign (%). Within a search string, % means *match any number of occurrences of any character*. For example, to find all products that start with the word *jet*, you can issue the following SELECT statement:

▼ Input

```
SELECT prod_id, prod_name
FROM products
WHERE prod_name LIKE 'jet%';
```

▼ Output

```
+---------+---------------+
| prod_id | prod_name     |
+---------+---------------+
| JP1000  | JetPack 1000  |
| JP2000  | JetPack 2000  |
+---------+---------------+
```

▼ Analysis

This example uses a search pattern of 'jet%'. When this clause is evaluated, any value that starts with jet is retrieved. The % tells MariaDB to accept any characters after the word jet, regardless of how many characters there are.

> **Note**
>
> **Case-Sensitivity** Depending on how the column is defined in MariaDB, searches might be case-sensitive, in which case 'jet%' would not match JetPack 1000.

Wildcards can be used anywhere within the search pattern, and multiple wildcards can be used as well. The following example uses two wildcards, one at either end of the pattern:

▼ Input

```
SELECT prod_id, prod_name
FROM products
WHERE prod_name LIKE '%anvil%';
```

▼ Output

```
+---------+--------------+
| prod_id | prod_name    |
+---------+--------------+
| ANV01   | .5 ton anvil |
| ANV02   | 1 ton anvil  |
| ANV03   | 2 ton anvil  |
+---------+--------------+
```

▼ Analysis

The search pattern '%anvil%' means *match any value that contains the text* anvil *anywhere within it, regardless of any characters before or after that text*.

Wildcards can also be used in the middle of a search pattern, although that is rarely useful. The following example finds all products that begin with an s and end with an e:

▼ Input

```
SELECT prod_name
FROM products
WHERE prod_name LIKE 's%e';
```

> **Tip**
>
> **Searching For Partial Email Addresses** There is one situation in which wildcards may indeed be useful in the middle of a search pattern, and that is looking for email address-es based on a partial address, such as WHERE email LIKE 'b%@forta.com'.

It is important to note that, in addition to matching one or more characters, % also matches zero characters. % represents zero, one, or more characters at the specified location in the search pattern.

> **Note**
>
> **Watch for Trailing Spaces** Trailing spaces can interfere with wildcard matching. For example, if any of the anvils had been saved with one or more spaces after the word anvil, the clause WHERE prod_name LIKE '%anvil' would not have matched them as there would have been additional characters after the final l. One simple solution to this problem is to always append a final % to the search pattern. A better solution is to trim the spaces using functions, as discussed in Chapter 11, "Using Data Manipulation Functions."

> **Caution**
>
> **Watch for NULL** While it may seem that the % wildcard matches anything, there is one exception, NULL. Not even the clause WHERE prod_name LIKE '%' will match a row with the value NULL as the product name.

The Underscore (_) Wildcard

Another useful wildcard is the underscore (_). The underscore is used just like %, but instead of matching multiple characters, the underscore matches just a single character.

Take a look at this example:

▼ Input
```
SELECT prod_id, prod_name
FROM products
WHERE prod_name LIKE '_ ton anvil';
```

▼ Output
```
+----------+--------------+
| prod_id  | prod_name    |
+----------+--------------+
| ANV02    | 1 ton anvil  |
| ANV03    | 2 ton anvil  |
+----------+--------------+
```

▼ Analysis

The search pattern used in this WHERE clause specifies a wildcard followed by literal text. The results shown are the only rows that match the search pattern: The underscore matches 1 in the first row and 2 in the second row. The .5 ton anvil product did not match because the search pattern matched a single character, not two. By contrast, the following SELECT statement uses the % wildcard and returns three matching products:

▼ Input
```
SELECT prod_id, prod_name
FROM products
WHERE prod_name LIKE '% ton anvil';
```

▼ Output
```
+----------+--------------+
| prod_id  | prod_name    |
+----------+--------------+
| ANV01    | .5 ton anvil |
| ANV02    | 1 ton anvil  |
| ANV03    | 2 ton anvil  |
+----------+--------------+
```

Unlike %, which can match zero characters, _ always matches one character—no more and no less.

Tips for Using Wildcards

As you can see, MariaDB's wildcards are powerful. But that power comes with a price: Wildcard searches typically take far longer to process than any other search types discussed previously. Here are some tips to keep in mind when using wildcards:

- Don't overuse wildcards. If another search operator will do, use it instead.

- When you do use wildcards, try to not use them at the beginning of the search pattern unless absolutely necessary. Search patterns that begin with wildcards are the slowest to process.

- Pay careful attention to the placement of the wildcard symbols. If they are misplaced, you might not return the data you intended.

Having said that, wildcards are an important and useful search tool and one that you will use frequently.

Summary

In this chapter, you learned what wildcards are and how to use SQL wildcards within your WHERE clauses. You also learned that wildcards should be used carefully and never overused.

9

Searching Using Regular Expressions

In this chapter, you learn how to use regular expressions within MariaDB `WHERE` clauses for greater control over data filtering.

Understanding Regular Expressions

The filtering examples in the previous two chapters enabled you to locate data using matches, comparisons, and wildcard operators. For basic filtering (and even some not-so-basic filtering) this might be enough. But as the complexity of filtering conditions grows, so does the complexity of the `WHERE` clauses themselves.

And this is where regular expressions become useful. Regular expressions are part of a special language used to match text. If you needed to extract phone numbers from a text file, you might use a regular expression. If you needed to locate all files with digits in the middle of their names, you might use a regular expression. If you wanted to find all repeated words in a block of text, you might use a regular expression. And if you wanted to replace all URLs in a page with actual HTML links to those same URLs, yes, you might use a regular expression (or two, for this last example).

Regular expressions are supported in all sorts of programming languages, text editors, operating systems, and more. And savvy programmers and network managers have long regarded regular expressions as a vital component of their technical toolboxes.

Regular expressions are created using the regular expression language, a specialized language designed to do everything that was just discussed and much more. Like any language, regular expressions have a special syntax and instructions that you must learn.

> **Note**
>
> **To Learn More**   Full coverage of regular expressions is beyond the scope of this chapter. While the basics are covered here, for a more thorough introduction to regular expressions you might want to obtain a copy of my *Sams Teach Yourself Regular Expressions in 10 Minutes* (ISBN 0672325667).

Using Regular Expressions

So what does this have to do with MariaDB? As already explained, all regular expressions do is match text, comparing a pattern (the regular expression) with a string of text. MariaDB provides rudimentary support for regular expressions with WHERE clauses, allowing you to specify regular expressions that are used to filter data retrieved using SELECT.

> **Note**
>
> **Just a Subset of the Regular Expression Language**   If you are already familiar with regular expressions, take note. MariaDB supports only a small subset of what is supported in most regular expression implementations, and this chapter covers most of what is supported.

This will all become much clearer with some examples.

Basic Character Matching

We start with a simple example. The following statement retrieves all rows where column prod_name contains the text 1000:

▼ **Input**

```
SELECT prod_name
FROM products
WHERE prod_name REGEXP '1000'
ORDER BY prod_name;
```

▼ **Output**

```
+--------------+
| prod_name    |
+--------------+
| JetPack 1000 |
+--------------+
```

▼ Analysis

This statement looks much like the ones that used LIKE (in Chapter 8, "Using Wildcard Filtering"), except that the keyword LIKE has been replaced with REGEXP. This tells MariaDB that what follows is to be treated as a regular expression (one that just matches the literal text 1000).

So, why bother using a regular expression? Well, in the example just used, regular expressions really add no value (and probably hurt performance), but consider this next example:

▼ Input

```
SELECT prod_name
FROM products
WHERE prod_name REGEXP '.000'
ORDER BY prod_name;
```

▼ Output

```
+--------------+
| prod_name    |
+--------------+
| JetPack 1000 |
| JetPack 2000 |
+--------------+
```

▼ Analysis

Here the regular expression .000 was used. . is a special character in the regular expression language. It means *match any single character*, and so both 1000 and 2000 matched and were returned.

Of course, this particular example could also have been accomplished using LIKE and wildcards (as seen in Chapter 8).

> **Note**
>
> **LIKE Versus REGEXP**   There is one important difference between LIKE and REGEXP. Look at these two statements:
>
> ```
> SELECT prod_name
> FROM products
> WHERE prod_name LIKE '1000'
> ORDER BY prod_name;
> ```
> and
> ```
> SELECT prod_name
> FROM products
> WHERE prod_name REGEXP '1000'
> ORDER BY prod_name;
> ```

If you were to try them both you'd discover that the first returns no data and the second returns one row. Why is this?

As seen in Chapter 8, LIKE matches an entire column. If the text to be matched existed in the middle of a column value, LIKE would not find it and the row would not be returned (unless wildcard characters were used). REGEXP, on the other hand, looks for matches within column values, and so if the text to be matched existed in the middle of a column value, REGEXP would find it and the row would be returned. This is an important distinction.

So can REGEXP be used to match entire column values (so that it functions like LIKE)? Actually, yes, using the ^ and $ anchors, as explained later in this chapter.

> **Tip**
>
> **Matches Are Not Case-Sensitive** Regular expression matching in MariaDB is not case-sensitive (either case will be matched). To force case-sensitivity, you can use the BINARY keyword, as in WHERE prod_name REGEXP BINARY 'JetPack .000'

Performing OR Matches

To search for one of two strings (either one or the other), use | as seen here:

▼ Input

```
SELECT prod_name
FROM products
WHERE prod_name REGEXP '1000|2000'
ORDER BY prod_name;
```

▼ Output

```
+--------------+
| prod_name    |
+--------------+
| JetPack 1000 |
| JetPack 2000 |
+--------------+
```

▼ Analysis

Here the regular expression 1000|2000 was used. | is the regular expression OR operator. It means *match one or the other*, and so both 1000 and 2000 matched and were returned.

Using | is functionally similar to using OR statements in SELECT statements, with multiple OR conditions being consolidated into a single regular expression.

> **Tip**
>
> **More than Two OR Conditions**   More than two OR conditions may be specified. For
> example, `'1000|2000|3000'` would match `1000` or `2000` or `3000`.

Matching One of Several Characters

. matches any single character. But what if you wanted to match only specific characters? You can do this by specifying a set of characters enclosed within [and], as seen here:

▼ Input

```
SELECT prod_name
FROM products
WHERE prod_name REGEXP '[123] Ton'
ORDER BY prod_name;
```

▼ Output

```
+-------------+
| prod_name   |
+-------------+
| 1 ton anvil |
| 2 ton anvil |
+-------------+
```

▼ Analysis

Here the regular expression [123] Ton was used. [123] defines a set of characters, and here it means *match 1 or 2 or 3*, so both 1 ton and 2 ton matched and were returned (there was no 3 ton).

As you have just seen, [] is another form of OR statement. In fact, the regular expression [123] Ton is shorthand for [1|2|3] Ton, which also would have worked. But the [] characters are needed to define what the OR statement is looking for. To better understand this, look at the next example:

▼ Input

```
SELECT prod_name
FROM products
WHERE prod_name REGEXP '1|2|3 Ton'
ORDER BY prod_name;
```

▼ Output

```
+---------------+
| prod_name     |
+---------------+
| 1 ton anvil   |
| 2 ton anvil   |
| JetPack 1000  |
| JetPack 2000  |
| TNT (1 stick) |
+---------------+
```

▼ Analysis

Well, that did not work. The two required rows were retrieved, but so were three others. This happened because MariaDB assumed that you meant '1' or '2' or '3 ton'. The | character applies to the entire string unless it is enclosed with a set.

Sets of characters can also be negated. That is, they'll match anything *but* the specified characters. To negate a character set, place a ^ at the start of the set. So, whereas [123] matches characters 1, 2, or 3, [^123] matches anything but those characters.

Matching Ranges

Sets can be used to define one or more characters to be matched. For example, the following matches digits 0 through 9:

```
[0123456789]
```

To simplify this type of set, - can be used to define a range. The following is functionally identical to the list of digits just seen:

```
[0-9]
```

Ranges are not limited to complete sets—[1-3] and [6-9] are valid ranges, too. In addition, ranges need not be numeric, and so [a-z] matches any alphabetical character.

Here is an example:

▼ Input

```
SELECT prod_name
FROM products
WHERE prod_name REGEXP '[1-5] Ton'
ORDER BY prod_name;
```

▼ Output

```
+--------------+
| prod_name    |
+--------------+
| .5 ton anvil |
| 1 ton anvil  |
| 2 ton anvil  |
+--------------+
```

▼ Analysis

Here the regular expression [1-5] Ton was used. [1-5] defines a range, and so this expression means *match 1 through 5*, and so three matches were returned. .5 ton was returned because 5 ton matched (without the . character).

Matching Special Characters

The regular expression language is made up of special characters that have specific meanings. You've already seen ., [], |, and -, and there are others, too. Which begs the question, if you needed to match those characters, how would you do so? For example, if you wanted to find values that contain the . character, how would you search for it? Look at this example:

▼ Input

```
SELECT vend_name
FROM vendors
WHERE vend_name REGEXP '.'
ORDER BY vend_name;
```

▼ Output

```
+----------------+
| vend_name      |
+----------------+
| ACME           |
| Anvils R Us    |
| Furball Inc.   |
| Jet Set        |
| Jouets Et Ours |
| LT Supplies    |
+----------------+
```

▼ Analysis

That did not work. . matches any character, and so every row was retrieved.

To match special characters they must be preceded by \\. So, \\- means find – and \\. means find .

▼ Input

```
SELECT vend_name
FROM vendors
WHERE vend_name REGEXP '\\.'
ORDER BY vend_name;
```

▼ Output

```
+--------------+
| vend_name    |
+--------------+
| Furball Inc. |
+--------------+
```

▼ Analysis

That worked. \\. matches ., and so only a single row was retrieved. This process is known as *escaping*, and all characters that have special significance within regular expressions must be escaped this way. This includes ., |, [], and all the other special characters used thus far.

\\ is also used to refer to metacharacters (characters that have specific meanings), as listed in Table 9.1.

Table 9.1   **Whitespace Metacharacters**

Metacharacter	Description
\\f	Form feed
\\n	Line feed
\\r	Carriage return
\\t	Tab
\\v	Vertical tab

> **Tip**
>
> **To Match **   To match the backslash character itself (\\), you need to use \\\\.

> **Note**
>
> **\\ or \\\\?**   Most regular expression implementations use a single backslash to escape special characters to be able to use them as literals. MariaDB, however, requires two backslashes (MariaDB itself interprets one, and the regular expression library interprets the other).

Matching Character Classes

There are matches that you'll find yourself using frequently—digits, or all alphabetical characters, or all alphanumerical characters, and so on. To make working with these easier, you may use predefined character sets known as *character classes*. Table 9.2 lists the character classes and what they mean.

Table 9.2   **Character Classes**

Class	Description
`[:alnum:]`	Any letter or digit, (same as `[a-zA-Z0-9]`)
`[:alpha:]`	Any letter (same as `[a-zA-Z]`)
`[:blank:]`	Space or tab (same as `[\\t ]`)
`[:cntrl:]`	ASCII control characters (ASCII 0 through 31 and 127)
`[:digit:]`	Any digit (same as `[0-9]`)
`[:graph:]`	Same as `[:print:]` but excludes space
`[:lower:]`	Any lowercase letter (same as `[a-z]`)
`[:print:]`	Any printable character
`[:punct:]`	Any character that is neither in `[:alnum:]` nor `[:cntrl:]`
`[:space:]`	Any whitespace character including the space (same as `[\\f\\n\\r\\t\\v ]`)
`[:upper:]`	Any uppercase letter (same as `[A-Z]`)
`[:xdigit:]`	Any hexadecimal digit (same as `[a-fA-F0-9]`)

Matching Multiple Instances

All the regular expressions used thus far attempt to match a single occurrence. If there is a match, the row is retrieved, and if not, nothing is retrieved. But sometimes you require greater control over the number of matches. For example, you might want to locate all numbers regardless of how many digits the number contains, or you might want to locate a word but also be able to accommodate a trailing s if one exists, and so on.

This can be accomplished using the regular expressions repetition metacharacters, listed in Table 9.3.

Table 9.3   **Repetition Metacharacters**

Metacharacter	Description
*	0 or more matches
+	1 or more matches (equivalent to {1, })
?	0 or 1 match (equivalent to {0,1})
{n}	Specific number of matches
{n, }	No less than a specified number of matches
{n,m}	Range of matches (m not to exceed 255)

Following are some examples.

▼ Input

```
SELECT prod_name
FROM products
WHERE prod_name REGEXP '\\([0-9] sticks?\\)'
ORDER BY prod_name;
```

▼ Output

```
+----------------+
| prod_name      |
+----------------+
| TNT (1 stick)  |
| TNT (5 sticks) |
+----------------+
```

▼ Analysis

Regular expression \\([0-9] sticks?\\) requires some explanation. \\
(matches (, [0-9] matches any digit (1 and 5 in this example), sticks?
matches stick and sticks (the ? after the s makes that s optional because ?
matches 0 or 1 occurrence of whatever it follows), and \\) matches the closing
). Without ? it would have been difficult to match both stick and sticks.

Here's another example. This time we try to match four consecutive digits:

▼ Input

```
SELECT prod_name
FROM products
WHERE prod_name REGEXP '[[:digit:]]{4}'
ORDER BY prod_name;
```

▼ Output

```
+--------------+
| prod_name    |
+--------------+
| JetPack 1000 |
| JetPack 2000 |
+--------------+
```

▼ Analysis

As explained previously, [:digit:] matches any digit, and so [[:digit:]] is a set of digits. {4} requires exactly four occurrences of whatever it follows (any digit), and so [[:digit:]]{4} matches any four consecutive digits.

It is worth noting that when using regular expressions there is almost always more than one way to write a specific expression. The previous example could have also been written as follows:

▼ Input

```
SELECT prod_name
FROM products
WHERE prod_name REGEXP '[0-9][0-9][0-9][0-9]'
ORDER BY prod_name;
```

Actually, it could also have been written as

▼ Input

```
SELECT prod_name
FROM products
WHERE prod_name REGEXP '[0-9]{4}'
ORDER BY prod_name;
```

Anchors

All the examples thus far have matched text anywhere within a string. To match text at specific locations, you need to use anchors as listed in Table 9.4.

Table 9.4 **Anchor Metacharacters**

Metacharacter	Description
^	Start of text
$	End of text
[[:<:]]	Start of word
[[:>:]]	End of word

For example, what if you wanted to find all products that started with a number (including numbers starting with a decimal point)? A simple search for [0-9\\.] (or [[:digit:]\\.]) would not work because it would find matches anywhere within the text. The solution is to use the ^ anchor, as seen here:

▼ Input

```
SELECT prod_name
FROM products
WHERE prod_name REGEXP '^[0-9\\.]'
ORDER BY prod_name;
```

▼ Output

```
+--------------+
| prod_name    |
+--------------+
| .5 ton anvil |
| 1 ton anvil  |
| 2 ton anvil  |
+--------------+
```

▼ Analysis

^ matches the start of a string. As such, ^[0-9\\.] matches . or any digit only if they are the first characters within a string. Without the ^, four other rows would have been retrieved, too (those that have digits in the middle).

> **Note**
>
> **The Dual Purpose ^**   ^ has two uses. Within a set (defined using [and]) it is used to negate that set. Otherwise, it is used to refer to the start of a string.

> **Note**
>
> **Making REGEXP Behave like LIKE**   Earlier in this chapter I mentioned that LIKE and REGEXP behaved differently in that LIKE matched an entire string and REGEXP matched substrings, too. Using anchors, REGEXP can be made to behave just like LIKE by simply starting each expression with ^ and ending it with $.

> **Tip**
>
> **Simple Regular Expression Testing**   You can use SELECT to test regular expressions without using database tables. REGEXP checks always return 0 (not a match) or 1 (match). You can use REGEXP with literal strings to test expressions and to experiment with them. The syntax would look like this:
>
> SELECT 'hello' REGEXP '[0-9]';
>
> This example would obviously return 0 (as there are no digits in the text hello).

Summary

In this chapter, you learned the basics of regular expressions and how to use them in MariaDB SELECT statements via the REGEXP keyword.

10

Creating Calculated Fields

In this chapter, you learn what calculated fields are, how to create them, and how to use aliases to refer to them from within your application.

Understanding Calculated Fields

Data stored within a database's tables is often not available in the exact format needed by your applications. Here are some examples:

- You need to display a field containing the name of a company along with the company's location, but that information is stored in separate table columns.

- City, state, and ZIP Code are stored in separate columns (as they should be), but your mailing label printing program needs them retrieved as one correctly formatted field.

- Column data is in mixed upper- and lowercase, and your report needs all data presented in uppercase.

- An order items table stores item price and quantity but not the expanded price (price multiplied by quantity) of each item. To print invoices, you need that expanded price.

- You need total, averages, or other calculations based on table data.

In each of these examples, the data stored in the table is not exactly what your application needs. Rather than retrieve the data as it is and then reformat it within your client application or report, what you really want is to retrieve converted, calculated, or reformatted data directly from the database.

This is where calculated fields come in. Unlike all the columns we retrieved in the chapters thus far, calculated fields don't actually exist in database tables. Rather, a calculated field is created on-the-fly within a SQL SELECT statement.

> **New Term**
>
> **Field**   Essentially means the same thing as *column* and often is used interchangeably, although database columns are typically called *columns* and the term *fields* is normally used in conjunction with calculated fields.

It is important to note that only the database knows which columns in a SELECT statement are actual table columns and which are calculated fields. From the perspective of a client (for example, your application), a calculated field's data is returned in the same way as data from any other column.

> **Tip**
>
> **Client Versus Server Formatting**   Many of the conversions and reformatting that can be performed within SQL statements can also be performed directly in your client application. However, as a rule, it is far quicker to perform these operations on the database server than it is to perform them within the client because DBMSs are built to perform this type of processing quickly and efficiently.

Concatenating Fields

To demonstrate working with calculated fields, let's start with a simple example—creating a title made up of two columns.

The vendors table contains vendor name and address information. Imagine you are generating a vendor report and need to list the vendor location as part of the vendor name in the format name (location).

The report wants a single value, and the data in the table is stored in two columns: vend_name and vend_country. In addition, you need to surround vend_country with parentheses, and those are definitely not stored in the database table. The SELECT statement that returns the vendor names and locations is simple enough, but how would you create this combined value?

> **New Term**
>
> **Concatenate**   Joining values together (by appending them to each other) to form a single long value.

The solution is to concatenate the two columns. In MariaDB SELECT statements, you can concatenate columns using the Concat() function.

> **Tip**
>
> **MariaDB Is Different**   Most DBMSs use operators + or || for concatenation; MariaDB (like MySQL) uses the Concat() function. Keep this in mind when converting SQL statements to MariaDB (and MySQL).

▼ Input

```
SELECT Concat(vend_name, ' (', vend_country, ')')
FROM vendors
ORDER BY vend_name;
```

▼ Output

```
+----------------------------------------------+
| Concat(vend_name, ' (', vend_country, ')') |
+----------------------------------------------+
| ACME (USA)                                   |
| Anvils R Us (USA)                            |
| Furball Inc. (USA)                           |
| Jet Set (England)                            |
| Jouets Et Ours (France)                      |
| LT Supplies (USA)                            |
+----------------------------------------------+
```

▼ Analysis

Concat() concatenates strings, appending them to each other to create one bigger string. Concat() requires one or more values to be specified, each separated by commas. The previous SELECT statements concatenate four elements:

- The name stored in the vend_name column

- A string containing a space and an open parenthesis

- The state stored in the vend_country column

- A string containing the close parenthesis

As you can see in the output shown previously, the SELECT statement returns a single column (a calculated field) containing all four of these elements as one unit.

Back in Chapter 8, "Using Wildcard Filtering," I mentioned the need to trim data so as to remove any trailing spaces. This can be done using the MariaDB RTrim() function, as follows:

▼ Input

```
SELECT Concat(RTrim(vend_name), ' (', RTrim(vend_country), ')')
FROM vendors
ORDER BY vend_name;
```

▼ Analysis

The RTrim() function trims all spaces from the right of a value. By using RTrim(), the individual columns are all trimmed properly.

> **Note**
>
> **The Trim() Functions** In addition to RTrim() (which, as just seen, trims the right side of a string), MariaDB supports the use of LTrim() (which trims the left side of a string), and Trim() (which trims both the right and left).

Using Aliases

The SELECT statement used to concatenate the address field works well, as seen in the previous output. But what is the name of this new calculated column? Well, the truth is, it has no name; it is simply a value. Although this can be fine if you are just looking at the results in a SQL query tool, an unnamed column cannot be used within a client application because the client has no way to refer to that column.

To solve this problem, SQL supports column aliases. An *alias* is just that, an alternative name for a field or value. Aliases are assigned with the AS keyword. Take a look at the following SELECT statement:

▼ Input

```
SELECT Concat(RTrim(vend_name), ' (', RTrim(vend_country), ')') AS vend_
title
FROM vendors
ORDER BY vend_title;
```

▼ Output

```
+--------------------------+
| vend_title               |
+--------------------------+
| ACME (USA)               |
| Anvils R Us (USA)        |
| Furball Inc. (USA)       |
| Jet Set (England)        |
| Jouets Et Ours (France)  |
| LT Supplies (USA)        |
+--------------------------+
```

▼ Analysis

The SELECT statement itself is the same as the one used in the previous code snippet, except that here the calculated field is followed by the text AS vend_ title. This instructs SQL to create a calculated field named vend_title containing the results of the specified calculation. As you can see in the output, the results are the same as before, but the column is now named vend_title and any client application can refer to this column by name, just as it would to any actual table column. Indeed, the ORDER BY itself uses the calculated vend_title.

> **Tip**
>
> **Other Uses for Aliases** Aliases have other uses, too. Some common uses include renaming a column if the real table column name contains illegal characters (for example, spaces) and expanding column names if the original names are either ambiguous or easily misread.

> **Note**
>
> **Derived Columns** Aliases are also sometimes referred to as *derived columns*, so regardless of the term you run across, they mean the same thing.

Performing Mathematical Calculations

Another frequent use for calculated fields is performing mathematical calculations on retrieved data. Let's take a look at an example. The orders table contains all orders received, and the orderitems table contains the individual items within each order. The following SQL statement retrieves all the items in order number 20005:

▼ Input

```
SELECT prod_id, quantity, item_price
FROM orderitems
WHERE order_num = 20005;
```

▼ Output

```
+---------+----------+------------+
| prod_id | quantity | item_price |
+---------+----------+------------+
| ANV01   |       10 |       5.99 |
| ANV02   |        3 |       9.99 |
| TNT2    |        5 |      10.00 |
| FB      |        1 |      10.00 |
+---------+----------+------------+
```

The item_price column contains the per unit price for each item in an order. To expand the item price (item price multiplied by quantity ordered), you simply do the following:

▼ Input

```
SELECT prod_id,
       quantity,
       item_price,
       quantity*item_price AS expanded_price
FROM orderitems
WHERE order_num = 20005;
```

▼ Output

```
+---------+----------+------------+----------------+
| prod_id | quantity | item_price | expanded_price |
+---------+----------+------------+----------------+
| ANV01   |       10 |       5.99 |          59.90 |
| ANV02   |        3 |       9.99 |          29.97 |
| TNT2    |        5 |      10.00 |          50.00 |
| FB      |        1 |      10.00 |          10.00 |
+---------+----------+------------+----------------+
```

▼ Analysis

The expanded_price column shown in the previous output is a calculated field; the calculation is simply quantity*item_price. The client application can now use this new calculated column just as it would any other column.

MariaDB supports the basic mathematical operators listed in Table 10.1. In addition, parentheses can be used to establish order of precedence. Refer to Chapter 7, "Advanced Data Filtering," for an explanation of precedence.

Table 10.1 **MariaDB Mathematical Operators**

Operator	Description
+	Addition
-	Subtraction
*	Multiplication
/	Division

> **Tip**
>
> **How to Test Calculations** SELECT provides a great way to test and experiment with functions and calculations. Although SELECT is usually used to retrieve data from a table, the FROM clause may be omitted to simply access and work with expressions. For example, SELECT 3 * 2; would return 6, SELECT Trim(' abc '); would return abc, and SELECT Now(); uses the Now() function to return the current date and time. You get the idea—use SELECT to experiment as needed.

Summary

In this chapter, you learned what calculated fields are and how to create them. We used examples demonstrating the use of calculated fields for both string concatenation and mathematical operations. In addition, you learned how to create and use aliases so your application can refer to calculated fields.

11

Using Data Manipulation Functions

In this chapter, you learn what functions are, what types of functions MariaDB supports, and how to use these functions.

Understanding Functions

Like almost any other computer language, SQL supports the use of functions to manipulate data. Functions are operations usually performed on data, usually to facilitate conversion and manipulation.

An example of a function is the `RTrim()` that we used in the last chapter to trim any spaces from the end of a string.

> **Note**
>
> **Functions Are Less Portable Than SQL** Code that runs on multiple systems is said to be *portable*. Most SQL statements are relatively portable, and when differences between SQL implementations do occur they are usually not that difficult to deal with. Functions, on the other hand, tend to be far less portable. Just about every major DBMS supports functions that others don't, and sometimes the differences are significant.
>
> With code portability in mind, many SQL programmers opt not to use any implementation-specific features. Although this is a somewhat noble and idealistic view, it is not always in the best interests of application performance. If you opt not to use these functions, you make your application code work harder. It must use other methods to do what the DBMS could have done more efficiently.
>
> If you do decide to use functions, make sure you comment your code well, so that at a later date you (or another developer) will know exactly to which SQL implementation you were writing. Code commenting was introduced back in Chapter 4, "Retrieving Data."

Using Functions

Most SQL implementations support the following types of functions:

- Text functions are used to manipulate strings of text (for example, trimming or padding values and converting values to upper- and lowercase).

- Numeric functions are used to perform mathematical operations on numeric data (for example, returning absolute numbers and performing algebraic calculations).

- Date and time functions are used to manipulate date and time values and to extract specific components from these values (for example, returning differences between dates and checking date validity).

- System functions return information specific to the DBMS being used (for example, returning user login information or checking version specifics).

Text Manipulation Functions

You've already seen an example of text-manipulation functions in the last chapter—the RTrim() function was used to trim white space from the end of a column value. Here is another example, this time using the Upper() function:

▼ **Input**
```
SELECT vend_name, UPPER(vend_name) AS vend_name_upcase
FROM vendors
ORDER BY vend_name;
```

▼ **Output**
```
+----------------+--------------------+
| vend_name      | vend_name_upcase   |
+----------------+--------------------+
| ACME           | ACME               |
| Anvils R Us    | ANVILS R US        |
| Furball Inc.   | FURBALL INC.       |
| Jet Set        | JET SET            |
| Jouets Et Ours | JOUETS ET OURS     |
| LT Supplies    | LT SUPPLIES        |
+----------------+--------------------+
```

▼ Analysis

As you can see, Upper() converts text to uppercase and so in this example each vendor is listed twice, first exactly as stored in the vendors table, and then converted to uppercase as column vend_name_upcase.

Table 11.1 lists some commonly used text-manipulation functions.

Table 11.1   **Commonly Used Text-Manipulation Functions**

Function	Description
Left()	Returns characters from left of string
Length()	Returns the length of a string
Locate()	Finds a substring within a string
Lower()	Converts string to lowercase
LTrim()	Trims white space from left of string
Right()	Returns characters from right of string
RTrim()	Trims white space from right of string
Soundex()	Returns a string's SOUNDEX value
SubString()	Returns characters from within a string
Upper()	Converts string to uppercase

One item in Table 11.1 requires further explanation. SOUNDEX is an algo-rithm that converts any string of text into an alphanumeric pattern describing the phonetic representation of that text. SOUNDEX takes into account similar sounding characters and syllables, enabling strings to be compared by how they sound rather than how they have been typed. Although SOUNDEX is not a SQL concept, MariaDB (like many other DBMSs) offers SOUNDEX support.

Here's an example using the Soundex() function. Customer Coyote Inc. is in the customers table and has a contact named Y. Lee. But what if that were a typo, and the contact actually was supposed to have been Y. Lie? Obviously, searching by the correct contact name would return no data, as shown here:

▼ Input

```
SELECT cust_name, cust_contact
FROM customers
WHERE cust_contact = 'Y. Lie';
```

▼ Output

```
+-------------+---------------+
| cust_name   | cust_contact  |
+-------------+---------------+
```

Now try the same search using the Soundex() function to match all contact names that sound similar to Y. Lie:

▼ Input

```
SELECT cust_name, cust_contact
FROM customers
WHERE Soundex(cust_contact) = Soundex('Y Lie');
```

▼ Output

```
+--------------+---------------+
| cust_name    | cust_contact  |
+--------------+---------------+
| Coyote Inc.  | Y Lee         |
+--------------+---------------+
```

▼ Analysis

In this example, the WHERE clause uses the Soundex() function to convert both the cust_contact column value and the search string to their SOUNDEX values. Because Y. Lee and Y. Lie sound alike, their SOUNDEX values match, and so the WHERE clause correctly filtered the desired data.

Date and Time Manipulation Functions

Date and times are stored in tables using special datatypes using special internal formats so they may be sorted or filtered quickly and efficiently, as well as to save physical storage space.

The format used to store dates and times is usually of no use to your applications, and so date and time functions are almost always used to read, expand, and manipulate these values. Because of this, date and time manipulation functions are some of the most important functions in the MariaDB SQL language.

Table 11.2 lists some commonly used date and time manipulation functions.

Table 11.2　Commonly Used Date and Time Manipulation Functions

Function	Description
AddDate()	Add to a date (days, weeks, and so on)
AddTime()	Add to a time (hours, minutes, and so on)
CurDate()	Returns the current date
CurTime()	Returns the current time
Date()	Returns the date portion of a date time
DateDiff()	Calculates the difference between two dates

Table 11.2   **Continued**

Function	Description
Date_Add()	Highly flexible date arithmetic function
Date_Format()	Returns a formatted date or time string
Day()	Returns the day portion of a date
DayOfWeek()	Returns the day of week for a date
Hour()	Returns the hour portion of a time
Minute()	Returns the minute portion of a time
Month()	Returns the month portion of a date
Now()	Returns the current date and time
Second()	Returns the second portion of a time
Time()	Returns the time portion of a date time
Year()	Returns the year portion of a date

This would be a good time to revisit data filtering using WHERE. Thus far we have filtered data using WHERE clauses that compared numbers and text, but frequently data needs to be filtered by date. Filtering by date requires some extra care and the use of special MariaDB SQL functions.

The first thing to keep in mind is the date format used by MariaDB. Whenever you specify a date, be it inserting or updating table values, or filtering using WHERE clauses, the date must be in the format yyyy-mm-dd. So, for September 1st, 2011, specify 2011-09-01. Although other date formats might be recognized, this is the preferred date format because it eliminates ambiguity (after all, is 04/05/06 May 4th 2006, or April 5th 2006, or May 6th 2004, or... you get the idea).

> **Tip**
>
> **Always Use Four-Digit Years**   Two-digit years are supported, and MariaDB treats years 00-69 as 2000-2069 and 70-99 as 1970-1999. While these might in fact be the intended years, it is far safer to always use a full four-digit year so MariaDB does not have to make any assumptions for you.

As such, a basic date comparison should be simple enough:

▼ **Input**

```
SELECT cust_id, order_num
FROM orders
WHERE order_date = '2011-09-01';
```

▼ Output

```
+---------+-----------+
| cust_id | order_num |
+---------+-----------+
|   10001 |     20005 |
+---------+-----------+
```

▼ Analysis

That SELECT statement worked; it retrieved a single order record, one with an order_date of 2011-09-01.

But is using WHERE order_date = '2011-09-01' safe? order_date has a datatype of *datetime*. This type stores dates along with time values. The values in our example tables all have times of 00:00:00, but that might not always be the case. What if order dates were stored using the current date and time (so you'd not only know the order date but also the time of day that the order was placed)? Then WHERE order_date = '2011-09-01' fails if, for example, the stored order_date value is 2011-09-01 11:30:05. Even though a row with that date is present, it is not retrieved because the WHERE match failed.

The solution is to instruct MariaDB to only compare the specified date to the date portion of the column instead of using the entire column value. To do this you must use the Date() function. Date(order_date) instructs MariaDB to extract just the date part of the column, and so a safer SELECT statement is

▼ Input

```
SELECT cust_id, order_num
FROM orders
WHERE Date(order_date) = '2011-09-01';
```

> **Tip**
>
> **If You Mean Date Use Date()** It's a good practice to use Date() if what you want is just the date, even if you know that the column only contains dates. This way, if somehow a date time value ends up in the table in the future, your SQL won't break. Oh, and yes, there is a Time() function, too, and it should be used when you want the time.

Now that you know how to use dates to test for equality, using all the other operators (introduced in Chapter 6, "Filtering Data") should be self-explanatory.

But one other type of date comparison warrants explanation. What if you wanted to retrieve all orders placed in September 2011? A simple equality test does not work as it matches the day of the month, too. There are several solutions, one of which follows:

▼ **Input**
```
SELECT cust_id, order_num
FROM orders
WHERE Date(order_date) BETWEEN '2011-09-01' AND '2011-09-30';
```

▼ **Output**
```
+----------+------------+
| cust_id  | order_num  |
+----------+------------+
|   10001  |    20005   |
|   10003  |    20006   |
|   10004  |    20007   |
+----------+------------+
```

▼ **Analysis**

Here a BETWEEN operator is used to define 2011-09-01 and 2011-09-30 as the range of dates to match.

Here's another solution (one that won't require you to remember how many days are in each month, or worry about February in leap years):

▼ **Input**
```
SELECT cust_id, order_num
FROM orders
WHERE Year(order_date) = 2011 AND Month(order_date) = 9;
```

▼ **Analysis**

Year() is a function that returns the year from a date (or a date time). Similarly, Month() returns the month from a date. WHERE Year(order_date) = 2011 AND Month(order_date) = 9 thus retrieves all rows that have an order_date in year 2011 and in month 9.

> **Note**
>
> **Support For Microseconds** MariaDB 5.3 adds support for microseconds when working with date and time values.

Numeric Manipulation Functions

Numeric manipulation functions do just that—manipulate numeric data. These functions tend to be used primarily for algebraic, trigonometric, or geometric calculations and, therefore, are not as frequently used as string or date and time manipulation functions.

The ironic thing is that of all the functions found in the major DBMSs, the numeric functions are the ones that are most uniform and consistent. Table 11.3 lists some of the more commonly used numeric manipulation functions.

Table 11.3   Commonly Used Numeric Manipulation Functions

Function	Description
Abs()	Returns a number's absolute value
Cos()	Returns the trigonometric cosine of a specified angle
Exp()	Returns the exponential value of a specific number
Mod()	Returns the remainder of a division operation
Pi()	Returns the value of pi
Rand()	Returns a random number
Sin()	Returns the trigonometric sine of a specified angle
Sqrt()	Returns the square root of a specified number
Tan()	Returns the trigonometric tangent of a specified angle

Summary

In this chapter, you learned how to use SQL's data manipulation functions and paid special attention to working with dates.

12

Summarizing Data

In this chapter, you learn what the SQL aggregate functions are and how to use them to summarize table data.

Using Aggregate Functions

It is often necessary to summarize data without actually retrieving it all, and MariaDB provides special functions for this purpose. Using these functions, MariaDB queries are often used to retrieve data for analysis and reporting purposes. Examples of this type of retrieval are

- Determining the number of rows in a table (or the number of rows that meet some condition or contain a specific value)

- Obtaining the sum of a group of rows in a table

- Finding the highest, lowest, and average values in a table column (either for all rows or for specific rows)

In each of these examples, you want a summary of the data in a table, not the actual data itself. Therefore, returning the actual table data would be a waste of time and processing resources (not to mention bandwidth). To repeat, all you really want is the summary information.

To facilitate this type of retrieval, MariaDB features a set of aggregate functions, some of which are listed in Table 12.1. These functions enable you to perform all the types of retrieval just enumerated.

> **Note**
>
> **Aggregate functions** Functions that operate on a set of rows to calculate and return a single value.

Table 12.1   **SQL Aggregate Functions**

Function	Description
AVG()	Returns a column's average value
COUNT()	Returns the number of rows in a column
MAX()	Returns a column's highest value
MIN()	Returns a column's lowest value
SUM()	Returns the sum of a column's values

The use of each of these functions is explained in the following sections.

> **Note**
>
> **Standard Deviation**   A series of standard deviation aggregate functions are also supported by MariaDB but are not covered in the chapters.

The AVG() Function

AVG() is used to return the average value of a specific column by counting both the number of rows in the table and the sum of their values. AVG() can be used to return the average value of all columns or of specific columns or rows.

This first example uses AVG() to return the average price of all the products in the products table:

▼ Input

```
SELECT AVG(prod_price) AS avg_price
FROM products;
```

▼ Output

```
+-----------+
| avg_price |
+-----------+
| 16.133571 |
+-----------+
```

▼ Analysis

The previous SELECT statement returns a single value, avg_price, that contains the average price of all products in the products table. avg_price is an alias as explained in Chapter 10, "Creating Calculated Fields."

AVG() can also be used to determine the average value of specific columns or rows. The following example returns the average price of products offered by a specific vendor:

▼ Input

```
SELECT AVG(prod_price) AS avg_price
FROM products
WHERE vend_id = 1003;
```

▼ Output

```
+-----------+
| avg_price |
+-----------+
| 13.212857 |
+-----------+
```

▼ Analysis

This SELECT statement differs from the previous one only in that this one contains a WHERE clause. The WHERE clause filters only products with a vend_id of 1003, and, therefore, the value returned in avg_price is the average of just that vendor's products.

> **Caution**
>
> **Individual Columns Only** AVG() may only be used to determine the average of a specific numeric column, and that column name must be specified as the function parameter. To obtain the average value of multiple columns, multiple AVG() functions must be used.

> **Note**
>
> **NULL Values** Column rows containing NULL values are ignored by the AVG() function.

The COUNT() Function

COUNT() does just that: It counts. Using COUNT(), you can determine the number of rows in a table or the number of rows that match a specific criterion.

COUNT() can be used two ways:

- Use COUNT(*) to count the number of rows in a table, whether columns contain values or NULL values.

- Use COUNT(column) to count the number of rows that have values in a specific column, ignoring NULL values.

This first example returns the total number of customers in the customers table:

▼ Input

```
SELECT COUNT(*) AS num_cust
FROM customers;
```

▼ Output

```
+----------+
| num_cust |
+----------+
|        5 |
+----------+
```

▼ Analysis

In this example, COUNT(*) is used to count all rows, regardless of values. The count is returned in num_cust.

The following example counts just the customers with an e-mail address:

▼ Input

```
SELECT COUNT(cust_email) AS num_cust
FROM customers;
```

▼ Output

```
+----------+
| num_cust |
+----------+
|        3 |
+----------+
```

▼ Analysis

This SELECT statement uses COUNT(cust_email) to count only rows with a value in the cust_email column. In this example, cust_email is 3 (meaning that only three of the five customers have e-mail addresses).

> **Note**
>
> **NULL Values**   Column rows with NULL values in them are ignored by the COUNT() function if a column name is specified, but not if the asterisk (*) is used.

The MAX() Function

MAX() returns the highest value in a specified column. MAX() requires that the column name be specified, as seen here:

▼ Input

```
SELECT MAX(prod_price) AS max_price
FROM products;
```

▼ Output

```
+-----------+
| max_price |
+-----------+
|     55.00 |
+-----------+
```

▼ Analysis

Here MAX() returns the price of the most expensive.

> **Tip**
>
> **Using MAX ( ) with Non-Numeric Data**   Although MAX() is usually used to find the highest numeric or date values, MariaDB allows it to be used to return the highest value in any column including textual columns. When used with textual data, MAX() returns the row that would be the last if the data were sorted by that column.

> **Note**
>
> **NULL Values**   Column rows with NULL values in them are ignored by the MAX() function.

The MIN() Function

MIN() does the exact opposite of MAX(); it returns the lowest value in a specified column. Like MAX(), MIN() requires that the column name be specified, as seen here:

▼ Input

```
SELECT MIN(prod_price) AS min_price
FROM products;
```

▼ Output

```
+-----------+
| min_price |
+-----------+
| 2.50      |
+-----------+
```

▼ Analysis

Here MIN() returns the price of the least expensive item in the products table.

> **Tip**
>
> **Using MIN() with Non-Numeric Data**   As with the MAX() function, MariaDB allows MIN() to be used to return the lowest value in any columns including textual columns. When used with textual data, MIN() returns the row that would be first if the data were sorted by that column.

> **Note**
>
> **NULL Values**   Column rows with NULL values in them are ignored by the MIN() function.

The SUM() Function

SUM() is used to return the sum (total) of the values in a specific column.

Here is an example to demonstrate this. The orderitems table contains the actual items in an order, and each item has an associated quantity. The total number of items ordered (the sum of all the quantity values) can be retrieved as follows:

▼ Input

```
SELECT SUM(quantity) AS items_ordered
FROM orderitems
WHERE order_num = 20005;
```

▼ Output

```
+---------------+
| items_ordered |
+---------------+
| 19            |
+---------------+
```

▼ Analysis

The function SUM(quantity) returns the sum of all the item quantities in an order, and the WHERE clause ensures that just the right order items are included.

SUM() can also be used to total calculated values. In this next example the total order amount is retrieved by totaling item_price*quantity for each item:

▼ Input

```
SELECT SUM(item_price*quantity) AS total_price
FROM orderitems
WHERE order_num = 20005;
```

▼ Output

```
+-------------+
| total_price |
+-------------+
|      149.87 |
+-------------+
```

▼ Analysis

The function SUM(item_price*quantity) returns the sum of all the expanded prices in an order, and again the WHERE clause ensures that just the correct order items are included.

> **Tip**
>
> **Performing Calculations on Multiple Columns**   All the aggregate functions can be used to perform calculations on multiple columns using the standard mathematical operators, as shown in the example.

> **Note**
>
> **NULL Values**   Column rows with NULL values in them are ignored by the SUM() function.

Aggregates on Distinct Values

The five aggregate functions can all be used in two ways:

- To perform calculations on all rows, specify the ALL argument, or specify no argument at all (because ALL is the default behavior).
- To only include unique values, specify the DISTINCT argument.

> **Tip**
>
> **ALL Is Default**   The ALL argument need not be specified because it is the default behavior. If DISTINCT is not specified, ALL is assumed.

The following example uses the AVG() function to return the average product price offered by a specific vendor. It is the same SELECT statement used in the previous example, but here the DISTINCT argument is used so the average only takes into account unique prices:

▼ Input

```
SELECT AVG(DISTINCT prod_price) AS avg_price
FROM products
WHERE vend_id = 1003;
```

▼ Output

```
+-----------+
| avg_price |
+-----------+
| 15.998000 |
+-----------+
```

▼ Analysis

As you can see, in this example avg_price is higher when DISTINCT is used because there are multiple items with the same lower price. Excluding them raises the average price.

> **Caution**
>
> **Using DISTINCT With COUNT()**   DISTINCT may only be used with COUNT() if a column name is specified. DISTINCT may not be used with COUNT(*), and so COUNT(DISTINCT *) is not allowed and generates an error. Similarly, DISTINCT must be used with a column name and not with a calculation or expression.

> **Tip**
>
> **Using DISTINCT with MIN() and MAX()**   Although DISTINCT can technically be used with MIN() and MAX(), there is actually no value in doing so. The minimum and maximum values in a column are the same whether or not only distinct values are included.

Combining Aggregate Functions

All the examples of aggregate functions used thus far have involved a single function. But actually, SELECT statements may contain as few or as many aggregate functions as needed. Look at this example:

▼ Input

```
SELECT COUNT(*) AS num_items,
       MIN(prod_price) AS price_min,
       MAX(prod_price) AS price_max,
       AVG(prod_price) AS price_avg
FROM products;
```

▼ Output

```
+-----------+-----------+-----------+-----------+
| num_items | price_min | price_max | price_avg |
+-----------+-----------+-----------+-----------+
|        14 |      2.50 |     55.00 | 16.133571 |
+-----------+-----------+-----------+-----------+
```

▼ Analysis

Here a single SELECT statement performs four aggregate calculations in one step and returns four values (the number of items in the products table; and the highest, lowest, and average product prices).

> **Tip**
>
> **Naming Aliases**   When specifying alias names to contain the results of an aggregate function, try not to use the name of an actual column in the table. Although there is nothing actually illegal about doing so, using unique names makes your SQL easier to understand and work with (and troubleshoot in the future).

Summary

Aggregate functions are used to summarize data. MariaDB supports a range of aggregate functions, all of which can be used in multiple ways to return just the results you need. These functions are designed to be highly efficient, and they usually return results far more quickly than you could calculate them yourself within your own client application.

13

Grouping Data

In this chapter, you learn how to group data so you can summarize subsets of table contents. This involves two new SELECT statement clauses: the GROUP BY clause and the HAVING clause.

Understanding Data Grouping

In the last chapter, you learned that the SQL aggregate functions can be used to summarize data. This enables you to count rows, calculate sums and averages, and obtain high and low values without having to retrieve all the data.

All the calculations thus far were performed on all the data in a table or on data that matched a specific WHERE clause. As a reminder, the following example returns the number of products offered by vendor 1003:

▼ **Input**
```
SELECT COUNT(*) AS num_prods
FROM products
WHERE vend_id = 1003;
```

▼ **Output**
```
+-----------+
| num_prods |
+-----------+
|         7 |
+-----------+
```

But what if you want to return the number of products offered by each vendor? Or products offered by vendors who offer a single product, or only those who offer more than ten products?

This is where groups come into play. Grouping enables you to divide data into logical sets so you can perform aggregate calculations on each group.

Creating Groups

Groups are created using the GROUP BY clause in your SELECT statement. The best way to understand this is to look at an example:

▼ Input

```
SELECT vend_id, COUNT(*) AS num_prods
FROM products
GROUP BY vend_id;
```

▼ Output

```
+---------+-----------+
| vend_id | num_prods |
+---------+-----------+
|    1001 |         3 |
|    1002 |         2 |
|    1003 |         7 |
|    1005 |         2 |
+---------+-----------+
```

▼ Analysis

The previous SELECT statement specifies two columns, vend_id, which contains the ID of a product's vendor, and num_prods, which is a calculated field (created using the COUNT(*) function). The GROUP BY clause instructs MariaDB to sort the data and group it by vend_id. This causes num_prods to be calculated once per vend_id rather than once for the entire table. As you can see in the output, vendor 1001 has 3 products listed, vendor 1002 has 2 products listed, vendor 1003 has 7 products listed, and vendor 1005 has 2 products listed.

Because you used GROUP BY, you did not have to specify each group to be evaluated and calculated. That was done automatically. The GROUP BY clause instructs MariaDB to group the data and then perform the aggregate on each group rather than on the entire result set.

Before you use GROUP BY, here are some important rules about its use that you need to know:

- GROUP BY clauses can contain as many columns as you want. This enables you to nest groups, providing you with more granular control over how data is grouped.

- If you have nested groups in your GROUP BY clause, data is summarized at the last specified group. In other words, all the columns specified are evaluated together when grouping is established (so you won't get data back for each individual column level).

- Every column listed in GROUP BY must be a retrieved column or a valid expression (but not an aggregate function). If an expression is used in the SELECT, that same expression must be specified in GROUP BY. Aliases cannot be used.

- Aside from the aggregate calculations statements, every column in your SELECT statement should be present in the GROUP BY clause.

- If the grouping column contains a row with a NULL value, NULL will be returned as a group. If there are multiple rows with NULL values, they'll all be grouped together.

- The GROUP BY clause must come after any WHERE clause and before any ORDER BY clause.

> **Tip**
>
> **Using** ROLLUP   To obtain values at each group and at a summary level (for each group), use the WITH ROLLUP keyword, as seen here:
>
> ```
> SELECT vend_id, COUNT(*) AS num_prods
> FROM products
> GROUP BY vend_id WITH ROLLUP;
> ```

Filtering Groups

In addition to being able to group data using GROUP BY, MariaDB also allows you to filter which groups to include and which to exclude. For example, you might want a list of all customers who have made at least two orders. To obtain this data you must filter based on the complete group, not on individual rows.

You've already seen the WHERE clause in action (introduced back in Chapter 6, "Filtering Data.") But WHERE does not work here because WHERE filters specific rows, not groups. As a matter of fact, WHERE has no idea what a group is.

So what do you use instead of WHERE? MariaDB provides yet another clause for this purpose: the HAVING clause. HAVING is similar to WHERE. In fact, all types of WHERE clauses you learned about thus far can also be used with HAVING. The only difference is that WHERE filters rows and HAVING filters groups.

> **Tip**
>
> **HAVING Supports All of WHERE's Operators**   In Chapter 6 and Chapter 7, "Advanced Data Filtering," you learned about WHERE clause conditions (including wild-card conditions and clauses with multiple operators). All the techniques and options you learned about WHERE can be applied to HAVING. The syntax is identical; just the keyword is different.

So how do you filter rows? Look at the following example:

▼ Input

```
SELECT cust_id, COUNT(*) AS orders
FROM orders
GROUP BY cust_id
HAVING COUNT(*) >= 2;
```

▼ Output

```
+---------+--------+
| cust_id | orders |
+---------+--------+
|   10001 |      2 |
+---------+--------+
```

▼ Analysis

The first three lines of this SELECT statement are similar to the statements seen previously. The final line adds a HAVING clause that filters on those groups with a COUNT(*) >= 2—two or more orders.

As you can see, a WHERE clause does not work here because the filtering is based on the group aggregate value, not on the values of specific rows.

> **Note**
>
> **The Difference Between HAVING and WHERE** Here's another way to look at it: WHERE filters before data is grouped, and HAVING filters after data is grouped. This is an important distinction; rows that are eliminated by a WHERE clause are not included in the group. This could change the calculated values, which in turn could affect which groups are filtered based on the use of those values in the HAVING clause.

So is there ever a need to use both WHERE and HAVING clauses in one statement? Actually, yes, there is. Suppose you want to further filter the previous statement so it returns any customers who placed two or more orders in the past 12 months. To do that, you can add a WHERE clause that filters out just the orders placed in the past 12 months. You then add a HAVING clause to filter just the groups with two or more rows in them.

To better demonstrate this, look at the following example that lists all vendors who have 2 or more products priced at 10 or more:

▼ Input

```
SELECT vend_id, COUNT(*) AS num_prods
FROM products
WHERE prod_price >= 10
GROUP BY vend_id
HAVING COUNT(*) >= 2;
```

▼ Output

```
+---------+-----------+
| vend_id | num_prods |
+---------+-----------+
|    1003 |         4 |
|    1005 |         2 |
+---------+-----------+
```

▼ Analysis

This statement warrants an explanation. The first line is a basic SELECT using an aggregate function—much like the examples thus far. The WHERE clause filters all rows with a prod_price of at least 10. Data is then grouped by vend_id, and then a HAVING clause filters just those groups with a count of 2 or more. Without the WHERE clause two extra rows would have been retrieved (vendor 1002 that only sells products all priced under 10, and vendor 1001 that sells three products but only one of them is priced greater or equal to 10) as seen here:

▼ Input

```
SELECT vend_id, COUNT(*) AS num_prods
FROM products
GROUP BY vend_id
HAVING COUNT(*) >= 2;
```

▼ Output

```
+---------+-----------+
| vend_id | num_prods |
+---------+-----------+
|    1001 |         3 |
|    1002 |         2 |
|    1003 |         7 |
|    1005 |         2 |
+---------+-----------+
```

Grouping and Sorting

It is important to understand that GROUP BY and ORDER BY are different, even though they often accomplish the same thing. Table 13.1 summarizes the differences between them.

Table 13.1 ORDER BY **Versus** GROUP BY

ORDER BY	GROUP BY
Sorts generated output.	Groups rows. The output might not be in group order, however.
Any columns (even columns not selected) may be used.	Only selected columns or expressions columns may be used, and every selected column expression must be used.
Never required.	Required if using columns (or expressions) with aggregate functions.

The first difference listed in Table 13.1 is extremely important. More often than not, you will find that data grouped using GROUP BY will indeed be output in group order. But that is not always the case, and it is not actually required by the SQL specifications. Furthermore, you might actually want it sorted differently than it is grouped. Just because you group data one way (to obtain group-specific aggregate values) does not mean that you want the output sorted that same way. You should always provide an explicit ORDER BY clause as well, even if it is identical to the GROUP BY clause.

> **Tip**
>
> **Don't Forget** ORDER BY As a rule, anytime you use a GROUP BY clause, you should also specify an ORDER BY clause. That is the only way to ensure that data is sorted properly. Never rely on GROUP BY to sort your data.

To demonstrate the use of both GROUP BY and ORDER BY, let's look at an example. The following SELECT statement is similar to the ones seen previously. It retrieves the order number and total order price of all orders with a total price of 50 or more:

▼ Input

```
SELECT order_num, SUM(quantity*item_price) AS ordertotal
FROM orderitems
GROUP BY order_num
HAVING SUM(quantity*item_price) >= 50;
```

▼ Output

```
+-----------+------------+
| order_num | ordertotal |
+-----------+------------+
|     20005 | 149.87     |
|     20006 | 55.00      |
|     20007 | 1000.00    |
|     20008 | 125.00     |
+-----------+------------+
```

To sort the output by order total, all you need to do is add an ORDER BY clause, as follows:

▼ Input

```
SELECT order_num, SUM(quantity*item_price) AS ordertotal
FROM orderitems
GROUP BY order_num
HAVING SUM(quantity*item_price) >= 50
ORDER BY ordertotal;
```

▼ Output

```
+-----------+------------+
| order_num | ordertotal |
+-----------+------------+
|     20006 | 55.00      |
|     20008 | 125.00     |
|     20005 | 149.87     |
|     20007 | 1000.00    |
+-----------+------------+
```

▼ Analysis

In this example, the GROUP BY clause is used to group the data by order number (the order_num column) so that the SUM(*) function can return the total order price. The HAVING clause filters the data so that only orders with a total price of 50 or more are returned. Finally, the output is sorted using the ORDER BY clause.

SELECT **Clause Ordering**

This is probably a good time to review the order in which SELECT statement clauses are to be specified. Table 13.2 lists all the clauses you have learned thus far, in the order they must be used.

Table 13.2   SELECT **Clauses and Their Sequence**

Clause	Description	Required
SELECT	Columns or expressions to be returned	Yes
FROM	Table to retrieve data from	Only if selecting data from a table
WHERE	Row-level filtering	No
GROUP BY	Group specification	Only if calculating aggregates by group
HAVING	Group-level filtering	No
ORDER BY	Output sort order	No
LIMIT	Number of rows to retrieve	No

Summary

In Chapter 12, "Summarizing Data," you learned how to use the SQL aggregate functions to perform summary calculations on your data. In this chapter, you learned how to use the GROUP BY clause to perform these calculations on groups of data, returning results for each group. You saw how to use the HAVING clause to filter specific groups. You also learned the difference between ORDER BY and GROUP BY and between WHERE and HAVING.

14

Working with Subqueries

In this chapter, you learn what subqueries are and how to use them.

Understanding Subqueries

SELECT statements are SQL queries. All the SELECT statements you have seen thus far are simple queries: single statements retrieving data from individual database tables.

> **New Term**
>
> **Query** Any SQL statement. However, the term is usually used to refer to SELECT statements.

SQL also enables you to create *subqueries*: queries that are embedded into other queries. Why would you want to do this? The best way to understand this concept is to look at a couple of examples.

Filtering by Subquery

The database tables used in all the chapters in this book are relational tables. (See Appendix B, "The Example Tables," for a description of each of the tables and their relationships.) Order data is stored in two tables. The orders table stores a single row for each order containing order number, customer ID, and order date. The individual order items are stored in the related orderitems table. The orders table does not store customer information. It only stores a customer ID. The actual customer information is stored in the customers table.

Now suppose you wanted a list of all the customers who ordered item TNT2. What would you have to do to retrieve this information? Here are the steps:

1. Retrieve the order numbers of all orders containing item TNT2.

2. Retrieve the customer ID of all the customers who have orders listed in the order numbers returned in the previous step.

3. Retrieve the customer information for all the customer IDs returned in the previous step.

Each of these steps can be executed as a separate query. By doing so, you use the results returned by one SELECT statement to populate the WHERE clause of the next SELECT statement.

You can also use subqueries to combine all three queries into one single statement.

The first SELECT statement should be self-explanatory by now. It retrieves the order_num column for all order items with a prod_id of TNT2. The output lists the two orders containing this item:

▼ Input
```
SELECT order_num
FROM orderitems
WHERE prod_id = 'TNT2';
```

▼ Output
```
+-----------+
| order_num |
+-----------+
|     20005 |
|     20007 |
+-----------+
```

The next step is to retrieve the customer IDs associated with orders 20005 and 20007. Using the IN clause described in Chapter 7, "Advanced Data Filtering," you can create a SELECT statement as follows:

▼ Input
```
SELECT cust_id
FROM orders
WHERE order_num IN (20005,20007);
```

▼ Output
```
+---------+
| cust_id |
+---------+
|   10001 |
|   10004 |
+---------+
```

Now, combine the two queries by turning the first (the one that returned the order numbers) into a subquery. Look at the following SELECT statement:

▼ Input

```
SELECT cust_id
FROM orders
WHERE order_num IN (SELECT order_num
                    FROM orderitems
                    WHERE prod_id = 'TNT2');
```

▼ Output

```
+---------+
| cust_id |
+---------+
|   10001 |
|   10004 |
+---------+
```

▼ Analysis

Subqueries are always processed starting with the innermost SELECT statement and working outward. When the preceding SELECT statement is processed, MariaDB actually performs two operations.

First it runs the subquery:

```
SELECT order_num FROM orderitems WHERE prod_id='TNT2'
```

That query returns the two order numbers 20005 and 20007. Those two values are then passed to the WHERE clause of the outer query in the comma-delimited format required by the IN operator. The outer query now becomes

```
SELECT cust_id FROM orders WHERE order_num IN (20005,20007)
```

As you can see, the output is correct and exactly the same as the output returned by the previous hard-coded WHERE clause.

> **Tip**
>
> **Formatting Your SQL** SELECT statements containing subqueries can be difficult to read and debug, especially as they grow in complexity. Breaking up the queries over multiple lines and indenting the lines appropriately as shown here can greatly simplify working with subqueries.

You now have the IDs of all the customers who ordered item TNT2. The next step is to retrieve the customer information for each of those customer IDs. The SQL statement to retrieve the two columns is

▼ Input

```
SELECT cust_name, cust_contact
FROM customers
WHERE cust_id IN (10001,10004);
```

Instead of hard-coding those customer IDs, you can turn this WHERE clause into yet another subquery:

▼ Input

```
SELECT cust_name, cust_contact
FROM customers
WHERE cust_id IN (SELECT cust_id
                  FROM orders
                  WHERE order_num IN (SELECT order_num
                                      FROM orderitems
                                      WHERE prod_id = 'TNT2'));
```

▼ Output

```
+-----------------+---------------+
| cust_name       | cust_contact  |
+-----------------+---------------+
| Coyote Inc.     | Y Lee         |
| Yosemite Place  | Y Sam         |
+-----------------+---------------+
```

▼ Analysis

To execute this SELECT statement, MariaDB had to actually perform three SELECT statements. The innermost subquery returned a list of order numbers that were then used as the WHERE clause for the subquery above it. That sub-query returned a list of customer IDs that were used as the WHERE clause for the top-level query. The top-level query actually returned the desired data.

As you can see, using subqueries in a WHERE clause enables you to write pow-erful and flexible SQL statements. There is no limit imposed on the number of subqueries that can be nested, although in practice you will find that perfor-mance tells you when you are nesting too deeply.

> **Caution**
>
> **Columns Must Match**   When using a subquery in a WHERE clause (as seen here), make sure that the SELECT statement has the same number of columns as in the WHERE clause. Usually, a single column will be returned by the subquery and matched against a single column, but multiple columns may be used if needed.

Although usually used in conjunction with the IN operator, subqueries can also be used to test for equality (using =), nonequality (using <>), and so on.

> **Caution**
>
> **Subqueries and Performance**   The code shown here works, and it achieves the desired result. However, using subqueries is not always the most efficient way to perform this type of data retrieval, although it might be. More on this is in Chapter 15, "Joining Tables," where you revisit this same example.

Using Subqueries as Calculated Fields

Another way to use subqueries is in creating calculated fields. Suppose you want to display the total number of orders placed by every customer in your customers table. Orders are stored in the orders table along with the appropriate customer ID.

To perform this operation, follow these steps:

1. Retrieve the list of customers from the customers table.

2. For each customer retrieved, count the number of associated orders in the orders table.

As you learned in the previous two chapters, you can use SELECT COUNT(*) to count rows in a table, and by providing a WHERE clause to filter a specific customer ID, you can count just that customer's orders. For example, the following code counts the number of orders placed by customer 10001:

▼ **Input**

```
SELECT COUNT(*) AS orders
FROM orders
WHERE cust_id = 10001;
```

To perform that COUNT(*) calculation for each customer, use COUNT* as a subquery. Look at the following code:

▼ **Input**

```
SELECT cust_name,
       cust_state,
       (SELECT COUNT(*)
        FROM orders
        WHERE orders.cust_id = customers.cust_id) AS orders
FROM customers
ORDER BY cust_name;
```

▼ Output

```
+-----------------+-------------+--------+
| cust_name       | cust_state  | orders |
+-----------------+-------------+--------+
| Coyote Inc.     | MI          |      2 |
| E Fudd          | IL          |      1 |
| Mouse House     | OH          |      0 |
| Wascals         | IN          |      1 |
| Yosemite Place  | AZ          |      1 |
+-----------------+-------------+--------+
```

▼ Analysis

This SELECT statement returns three columns for every customer in the customers table: cust_name, cust_state, and orders. orders is a calculated field that is set by a subquery provided in parentheses. That subquery is executed once for every customer retrieved. In this example, the subquery is executed five times because five customers were retrieved.

The WHERE clause in the subquery is a little different from the WHERE clauses used previously because it uses fully qualified column names (first mentioned in Chapter 4, "Retrieving Data"). The following clause tells SQL to compare the cust_id in the orders table to the one currently being retrieved from the customers table:

```
WHERE orders.cust_id = customers.cust_id
```

> **New Term**
> **Correlated subquery** A subquery that refers to the outer query.

The type of subquery is called a *correlated subquery*. This syntax—the table name and the column name separated by a period—must be used whenever there is possible ambiguity about column names. Why? Well, let's look at what happens if fully qualified column names are not used:

▼ Input

```
SELECT cust_name,
       cust_state,
       (SELECT COUNT(*)
        FROM orders
        WHERE cust_id = cust_id) AS orders
FROM customers
ORDER BY cust_name;
```

▼ Output

```
+----------------+------------+--------+
| cust_name      | cust_state | orders |
+----------------+------------+--------+
| Coyote Inc.    | MI         |      5 |
| E Fudd         | IL         |      5 |
| Mouse House    | OH         |      5 |
| Wascals        | IN         |      5 |
| Yosemite Place | AZ         |      5 |
+----------------+------------+--------+
```

▼ Analysis

Obviously the returned results are incorrect (compare them to the previous results), but why did this happen? There are two cust_id columns, one in customers and one in orders, and those two columns need to be compared to correctly match orders with their appropriate customers. Without fully qualifying the column names, MariaDB assumes you are comparing the cust_id in the orders table to itself. And

```
SELECT COUNT(*) FROM orders WHERE cust_id = cust_id;
```

always returns the total number of orders in the orders table (because MariaDB checks to see that every order's cust_id matches itself, which it always does, of course).

▼ Analysis

Although subqueries are useful in constructing this type of SELECT statement, care must be taken to properly qualify ambiguous column names.

> **Note**
>
> **Always More Than One Solution**   As explained earlier in this chapter, although the sample code shown here works, it is often not the most efficient way to perform this type of data retrieval. You revisit this example in a later chapter.

> **Tip**
>
> **Build Queries with Subqueries Incrementally**   Testing and debugging queries with subqueries can be tricky, particularly as these statements grow in complexity. The safest way to build (and test) queries with subqueries is to do so incrementally, in much the same way as MariaDB processes them. Build and test the innermost query first. Then build and test the outer query with hard-coded data, and only after you have verified that it is working embed the subquery. Then test it again. And keep repeating these steps as for each additional query. This takes just a little longer to construct your queries, but doing so saves you a lot of time later (when you try to figure out why queries are not working) and significantly increases the likelihood of them working the first time.

Summary

In this chapter, you learned what subqueries are and how to use them. The most common uses for subqueries are in WHERE clauses, in IN operators, and for populating calculated columns. You saw examples of both of these types of operations.

15

Joining Tables

In this chapter, you learn what joins are, why they are used, and how to create SELECT statements using them.

Understanding Joins

One of SQL's most powerful features is the capability to join tables on-the-fly within data retrieval queries. Joins are one of the most important operations you can perform using SQL SELECT, and a good understanding of joins and join syntax is an extremely important part of learning SQL.

Before you can effectively use joins, you must understand relational tables and the basics of relational database design. What follows is by no means a complete coverage of the subject, but it should be enough to get you up and running.

Understanding Relational Tables

The best way to understand relational tables is to look at a real-world example.

Suppose you had a database table containing a product catalog, with each catalog item in its own row. The kind of information you would store with each item would include a product description and price, along with vendor information about the company that creates the product.

Now suppose you had multiple catalog items created by the same vendor. Where would you store the vendor information (things such as vendor name, address, and contact information)? You wouldn't want to store that data along with the products for several reasons:

- Because the vendor information is the same for each product that vendor produces, repeating the information for each product is a waste of time and storage space.

- If vendor information changes (for example, if the vendor moves or his area code changes), you would need to update every occurrence of the vendor information.

- When data is repeated (that is, the vendor information is used with each product), there is a high likelihood that the data will not be entered exactly the same way each time. Inconsistent data is extremely difficult to use in reporting.

The key here is that having multiple occurrences of the same data is never a good thing, and that principle is the basis for relational database design. Relational tables are designed so information is split into multiple tables, one for each data type. The tables are related to each other through common values (and thus the *relational* in relational design).

In our example, you can create two tables, one for vendor information and one for product information. The vendors table contains all the vendor information, one table row per vendor, along with a unique identifier for each vendor. This value, called a *primary key*, can be a vendor ID, or any other unique value. (Primary keys were first mentioned in Chapter 1, "Understanding SQL").

The products table stores only product information, and no vendor specific information other than the vendor ID (the vendors table's primary key). This key, called a *foreign key*, relates the vendors table to the products table, and using this vendor ID enables you to use the vendors table to find the details about the appropriate vendor.

> **New Term**
>
> **Foreign key**   A column in one table that contains the primary key values from another table, thus defining the relationships between tables.

What does this do for you? Well, consider the following:

- Vendor information is never repeated, and so time and space are not wasted.

- If vendor information changes, you can update a single record in the vendors table. Data in related tables does not change.

- As no data is repeated, the data used is obviously consistent, making data reporting and manipulation much simpler.

The bottom line is that relational data can be stored efficiently and manipulated easily. Because of this, relational databases scale far better than nonrelational databases.

> **New Term**
>
> **Scale**   Able to handle an increasing load without failing. A well-designed database or application is said to *scale well.*

Why Use Joins?

As just explained, breaking data into multiple tables enables more efficient storage, easier manipulation, and greater scalability. But these benefits come with a price.

If data is stored in multiple tables, how can you retrieve that data with a single SELECT statement?

The answer is to use a join. Simply put, a join is a mechanism used to associate tables within a SELECT statement (and thus the name join). Using a special syntax, multiple tables can be joined so a single set of output is returned, and the join associates the correct rows in each table on-the-fly.

> **Note**
>
> **Maintaining Referential Integrity**   It is important to understand that a join is not a physical entity—in other words, it does not exist in the actual database tables. A join is created by MariaDB as needed, and it persists for the duration of the query execution.
>
> When using relational tables, it is important that only valid data is inserted into relational columns. Going back to the example, if products were stored in the products table with an invalid vendor ID (one not present in the vendors table), those products would be inaccessible because they would not be related to any vendor.
>
> To prevent this from occurring, MariaDB can be instructed to only allow valid values (ones present in the vendors table) in the vendor ID column in the products table. This is known as maintaining *referential integrity* and is achieved by specifying the primary and foreign keys as part of the table definitions (as explained in Chapter 21, "Creating and Manipulating Tables").
>
> For an example of this, see the create.sql script used to create the crashcourse database tables. The ALTER TABLE statements at the end of the file are defining constraints to enforce referential integrity.

Creating a Join

Creating a join is simple. You must specify all the tables to be included and how they are related to each other. Look at the following example:

▼ Input

```
SELECT vend_name, prod_name, prod_price
FROM vendors, products
WHERE vendors.vend_id = products.vend_id
ORDER BY vend_name, prod_name;
```

▼ Output

```
+-------------+-----------------+------------+
| vend_name   | prod_name       | prod_price |
+-------------+-----------------+------------+
| ACME        | Bird seed       | 10.00      |
| ACME        | Carrots         | 2.50       |
| ACME        | Detonator       | 13.00      |
| ACME        | Safe            | 50.00      |
| ACME        | Sling           | 4.49       |
| ACME        | TNT (1 stick)   | 2.50       |
| ACME        | TNT (5 sticks)  | 10.00      |
| Anvils R Us | .5 ton anvil    | 5.99       |
| Anvils R Us | 1 ton anvil     | 9.99       |
| Anvils R Us | 2 ton anvil     | 14.99      |
| Jet Set     | JetPack 1000    | 35.00      |
| Jet Set     | JetPack 2000    | 55.00      |
| LT Supplies | Fuses           | 3.42       |
| LT Supplies | Oil can         | 8.99       |
+-------------+-----------------+------------+
```

▼ Analysis

Take a look at the preceding code. The SELECT statement starts in the same way as all the statements you've looked at thus far, by specifying the columns to be retrieved. The big difference here is that two of the specified columns (prod_name and prod_price) are in one table, whereas the other (vend_name) is in another table.

Now look at the FROM clause. Unlike all the prior SELECT statements, this one has two tables listed in the FROM clause, vendors and products. These are the names of the two tables that are being joined in this SELECT statement. The tables are correctly joined with a WHERE clause that instructs MariaDB to match vend_id in the vendors table with vend_id in the products table.

Notice that the columns are specified as vendors.vend_id and products. vend_id. This fully qualified column name is required here because if you just specified vend_id, MariaDB cannot tell which vend_id columns you are referring to (as there are two of them, one in each table).

> **Caution**
>
> **Fully Qualifying Column Names** You must use the fully qualified column name (table and column separated by a period) whenever there is possible ambiguity about to which column you are referring. MariaDB returns an error message if you refer to an ambiguous column name without fully qualifying it with a table name.

The Importance of the WHERE Clause

It might seem strange to use a WHERE clause to set the join relationship, but actually, there is a good reason for this. Remember, when tables are joined in a SELECT statement, that relationship is constructed on-the-fly. Nothing in the database table definitions can instruct MariaDB how to join the tables. You have to do that yourself. When you join two tables, what you are actually doing is pairing every row in the first table with every row in the second table. The WHERE clause acts as a filter to only include rows that match the specified filter condition—the join condition, in this case. Without the WHERE clause, every row in the first table is paired with every row in the second table, regardless of whether they logically go together.

> **New Term**
>
> **Cartesian product**   The results returned by a table relationship without a join condition. The number of rows retrieved is the number of rows in the first table multiplied by the number of rows in the second table.

To understand this, look at the following SELECT statement and output:

▼ Input

```
SELECT vend_name, prod_name, prod_price
FROM vendors, products
ORDER BY vend_name, prod_name;
```

▼ Output

```
+----------------+----------------+------------+
| vend_name      | prod_name      | prod_price |
+----------------+----------------+------------+
| ACME           | .5 ton anvil   | 5.99       |
| ACME           | 1 ton anvil    | 9.99       |
| ACME           | 2 ton anvil    | 14.99      |
| ACME           | Bird seed      | 10.00      |
| ACME           | Carrots        | 2.50       |
| ACME           | Detonator      | 13.00      |
| ACME           | Fuses          | 3.42       |
| ACME           | JetPack 1000   | 35.00      |
| ACME           | JetPack 2000   | 55.00      |
| ACME           | Oil can        | 8.99       |
| ACME           | Safe           | 50.00      |
| ACME           | Sling          | 4.49       |
| ACME           | TNT (1 stick)  | 2.50       |
| ACME           | TNT (5 sticks) | 10.00      |
| Anvils R Us    | .5 ton anvil   | 5.99       |
| Anvils R Us    | 1 ton anvil    | 9.99       |
```

```
| Anvils R Us     | 2 ton anvil     | 14.99 |     |
| Anvils R Us     | Bird seed       | 10.00 |     |
| Anvils R Us     | Carrots         | 2.50  |     |
| Anvils R Us     | Detonator       | 13.00 |     |
| Anvils R Us     | Fuses           | 3.42  |     |
| Anvils R Us     | JetPack 1000    | 35.00 |     |
| Anvils R Us     | JetPack 2000    | 55.00 |     |
| Anvils R Us     | Oil can         | 8.99  |     |
| Anvils R Us     | Safe            | 50.00 |     |
| Anvils R Us     | Sling           | 4.49  |     |
| Anvils R Us     | TNT (1 stick)   | 2.50  |     |
| Anvils R Us     | TNT (5 sticks)  | 10.00 |     |
| Furball Inc.    | .5 ton anvil    | 5.99  |     |
| Furball Inc.    | 1 ton anvil     | 9.99  |     |
| Furball Inc.    | 2 ton anvil     | 14.99 |     |
| Furball Inc.    | Bird seed       | 10.00 |     |
| Furball Inc.    | Carrots         | 2.50  |     |
| Furball Inc.    | Detonator       | 13.00 |     |
| Furball Inc.    | Fuses           | 3.42  |     |
| Furball Inc.    | JetPack 1000    | 35.00 |     |
| Furball Inc.    | JetPack 2000    | 55.00 |     |
| Furball Inc.    | Oil can         | 8.99  |     |
| Furball Inc.    | Safe            | 50.00 |     |
| Furball Inc.    | Sling           | 4.49  |     |
| Furball Inc.    | TNT (1 stick)   | 2.50  |     |
| Furball Inc.    | TNT (5 sticks)  | 10.00 |     |
| Jet Set         | .5 ton anvil    | 5.99  |     |
| Jet Set         | 1 ton anvil     | 9.99  |     |
| Jet Set         | 2 ton anvil     | 14.99 |     |
| Jet Set         | Bird seed       | 10.00 |     |
| Jet Set         | Carrots         | 2.50  |     |
| Jet Set         | Detonator       | 13.00 |     |
| Jet Set         | Fuses           | 3.42  |     |
| Jet Set         | JetPack 1000    | 35.00 |     |
| Jet Set         | JetPack 2000    | 55.00 |     |
| Jet Set         | Oil can         | 8.99  |     |
| Jet Set         | Safe            | 50.00 |     |
| Jet Set         | Sling           | 4.49  |     |
| Jet Set         | TNT (1 stick)   | 2.50  |     |
| Jet Set         | TNT (5 sticks)  | 10.00 |     |
| Jouets Et Ours  | .5 ton anvil    | 5.99  |     |
| Jouets Et Ours  | 1 ton anvil     | 9.99  |     |
| Jouets Et Ours  | 2 ton anvil     | 14.99 |     |
| Jouets Et Ours  | Bird seed       | 10.00 |     |
| Jouets Et Ours  | Carrots         | 2.50  |     |
| Jouets Et Ours  | Detonator       | 13.00 |     |
| Jouets Et Ours  | Fuses           | 3.42  |     |
| Jouets Et Ours  | JetPack 1000    | 35.00 |     |
| Jouets Et Ours  | JetPack 2000    | 55.00 |     |
```

```
| Jouets Et Ours | Oil can         | 8.99  |
| Jouets Et Ours | Safe            | 50.00 |
| Jouets Et Ours | Sling           | 4.49  |
| Jouets Et Ours | TNT (1 stick)   | 2.50  |
| Jouets Et Ours | TNT (5 sticks)  | 10.00 |
| LT Supplies    | .5 ton anvil    | 5.99  |
| LT Supplies    | 1 ton anvil     | 9.99  |
| LT Supplies    | 2 ton anvil     | 14.99 |
| LT Supplies    | Bird seed       | 10.00 |
| LT Supplies    | Carrots         | 2.50  |
| LT Supplies    | Detonator       | 13.00 |
| LT Supplies    | Fuses           | 3.42  |
| LT Supplies    | JetPack 1000    | 35.00 |
| LT Supplies    | JetPack 2000    | 55.00 |
| LT Supplies    | Oil can         | 8.99  |
| LT Supplies    | Safe            | 50.00 |
| LT Supplies    | Sling           | 4.49  |
| LT Supplies    | TNT (1 stick)   | 2.50  |
| LT Supplies    | TNT (5 sticks)  | 10.00 |
+----------------+----------------+-----------+
```

▼ Analysis

As you can see in the preceding output, the Cartesian product is seldom what you want. The data returned here has matched every product with every vendor, including products with the incorrect vendor (and even vendors with no products at all).

> **Caution**
>
> **Don't Forget the WHERE Clause** Make sure all your joins have WHERE clauses, or MariaDB returns far more data than you want. Similarly, make sure your WHERE clauses are correct. An incorrect filter condition causes MariaDB to return incorrect data.

> **Tip**
>
> **Cross Joins** Sometimes you'll hear the type of join that returns a Cartesian product referred to as a *cross join*.

Inner Joins

The join you have been using so far is called an *equijoin*—a join based on the testing of equality between two tables. This kind of join is also called an *inner join*. In fact, you may use a slightly different syntax for these joins, specifying the type of join explicitly. The following SELECT statement returns the exact same data as the preceding example:

▼ Input

```
SELECT vend_name, prod_name, prod_price
FROM vendors INNER JOIN products
 ON vendors.vend_id = products.vend_id;
```

▼ Analysis

The SELECT in the statement is the same as the preceding SELECT statement, but the FROM clause is different. Here the relationship between the two tables is part of the FROM clause specified as INNER JOIN. When using this syntax the join condition is specified using the special ON clause instead of a WHERE clause. The actual condition passed to ON is the same as would be passed to WHERE.

> **Note**
>
> **Which Syntax To Use?** Per the ANSI SQL specification, use of the INNER JOIN syntax is preferable. Furthermore, while the using the WHERE clause to define joins is indeed simpler, using explicit join syntax ensures that you will never forget the join condition and can impact performance, too (in some cases).

Joining Multiple Tables

SQL imposes no limit to the number of tables that may be joined in a SELECT statement. The basic rules for creating the join remain the same. First list all the tables, and then define the relationship between each. Here is an example:

▼ Input

```
SELECT prod_name, vend_name, prod_price, quantity
FROM orderitems, products, vendors
WHERE products.vend_id = vendors.vend_id
  AND orderitems.prod_id = products.prod_id
  AND order_num = 20005;
```

▼ Output

prod_name	vend_name	prod_price	quantity
.5 ton anvil	Anvils R Us	5.99	10
1 ton anvil	Anvils R Us	9.99	3
TNT (5 sticks)	ACME	10.00	5
Bird seed	ACME	10.00	1

▼ Analysis

This example displays the items in order number 20005. Order items are stored in the orderitems table. Each product is stored by its product ID, which refers to a product in the products table. The products are linked to the appropriate vendor in the vendors table by the vendor ID, which is stored with each product record. The FROM clause here lists the three tables, and the WHERE clause defines both of those join conditions. An additional WHERE condition is then used to filter just the items for order 20005.

> **Caution**
>
> **Performance Considerations**   MariaDB processes joins at runtime, relating each table as specified. This process can become resource intensive, so be careful not to join tables unnecessarily. The more tables you join, the more performance degrades.

Now would be a good time to revisit the following example from Chapter 14, "Working with Subqueries." As you will recall, this SELECT statement returns a list of customers who ordered product TNT2:

▼ Input

```
SELECT cust_name, cust_contact
FROM customers
WHERE cust_id IN (SELECT cust_id
                  FROM orders
                  WHERE order_num IN (SELECT order_num
                                      FROM orderitems
                                      WHERE prod_id = 'TNT2'));
```

As mentioned in Chapter 14, subqueries might not always be the most efficient way to perform complex SELECT operations, and so as promised, here is the same query using joins:

▼ Input

```
SELECT cust_name, cust_contact
FROM customers, orders, orderitems
WHERE customers.cust_id = orders.cust_id
  AND orderitems.order_num = orders.order_num
  AND prod_id = 'TNT2';
```

▼ Output

```
+----------------+--------------+
| cust_name      | cust_contact |
+----------------+--------------+
| Coyote Inc.    | Y Lee        |
| Yosemite Place | Y Sam        |
+----------------+--------------+
```

▼ Analysis

As explained in Chapter 14, returning the data needed in this query requires the use of three tables. But instead of using them within nested subqueries, here two joins are used to connect the tables. There are three WHERE clause conditions here. The first two connect the tables in the join, and the last one filters the data for product TNT2.

> **Tip**
>
> **It Pays to Experiment**   As you can see, there is often more than one way to perform any given SQL operation. And there is rarely a definitive right or wrong way. Performance can be affected by the type of operation, the amount of data in the tables, whether indexes and keys are present, and a whole slew of other criteria. Therefore, it is often worth experimenting with different selection mechanisms to find the one that works best for you.

Summary

Joins are one of the most important and powerful features in SQL, and using them effectively requires a basic understanding of relational database design. In this chapter, you learned some of the basics of relational database design as an introduction to learning about joins. You also learned how to create an equi-join (also known as an inner join), which is the most commonly used form of join. In the next chapter you learn how to create other types of joins.

Creating Advanced Joins

In this chapter, you learn all about additional join types—what they are and how to use them. You also learn how to use table aliases and how to use aggregate functions with joined tables.

Using Table Aliases

Back in Chapter 10, "Creating Calculated Fields," you learned how to use aliases to refer to retrieved table columns. The syntax to alias a column looks like this:

▼ **Input**
```
SELECT Concat(RTrim(vend_name), ' (', RTrim(vend_country), ')')
       AS vend_title
FROM vendors
ORDER BY vend_name;
```

In addition to using aliases for column names and calculated fields, SQL also enables you to alias table names. There are two primary reasons to do this:

- To shorten the SQL syntax
- To enable multiple uses of the same table within a single SELECT statement

Take a look at the following SELECT statement. It is basically the same statement as an example used in the previous chapter, but it has been modified to use aliases:

▼ **Input**
```
SELECT cust_name, cust_contact
FROM customers AS c, orders AS o, orderitems AS oi
WHERE c.cust_id = o.cust_id
  AND oi.order_num = o.order_num
  AND prod_id = 'TNT2';
```

▼ Analysis

Notice that the three tables in the FROM clauses all have aliases. customers AS c establishes c as an alias for customers, and so on. This enables you to use the abbreviated c instead of the full text customers. In this example, the table aliases were used only in the WHERE clause, but aliases are not limited to just WHERE. You can use aliases in the SELECT list, the ORDER BY clause, and in any other part of the statement as well.

It is also worth noting that table aliases are only used during query execution. Unlike column aliases, table aliases are never returned to the client.

Using Different Join Types

So far, you have used only simple joins known as inner joins or *equijoins*. You now take a look at three additional join types: the self join, the natural join, and the outer join.

Self Joins

As mentioned earlier, one of the primary reasons to use table aliases is to be able to refer to the same table more than once in a single SELECT statement. An example demonstrates this.

Suppose that a problem was found with a product (item id DTNTR), and you therefore wanted to know all of the products made by the same vendor to determine whether the problem applied to them, too. This query requires that you first find out which vendor creates item DTNTR, and next find which other products are made by the same vendor. The following is one way to approach this problem:

▼ Input

```
SELECT prod_id, prod_name
FROM products
WHERE vend_id = (SELECT vend_id
                 FROM products
                 WHERE prod_id = 'DTNTR');
```

▼ Output

```
+---------+----------------+
| prod_id | prod_name      |
+---------+----------------+
| DTNTR   | Detonator      |
| FB      | Bird seed      |
| FC      | Carrots        |
| SAFE    | Safe           |
| SLING   | Sling          |
| TNT1    | TNT (1 stick)  |
| TNT2    | TNT (5 sticks) |
+---------+----------------+
```

▼ Analysis

This first solution uses subqueries. The inner SELECT statement does a simple retrieval to return the vend_id of the vendor that makes item DTNTR. That ID is the one used in the WHERE clause of the outer query so all items produced by that vendor are retrieved. (You learned all about subqueries in Chapter 14, "Working with Subqueries." Refer to that chapter for more information.)

Now look at the same query using a join:

▼ Input

```
SELECT p1.prod_id, p1.prod_name
FROM products AS p1, products AS p2
WHERE p1.vend_id = p2.vend_id
  AND p2.prod_id = 'DTNTR';
```

▼ Output

```
+---------+----------------+
| prod_id | prod_name      |
+---------+----------------+
| DTNTR   | Detonator      |
| FB      | Bird seed      |
| FC      | Carrots        |
| SAFE    | Safe           |
| SLING   | Sling          |
| TNT1    | TNT (1 stick)  |
| TNT2    | TNT (5 sticks) |
+---------+----------------+
```

▼ Analysis

The two tables needed in this query are actually the same table, and so the products table appears in the FROM clause twice. Although this is perfectly legal, any references to table products would be ambiguous because MariaDB could not know to which instance of the products table you are referring.

To resolve this problem, table aliases are used. The first occurrence of products has an alias of p1, and the second has an alias of p2. Now those aliases can be used as table names. The SELECT statement, for example, uses the p1 prefix to explicitly state the full name of the desired columns. If it did not, MariaDB would return an error because there are two columns named prod_id and prod_name. It cannot know which one you want (even though, in truth, they are one and the same). The WHERE clause first joins the tables (by matching vend_id in p1 to vend_id in p2), and then it filters the data by prod_id in the second table to return only the desired data.

> **Tip**
>
> **Self Joins Instead of Subqueries**   Self joins are often used to replace statements using subqueries that retrieve data from the same table as the outer statement. Although the end result is the same, sometimes these joins execute far more quickly than do subqueries. It is usually worth experimenting with both to determine which performs better.

Natural Joins

Whenever tables are joined, at least one column appears in more than one table (the columns being joined). Standard joins (the inner joins you learned about in the previous chapter) return all data, even multiple occurrences of the same column. A *natural join* simply eliminates those multiple occurrences so only one of each column is returned.

How does it do this? The answer is it doesn't—you do it. A natural join is a join in which you select only columns that are unique. This is typically done using a wildcard (SELECT *) for one table and explicit subsets of the columns for all other tables. The following is an example:

▼ Input

```
SELECT c.*, o.order_num, o.order_date,
       oi.prod_id, oi.quantity, OI.item_price
FROM customers AS c, orders AS o, orderitems AS oi
WHERE c.cust_id = o.cust_id
  AND oi.order_num = o.order_num
  AND prod_id = 'FB';
```

▼ Analysis

In this example, a wildcard is used for the first table only. All other columns are explicitly listed so no duplicate columns are retrieved.

The truth is, every inner join you have created thus far is actually a natural join, and you will probably never even need an inner join that is not a natural join.

Outer Joins

Most joins relate rows in one table with rows in another. But occasionally, you want to include rows that have no related rows. For example, you might use joins to accomplish the following tasks:

- Count how many orders each customer placed, including customers who have yet to place an order

- List all products with order quantities, including products not ordered by anyone

- Calculate average sale sizes, taking into account customers who have not yet placed an order

In each of these examples, the join includes table rows that have no associated rows in the related table. This type of join is called an *outer join*.

The following SELECT statement is a simple inner join. It retrieves a list of all customers and their orders:

▼ Input

```
SELECT customers.cust_id, orders.order_num
FROM customers INNER JOIN orders
 ON customers.cust_id = orders.cust_id;
```

Outer join syntax is similar. To retrieve a list of all customers, including those who have placed no orders, you can do the following:

▼ Input

```
SELECT customers.cust_id, orders.order_num
FROM customers LEFT OUTER JOIN orders
 ON customers.cust_id = orders.cust_id;
```

▼ Output

```
+---------+-----------+
| cust_id | order_num |
+---------+-----------+
|   10001 |     20005 |
|   10001 |     20009 |
|   10002 |      NULL |
|   10003 |     20006 |
|   10004 |     20007 |
|   10005 |     20008 |
+---------+-----------+
```

▼ Analysis

Like the inner join seen in the previous chapter, this SELECT statement uses the keywords OUTER JOIN to specify the join type (instead of specifying it in the WHERE clause). But unlike inner joins, which relate rows in both tables, outer joins also include rows with no related rows. When using OUTER JOIN syntax you must use the RIGHT or LEFT keywords to specify the table from which to include all rows (RIGHT for the one on the right of OUTER JOIN, and LEFT for the one on the left). The previous example uses LEFT OUTER JOIN to select all the rows from the table on the left in the FROM clause (the customers table). To select all the rows from the table on the right, you use a RIGHT OUTER JOIN as seen in this example:

▼ Input

```
SELECT customers.cust_id, orders.order_num
FROM customers RIGHT OUTER JOIN orders
 ON orders.cust_id = customers.cust_id;
```

> **Note**
>
> **No *=**   MariaDB does not support the use of the simplified *= and =* syntax popularized by other DBMSs.

> **Tip**
>
> **Outer Join Types**   There are two basic forms of outer joins—the left outer join and the right outer join. The only difference between them is the order of the tables they are relating. In other words, a left outer join can be turned into a right outer join simply by reversing the order of the tables in the FROM or WHERE clause. As such, the two types of outer join can be used interchangeably, and the decision about which one is used is based purely on convenience.

Using Joins with Aggregate Functions

As you learned in Chapter 12, "Summarizing Data," aggregate functions are used to summarize data. Although all the examples of aggregate functions thus far summarized data from a single table only, these functions can also be used with joins.

To demonstrate this, let's look at an example. You want to retrieve a list of all customers and the number of orders that each has placed. The following code uses the COUNT() function to achieve this:

▼ Input

```
SELECT customers.cust_name,
       customers.cust_id,
       COUNT(orders.order_num) AS num_ord
FROM customers INNER JOIN orders
 ON customers.cust_id = orders.cust_id
GROUP BY customers.cust_id;
```

▼ Output

```
+----------------+---------+---------+
| cust_name      | cust_id | num_ord |
+----------------+---------+---------+
| Coyote Inc.    |   10001 |       2 |
| Wascals        |   10003 |       1 |
| Yosemite Place |   10004 |       1 |
| E Fudd         |   10005 |       1 |
+----------------+---------+---------+
```

▼ Analysis

This SELECT statement uses INNER JOIN to relate the customers and orders tables to each other. The GROUP BY clause groups the data by customer, and so the function call COUNT(orders.order_num) counts the number of orders for each customer and returns it as num_ord.

Aggregate functions can be used just as easily with other join types. See the following example:

▼ Input

```
SELECT customers.cust_name,
       customers.cust_id,
       COUNT(orders.order_num) AS num_ord
FROM customers LEFT OUTER JOIN orders
 ON customers.cust_id = orders.cust_id
GROUP BY customers.cust_id;
```

▼ **Output**

```
+----------------+---------+---------+
| cust_name      | cust_id | num_ord |
+----------------+---------+---------+
| Coyote Inc.    |   10001 |       2 |
| Mouse House    |   10002 |       0 |
| Wascals        |   10003 |       1 |
| Yosemite Place |   10004 |       1 |
| E Fudd         |   10005 |       1 |
+----------------+---------+---------+
```

▼ **Analysis**

This example uses a left outer join to include all customers, even those who have not placed any orders. The results show that customer Mouse House (with 0 orders) is also included this time.

Using Joins and Join Conditions

Before wrapping up this two chapter discussion on joins, it is worthwhile to summarize some key points regarding joins and their use:

- Pay careful attention to the type of join being used. More often than not, you'll want an inner join, but there are often valid uses for outer joins, too.

- Make sure you use the correct join condition, or you'll return incorrect data.

- Make sure you always provide a join condition, or you'll end up with the Cartesian product.

- You may include multiple tables in a join and even have different join types for each. Although this is legal and often useful, make sure you test each join separately before testing them together. This makes troubleshooting far simpler.

Summary

This chapter was a continuation of the previous chapter on joins. This chapter started by teaching you how and why to use aliases, and then continued with a discussion on different join types and various forms of syntax used with each. You also learned how to use aggregate functions with joins, and some important do's and don'ts to keep in mind when working with joins.

17

Combining Queries

In this chapter you learn how to use the UNION operator to combine multiple SELECT statements into one result set.

Understanding Combined Queries

Most SQL queries contain a single SELECT statement that returns data from one or more tables. MariaDB also enables you to perform multiple queries (multiple SELECT statements) and return the results as a single query result set. These combined queries are usually known as *unions* or *compound queries*.

There are basically two scenarios in which you'd use combined queries:

- To return similarly structured data from different tables in a single query

- To perform multiple queries against a single table returning the data as one query

> **Tip**
>
> **Combining Queries and Multiple WHERE Conditions**   For the most part, combining two queries to the same table accomplishes the same thing as a single query with multiple WHERE clause conditions. In other words, any SELECT statement with multiple WHERE clauses can also be specified as a combined query, as you see in the section that follows. However, the performance of each of the two techniques can vary based on the queries used. As such, it is always good to experiment to determine which is preferable for specific queries.

Creating Combined Queries

SQL queries are combined using the UNION operator. Using UNION, multiple SELECT statements can be specified, and their results can be combined into a single result set.

Using UNION

Using UNION is simple enough. All you do is specify each SELECT statement and place the keyword UNION between each.

Let's look at an example. You need a list of all products costing 5 or less. You also want to include all products made by vendors 1001 and 1002, regardless of price. Of course, you can create a WHERE clause that does this, but this time we use a UNION instead.

As just explained, creating a UNION involves writing multiple SELECT statements. First look at the individual statements:

▼ **Input**
```
SELECT vend_id, prod_id, prod_price
FROM products
WHERE prod_price <= 5;
```

▼ **Output**
```
+---------+---------+------------+
| vend_id | prod_id | prod_price |
+---------+---------+------------+
|    1003 | FC      |       2.50 |
|    1002 | FU1     |       3.42 |
|    1003 | SLING   |       4.49 |
|    1003 | TNT1    |       2.50 |
+---------+---------+------------+
```

▼ **Input**
```
SELECT vend_id, prod_id, prod_price
FROM products
WHERE vend_id IN (1001,1002);
```

▼ **Output**
```
+---------+---------+------------+
| vend_id | prod_id | prod_price |
+---------+---------+------------+
|    1001 | ANV01   |       5.99 |
|    1001 | ANV02   |       9.99 |
|    1001 | ANV03   |      14.99 |
|    1002 | FU1     |       3.42 |
|    1002 | OL1     |       8.99 |
+---------+---------+------------+
```

▼ Analysis

The first SELECT retrieves all products with a price of no more than 5. The second SELECT uses IN to find all products made by vendors 1001 and 1002.

To combine these two statements, do the following:

▼ Input

```
SELECT vend_id, prod_id, prod_price
FROM products
WHERE prod_price <= 5
UNION
SELECT vend_id, prod_id, prod_price
FROM products
WHERE vend_id IN (1001,1002);
```

▼ Output

```
+---------+---------+------------+
| vend_id | prod_id | prod_price |
+---------+---------+------------+
|    1003 | FC      | 2.50       |
|    1002 | FU1     | 3.42       |
|    1003 | SLING   | 4.49       |
|    1003 | TNT1    | 2.50       |
|    1001 | ANV01   | 5.99       |
|    1001 | ANV02   | 9.99       |
|    1001 | ANV03   | 14.99      |
|    1002 | OL1     | 8.99       |
+---------+---------+------------+
```

▼ Analysis

The preceding statements are made up of both of the previous SELECT statements separated by the UNION keyword. UNION instructs MariaDB to execute both SELECT statements and combine the output into a single query result set.

As a point of reference, here is the same query using multiple WHERE clauses instead of a UNION:

▼ Input

```
SELECT vend_id, prod_id, prod_price
FROM products
WHERE prod_price <= 5
  OR vend_id IN (1001,1002);
```

In this simple example, the UNION might actually be more complicated than using a WHERE clause. But with more complex filtering conditions, or if the data is being retrieved from multiple tables (and not just a single table), the UNION could have made the process much simpler.

UNION **Rules**

As you can see, unions are easy to use. But a few rules govern exactly which can be combined:

- A UNION must be comprised of two or more SELECT statements, each separated by the keyword UNION (so, if combining four SELECT statements, three UNION keywords would be used).

- Each query in a UNION must contain the same columns, expressions, or aggregate functions (although columns need not be listed in the same order).

- Column datatypes must be compatible: They need not be the exact same type, but they must be of a type that MariaDB can implicitly convert (for example, different numeric types or different date types).

Aside from these basic rules and restrictions, unions can be used for any data retrieval tasks.

Including or Eliminating Duplicate Rows

Go back to the preceding section titled "Using UNION" and look at the sample SELECT statements used. Notice that when executed individually, the first SELECT statement returns four rows, and the second SELECT statement returns five rows. However, when the two SELECT statements are combined with a UNION, only eight rows are returned, not nine.

The UNION automatically removes any duplicate rows from the query result set (in other words, it behaves just as multiple WHERE clause conditions in a single SELECT would). Because vendor 1002 creates a product that costs less than 5, that row was returned by both SELECT statements. When the UNION was used, the duplicate row was eliminated.

This is the default behavior of UNION, but you can change this if you want. If you do, in fact, want all occurrences of all matches returned, you can use UNION ALL instead of UNION.

Look at the following example:

▼ Input

```
SELECT vend_id, prod_id, prod_price
FROM products
WHERE prod_price <= 5
UNION ALL
SELECT vend_id, prod_id, prod_price
FROM products
WHERE vend_id IN (1001,1002);
```

▼ Output

```
+---------+---------+------------+
| vend_id | prod_id | prod_price |
+---------+---------+------------+
|    1003 | FC      |       2.50 |
|    1002 | FU1     |       3.42 |
|    1003 | SLING   |       4.49 |
|    1003 | TNT1    |       2.50 |
|    1001 | ANV01   |       5.99 |
|    1001 | ANV02   |       9.99 |
|    1001 | ANV03   |      14.99 |
|    1002 | FU1     |       3.42 |
|    1002 | OL1     |       8.99 |
+---------+---------+------------+
```

▼ Analysis

Using UNION ALL, MariaDB does not eliminate duplicates. Therefore, the preceding example returns nine rows, one of them occurring twice.

> **Tip**
>
> **UNION Versus WHERE**   The beginning of this chapter said that UNION almost always accomplishes the same thing as multiple WHERE conditions. UNION ALL is the form of UNION that accomplishes what cannot be done with WHERE clauses. If you do, in fact, want all occurrences of matches for every condition (including duplicates), you must use UNION ALL and not WHERE.

Sorting Combined Query Results

SELECT statement output is sorted using the ORDER BY clause. When combining queries with a UNION, only one ORDER BY clause may be used, and it must occur after the final SELECT statement. There is little point in sorting part of a result set one way and part another way, and so multiple ORDER BY clauses are not allowed.

The following example sorts the results returned by the previously used UNION:

▼ Input

```
SELECT vend_id, prod_id, prod_price
FROM products
WHERE prod_price <= 5
UNION
SELECT vend_id, prod_id, prod_price
FROM products
WHERE vend_id IN (1001,1002)
ORDER BY vend_id, prod_price;
```

▼ Output

```
+---------+---------+------------+
| vend_id | prod_id | prod_price |
+---------+---------+------------+
|    1001 | ANV01   |       5.99 |
|    1001 | ANV02   |       9.99 |
|    1001 | ANV03   |      14.99 |
|    1002 | FU1     |       3.42 |
|    1002 | OL1     |       8.99 |
|    1003 | TNT1    |       2.50 |
|    1003 | FC      |       2.50 |
|    1003 | SLING   |       4.49 |
+---------+---------+------------+
```

▼ Analysis

This UNION takes a single ORDER BY clause after the final SELECT statement. Even though the ORDER BY appears to only be a part of that last SELECT statement, MariaDB in fact uses it to sort all the results returned by all the SELECT statements.

> **Note**
>
> **Combining Different Tables**   For the sake of simplicity, all the examples in this chapter combined queries using the same table. However, everything you learned here also applies to using UNION to combine queries of different tables.

Summary

In this chapter, you learned how to combine SELECT statements with the UNION operator. Using UNION, you can return the results of multiple queries as one combined query, either including or excluding duplicates. The use of UNION can greatly simplify complex WHERE clauses and retrieving data from multiple tables.

18

Full-Text Searching

In this chapter, you learn how to use MariaDB's full-text searching capabilities to perform sophisticated data querying and selection.

Understanding Full-Text Searching

> **Note**
>
> **Not All Engines Support Full-Text Searching** As explained in Chapter 21, "Creating and Manipulating Tables," MariaDB supports the use of several underlying database engines. The MariaDB ARIA engine supports full-text searching, and all the `crashcourse` tables were created to use the ARIA engine (by specifying `ENGINE=Aria`) in the `CREATE TABLE` statements in `create.sql`. Keep this in mind, if you need full-text searching functionality in your applications; you need to use an engine that supports this capability.

In Chapter 8, "Using Wildcard Filtering," you were introduced to the `LIKE` keyword that is used to match text (and partial text) using wildcard operators. Using `LIKE` it is possible to locate rows that contain specific values or parts of values, regardless of the location of those values within row columns.

In Chapter 9, "Searching Using Regular Expressions," text-based searching was taken one step further with the introduction to using regular expressions to match column values. Using regular expressions, it is possible to write sophisticated matching patterns to locate the desired rows.

But as useful as these search mechanisms are, they have several important limitations:

- **Performance**—Wildcard and regular expression matching usually requires that MariaDB try and match each and every row in a table (and table indexes are rarely of use in these searches). As such, these searches can be time-consuming as the number of rows to be searched grows.

- **Explicit control**—Using wildcard and regular expression matching, it is difficult (and not always possible) to explicitly control what is and what is not matched. An example of this is a search specifying a word that must be matched, a word that must not be matched, and a word that may or may not be matched but only if the first word is indeed matched.

- **Intelligent results**—Although wildcard- and regular expression–based searching provide for flexible searching, neither provides an intelligent way to select results. For example, searching for a specific word returns all rows that contain that word and does not distinguish between rows that contain a single match and those that contain multiple matches (ranking them as potentially better matches). Similarly, searches for a specific word does not find rows that do not contain that word but do contain other related words.

All these limitations and more are addressed by full-text searching. When full-text searching is used, MariaDB does not need to look at each row individually, analyzing and processing each word individually. Rather, an index of the words (in specified columns) is created by MariaDB, and searches can be made against those words. MariaDB can thus quickly and efficiently determine which words match (which rows contain them), which don't, how often they match, and so on.

Using Full-Text Searching

To perform full-text searches, the columns to be searched must be indexed and constantly reindexed as data changes. MariaDB handles all indexing and rein-dexing automatically after table columns have been appropriately designated.

After indexing, SELECT can be used with Match() and Against() to actually perform the searches.

Enabling Full-Text Searching Support

Generally, full-text searching is enabled when a table is created. The CREATE TABLE statement (which is introduced in Chapter 21) accepts a FULLTEXT clause, which is a comma-delimited list of the columns to be indexed.

The following CREATE statement demonstrates the use of the FULLTEXT clause:

▼ Input

```
CREATE TABLE productnotes
(
  note_id    int            NOT NULL AUTO_INCREMENT,
  prod_id    char(10)       NOT NULL,
  note_date datetime        NOT NULL,
  note_text  text           NULL ,
  PRIMARY KEY(note_id),
  FULLTEXT(note_text)
) ENGINE=Maria;
```

▼ Analysis

We look at the CREATE TABLE statement in detail in Chapter 21. For now, just note that this CREATE_TABLE statement defines table productnotes and lists the columns that it is to contain. One of those columns is named note_ text, and it is indexed by MariaDB for full-text searching as instructed by the clause FULLTEXT(note_text). Here FULLTEXT indexes a single column, but multiple columns may be specified if needed.

Once defined, MariaDB automatically maintains the index. When rows are added, updated, or deleted, the index is automatically updated accordingly.

FULLTEXT may be specified at table creation time, or later on (in which case all existing data would have to be immediately indexed).

> **Tip**
>
> **Don't Use FULLTEXT When Importing Data**   Updating indexes takes time—not a lot of time, but time nonetheless. If you are importing data into a new table, you should not enable FULLTEXT indexing at that time. Rather, first import all the data, and then modify the table to define FULLTEXT. This makes for a much faster data import (and the total time needed to index all data will be less than the sum of the time needed to index each row individually).

Performing Full-Text Searches

After indexing, full-text searches are performed using two functions: Match() to specify the columns to be searched and Against() to specify the search expression to be used.

Here is a basic example:

▼ Input

```
SELECT note_text
FROM productnotes
WHERE Match(note_text) Against('rabbit');
```

▼ Output

```
+-----------------------------------------------------------------------+
| note_text                                                             |
+-----------------------------------------------------------------------|
| Customer complaint: rabbit has been able to detect trap, food apparently |
| less effective now.                                                   |
| Quantity varies, sold by the sack load. All guaranteed to be bright and |
| orange, and suitable for use as rabbit bait.                          |
+-----------------------------------------------------------------------+
```

▼ Analysis

The SELECT statement retrieves a single column, note_text. For the WHERE clause, a full-text search is performed. Match(note_text) instructs MariaDB to perform the search against that named column, and Against('rabbit') specifies the word rabbit as the search text. As two rows contained the word rabbit, those two rows were returned.

> **Note**
>
> **Use Full Match() Specification**   The value passed to Match() must be the same as the one used in the FULLTEXT() definition. If multiple columns are specified, all of them must be listed (and in the correct order).

> **Note**
>
> **Searches Are Case Insensitive**   Full-text searches are case insensitive, unless BINARY mode (not covered in this chapter) is used.

The truth is that the search just performed could just as easily have used a LIKE clause, as seen here:

▼ Input

```
SELECT note_text
FROM productnotes
WHERE note_text LIKE '%rabbit%';
```

▼ Output

```
+-----------------------------------------------------------------------+
| note_text                                                             |
+-----------------------------------------------------------------------|
| Quantity varies, sold by the sack load. All guaranteed to be bright and |
| orange, and suitable for use as rabbit bait.                          |
| Customer complaint: rabbit has been able to detect trap, food apparently |
| less effective now.                                                   |
+-----------------------------------------------------------------------+
```

▼ Analysis

This SELECT retrieves the same two rows, but the order is different (although that may not always be the case).

Neither of the two SELECT statements contained an ORDER BY clause. The latter (using LIKE) returns data in no particularly useful order. But the former (using full-text searching) returns data ordered by how well the text matched. Both rows contained the word rabbit, but the row that contained the word rabbit as the third word ranked higher than the row that contained it as the twentieth word. This is important. An important part of full-text searching is the ranking of results. Rows with a higher rank are returned first (as there is a higher degree of likelihood that those are the ones you really wanted).

To demonstrate how ranking works, look at this example:

▼ Input

```
SELECT note_text,
       Match(note_text) Against('rabbit') AS rank
FROM productnotes;
```

▼ Output

```
+----------------------------------------------------------+----------------+
| note_text                                                | rank           |
+----------------------------------------------------------+----------------+
| Customer complaint: Sticks not individually wrapped, too |              0 |
| easy to mistakenly detonate all at once. Recommend       |                |
| individual wrapping.                                     |                |
| Can shipped full, refills not available. Need to order   |              0 |
| new can if refill needed.                                |                |
| Safe is combination locked, combination not provided     |              0 |
| with safe. This is rarely a problem as safes are         |                |
| typically blown up or dropped by customers               |                |
| Quantity varies, sold by the sack load. All guaranteed   | 1.5905543170914|
| to be bright and orange, and suitable for as rabbit bait.|                |
| Included fuses are short and have been known to detonate  |              0 |
| too quickly for some customers. Longer fuses are         |                |
| available (item FU1) and should be recommended.          |                |
| Matches not included, recommend purchase of matches or   |              0 |
| detonator (item DTNTR).                                  |                |
| Please note that no returns will be accepted if safe     |              0 |
| opened using explosives.                                 |                |
| Multiple customer returns, anvils failing to drop fast   |              0 |
| enough or falling backwards on purchaser. Recommend      |                |
| that customer considers using heavier anvils.            |                |
| Item is extremely heavy. Designed for dropping, not      |              0 |
| recommended for use with slings, ropes, pulleys, or      |                |
| tightropes.                                              |                |
```

```
| Customer complaint: rabbit has been able to detect trap, | 1.6408053837485|
| food apparently less effective now.                      |                |
| Shipped unassembled, requires common tools (including    |            0   |
| oversized hammer).                                       |                |
| Customer complaint: Circular hole in safe floor can      |            0   |
| apparently be easily cut with handsaw.                   |                |
| Customer complaint: Not heavy enough to generate flying  |            0   |
| stars around head of victim. If being purchased for      |                |
| dropping, recommend ANV02 or ANV03 instead.              |                |
| Call from individual trapped in safe plummeting to the   |            0   |
| ground, suggests an escape hatch be added. Comment       |                |
| forwarded to vendor.                                     |                |
+----------------------------------------------------------+----------------+
```

▼ Analysis

Here Match() and Against() are used in the SELECT instead of the WHERE clause. This causes all rows to be returned (as there is no WHERE clause). Match() and Against() are used to create a calculated column (with the alias rank), which contains the ranking value calculated by the full-text search. The ranking is calculated by MariaDB based on the number of words in the row, the number of unique words, the total number of words in the entire index, and the number of rows that contain the word. As you can see, the rows that do not contain the word rabbit have a rank of 0 (and were therefore not selected by the WHERE clause in the previous example). The two rows that do contain the word rabbit each have a rank value, and the one with the word earlier in the text has a higher rank value than the one in which the word appeared later. This helps demonstrate how full-text searching eliminates rows (those with a rank of 0), and how it sorts results (by rank in descending order).

> **Note**
>
> **Ranking Multiple Search Terms** If multiple search terms are specified, those that contain the most matching words will be ranked higher than those with less (or just a single match).

As you can see, full-text searching offers functionality not available with simple LIKE searches. And as data is indexed, full-text searches are considerably faster, too.

Using Query Expansion

Query expansion is used to try to widen the range of returned full-text search results. Consider the following scenario. You want to find all notes with references to anvils in them. Only one note contains the word anvils, but you also want any other rows that may be related to your search, even if the specific word anvils is not contained within them.

This is a job for query expansion. When query expansion is used, MariaDB makes two passes through the data and indexes to perform your search:

- First, a basic full-text search is performed to find all rows that match the search criteria.

- Next, MariaDB examines those matched rows and selects all useful words (we explain how MariaDB figures out what is useful and what is not shortly).

- Then, MariaDB performs the full-text search again, this time using not just the original criteria, but also all the useful words.

Using query expansion you can therefore find results that might be relevant, even if they don't contain the exact words for which you were looking.

Here is an example. First, a simple full-text search, without query expansion:

▼ Input

```
SELECT note_text
FROM productnotes
WHERE Match(note_text) Against('anvils');
```

▼ Output

```
+---------------------------------------------------------------------------+
| note_text                                                                 |
+---------------------------------------------------------------------------+
| Multiple customer returns, anvils failing to drop fast enough or falling  |
| backwards on purchaser. Recommend that customer considers using heavier   |
| anvils.                                                                   |
+---------------------------------------------------------------------------+
```

▼ Analysis

Only one row contains the word anvils, so only one row is returned.

Here is the same search, this time using query expansion:

▼ Input

```
SELECT note_text
FROM productnotes
WHERE Match(note_text) Against('anvils' WITH QUERY EXPANSION);
```

▼ Output

```
+------------------------------------------------------------------+
| note_text                                                        |
+------------------------------------------------------------------+
| Multiple customer returns, anvils failing to drop fast enough or falling |
| backwards on purchaser. Recommend that customer considers using heavier  |
| anvils.                                                          |
| Customer complaint: Sticks not individually wrapped, too easy to |
| mistakenly detonate all at once. Recommend individual wrapping.  |
| Customer complaint: Not heavy enough to generate flying stars around head |
| of victim. If being purchased for dropping, recommend ANV02 or ANV03 |
| instead.                                                         |
| Please note that no returns will be accepted if safe opened using |
| explosives.                                                      |
| Customer complaint: rabbit has been able to detect trap, food apparently |
| less effective now.                                              |
| Customer complaint: Circular hole in safe floor can apparently be easily |
| cut with handsaw.                                                |
| Matches not included, recommend purchase of matches or detonator (item |
| DTNTR).                                                          |
+------------------------------------------------------------------+
```

▼ Analysis

This time seven rows were returned. The first contains the word `anvils` and is thus ranked highest. The second row has nothing to do with `anvils`, but as it contains two words that are also in the first row (`customer` and `recommend`) it was retrieved, too. The third row also contains those same two words, but they are further into the text and further apart, and so it was included, but ranked third. And this third row does indeed refer to anvils (by their product name).

As you can see, query expansion greatly increases the number of rows returned, but in doing so also increases the number of returns that you might not actually want.

> **Tip**
>
> **The More Rows the Better** The more rows in your table (and the more text within those rows), the better the results returned when using query expansion.

Boolean Text Searches

MariaDB supports an additional form of full-text searching called *boolean mode*. In boolean mode you may provide specifics as to

- Words to be matched

- Words to be excluded (if a row contained this word it would not be returned, even though other specified words were matched)

- Ranking hints (specifying which words are more important than others so they can be ranked higher)

- Expression grouping

- And more

Tip

Useable Even Without a FULLTEXT Index   Boolean mode differs from the full-text search syntax used thus far in that it may be used even if no FULLTEXT index is defined. However, this would be a slow operation (and the performance would degrade further as data volume increased).

To demonstrate what IN BOOLEAN MODE does, here is a simple example:

▼ Input

```
SELECT note_text
FROM productnotes
WHERE Match(note_text) Against('heavy' IN BOOLEAN MODE);
```

▼ Output

```
+----------------------------------------------------------------------+
| note_text                                                            |
+----------------------------------------------------------------------+
| Item is extremely heavy. Designed for dropping, not recommended for use |
| with slings, ropes, pulleys, or tightropes.                          |
| Customer complaint: Not heavy enough to generate flying stars around head |
| of victim. If being purchased for dropping, recommend ANV02 or ANV03 |
| instead.                                                             |
+----------------------------------------------------------------------+
```

▼ Analysis

This full-text search retrieves all rows containing the word heavy (there are two of them). The keywords IN BOOLEAN MODE are specified, but no boolean operators are actually specified and so the results are just as if boolean mode had not been specified.

> **Note**
>
> **IN BOOLEAN MODE Behaves Differently**   Although the results in this example are the same as they would be without IN BOOLEAN MODE, there is an important difference in behavior (even if it did not manifest itself in this particular example). I point these out in the "Full-Text Search Usage Notes" section later in this chapter.

To match the rows that contain heavy but not any word beginning with rope, the following can be used:

▼ Input

```
SELECT note_text
FROM productnotes
WHERE Match(note_text) Against('heavy -rope*' IN BOOLEAN MODE);
```

▼ Output

```
+----------------------------------------------------------------------+
| note_text                                                            |
+----------------------------------------------------------------------+
| Customer complaint: Not heavy enough to generate flying stars around head |
| of victim. If being purchased for dropping, recommend ANV02 or ANV03 |
| instead.                                                             |
+----------------------------------------------------------------------+
```

▼ Analysis

This time only one row is returned. Again, the word heavy is matched, but this time -rope* instructs MariaDB to explicitly exclude any row that contains rope* (any word beginning with rope, including ropes, which is why one of the rows was excluded).

You have now seen two full-text search boolean operators: - excludes a word and * is the truncation operator (think of it as a wildcard used at the end of a word). Table 18.1 lists all the supported boolean operators.

Table 18.1 Full-Text Boolean Operators

Privilege	Description
+	Include, word must be present.
–	Exclude, word must not be present.
>	Include, and increase ranking value.
<	Include, and decrease ranking value.
( )	Group words into subexpressions (allowing them to be included, excluded, ranked, and so forth as a group).
~	Negate a word's ranking value.
*	Wildcard at end of word.
" "	Defines a phrase. (As opposed to a list of individual words, the entire phrase is matched for inclusion or exclusion.)

Here are some more examples to demonstrate the use of some of these operators:

▼ Input

```
SELECT note_text
FROM productnotes
WHERE Match(note_text) Against('+rabbit +bait' IN BOOLEAN MODE);
```

▼ Analysis

This search matches rows that contain both the words rabbit and bait.

▼ Input

```
SELECT note_text
FROM productnotes
WHERE Match(note_text) Against('rabbit bait' IN BOOLEAN MODE);
```

▼ Analysis

Without operators specified, this search matches rows that contain at least one of rabbit or bait.

▼ Input

```
SELECT note_text
FROM productnotes
WHERE Match(note_text) Against('"rabbit bait"' IN BOOLEAN MODE);
```

▼ Analysis

This search matches the phrase rabbit bait instead of the two words rabbit and bait.

▼ Input

```
SELECT note_text
FROM productnotes
WHERE Match(note_text) Against('>rabbit <carrot' IN BOOLEAN MODE);
```

▼ Analysis

Match both rabbit and carrot, increasing the rank of the former and decreasing the rank of the latter.

▼ Input

```
SELECT note_text
FROM productnotes
WHERE Match(note_text) Against('+safe +(<combination)' IN BOOLEAN MODE);
```

▼ Analysis

This search matches the words `safe` and `combination`, lowering the ranking of the latter.

> **Note**
>
> **Ranked, But Not Sorted**   In boolean mode, rows will not be returned sorted descending by ranking score.

Full-Text Search Usage Notes

Before finishing this chapter, here are some important notes pertaining to the use of full-text searching:

- When indexing full-text data, short words are ignored and are excluded from the index. Short words are defined as those having three or fewer characters (this number can be changed if needed).

- MariaDB comes with a built-in list of *stopwords*, words that are always ignored when indexing full-text data. This list can be overridden if needed. (Refer to the MariaDB documentation to learn how to accomplish this.)

- Many words appear so frequently that searching on them would be useless (too many results would be returned). As such, MariaDB honors a 50% rule—if a word appears in 50% or more of the rows, it is treated as a stopword and is effectively ignored. (The 50% rule is not used for IN BOOLEAN MODE).

- Full-text searching never returns any results if there are fewer than three rows in a table (because every word is always in at least 50% of the rows).

- Single quote characters in words are ignored. For example, `don't` is indexed as `dont`.

- Languages that don't have word delimiters (including Japanese and Chinese) will not return full-text results properly.

- As already noted, full-text searching is not supported in all database engines (it is supported in ARIA and MyISAM).

> **Note**
>
> **No Proximity Operators** One feature supported by many full-text search engines is proximity searching, the ability to search for words that are near each other (in the same sentence, in the same paragraph, or no more than a specific number of words apart, and so on). Proximity operators are not yet supported by MariaDB full-text searching, although this is planned for a future release.

Summary

In this chapter, you learned why full-text searching is used, and how to use the MariaDB Match() and Against() functions to perform these searches. You also learned about query expansion as a way to increase the chances of finding related matches, and how to use boolean mode for more granular lookup control.

19

Inserting Data

In this chapter, you learn how to insert data into tables using the SQL INSERT statement.

Understanding Data Insertion

SELECT is undoubtedly the most frequently used SQL statement (which is why the past 18 chapters were dedicated to it). But there are three other frequently used SQL statements that you should learn. The first one is INSERT. (You get to the other two in the next chapter.)

As its name suggests, INSERT is used to insert (add) rows to a database table. Insert can be used in several ways:

- To insert a single complete row
- To insert a single partial row
- To insert multiple rows
- To insert the results of a query

We look at each of these in the following sections.

> **Tip**
>
> **INSERT and System Security** Use of the INSERT statement can be disabled per table or per user using MariaDB security, as explained in Chapter 28, "Managing Security."

Inserting Complete Rows

The simplest way to insert data into a table is to use the basic INSERT syntax, which requires that you specify the table name and the values to be inserted into the new row. Here is an example of this:

▼ Input

```
INSERT INTO Customers
VALUES(NULL,
   'Pep E. LaPew',
   '100 Main Street',
   'Los Angeles',
   'CA',
   '90046',
   'USA',
   NULL,
   NULL);
```

> **Note**
>
> **No Output**   INSERT statements usually generate no output.

▼ Analysis

The preceding example inserts a new customer into the customers table. The data to be stored in each table column is specified in the VALUES clause, and a value must be provided for every column. If a column has no value (for example, the cust_contact and cust_email columns), the NULL value should be used (assuming the table allows no value to be specified for that column). The columns must be populated in the order in which they appear in the table definition. The first column, cust_id, is also NULL. This is because that column is automatically incremented by MariaDB each time a row is inserted. You'd not want to specify a value (that is MariaDB's job), and nor could you omit the column (as already stated, every column must be listed), and so a NULL value is specified (it is ignored by MariaDB, which inserts the next available cust_id value in its place).

Although this syntax is indeed simple, it is not at all safe and should generally be avoided at all costs. The previous SQL statement is highly dependent on the order in which the columns are defined in the table. It also depends on information about that order being readily available. Even if it is available, there is no guarantee that the columns will be in the exact same order the next time the table is reconstructed. Therefore, writing SQL statements that depend on specific column ordering is unsafe. If you do so, something will inevitably break at some point.

The safer (and unfortunately more cumbersome) way to write the INSERT statement is as follows:

▼ Input

```
INSERT INTO customers(cust_name,
    cust_address,
    cust_city,
    cust_state,
    cust_zip,
    cust_country,
    cust_contact,
    cust_email)
VALUES('Pep E. LaPew',
    '100 Main Street',
    'Los Angeles',
    'CA',
    '90046',
    'USA',
    NULL,
    NULL);
```

▼ Analysis

This example does the exact same thing as the previous INSERT statement, but this time the column names are explicitly stated in parentheses after the table name. When the row is inserted MariaDB matches each item in the columns list with the appropriate value in the VALUES list. The first entry in VALUES corresponds to the first specified column name. The second value corresponds to the second column name, and so on.

Because column names are provided, the VALUES must match the specified column names in the order in which they are specified, and not necessarily in the order that the columns appear in the actual table. The advantage of this is that, even if the table layout changes, the INSERT statement will still work correctly. You'll also notice that the NULL for cust_id was not needed; the cust_id column was not listed in the column list and so no value was needed.

The following INSERT statement populates all the row columns (just as before), but it does so in a different order. Because the column names are specified, the insertion works correctly:

▼ Input

```
INSERT INTO customers(cust_name,
    cust_contact,
    cust_email,
    cust_address,
    cust_city,
    cust_state,
    cust_zip,
```

```
    cust_country)
VALUES('Pep E. LaPew',
    NULL,
    NULL,
    '100 Main Street',
    'Los Angeles',
    'CA',
    '90046',
    'USA');
```

> **Tip**
>
> **Always Use a Columns List**   As a rule, never use INSERT without explicitly specifying the column list. This greatly increases the probability that your SQL will continue to function in the event that table changes occur.

> **Caution**
>
> **Use VALUES Carefully**   Regardless of the INSERT syntax being used, the correct number of VALUES must be specified. If no column names are provided, a value must be present for every table column. If columns names are provided, a value must be present for each listed column. If none is present, an error message will be generated, and the row will not be inserted.

Using this syntax, you can also omit columns. This means you provide values only for some columns, but not for others. (You've actually already seen an example of this, cust_id was omitted when column names were explicitly listed.)

> **Caution**
>
> **Omitting Columns**   You may omit columns from an INSERT operation if the table definition so allows. One of the following conditions must exist:
>
> ■ The column is defined as allowing NULL values (no value at all).
>
> ■ A default value is specified in the table definition. This means the default value will be used if no value is specified.
>
> If you omit a value from a table that does not allow NULL values and does not have a default, MariaDB generates an error message, and the row is not inserted.

> **Tip**
>
> **Improving Overall Performance**   Databases are frequently accessed by multiple clients, and it is MariaDB's job to manage which requests are processed and in which order. INSERT operations can be time consuming (especially if there are many indexes to be updated), and this can hurt the performance of SELECT statements waiting to be · processed.

If data retrieval is of utmost importance (as it usually is), you can instruct MariaDB to lower the priority of your INSERT statement by adding the keyword LOW_PRIORITY in between INSERT and INTO, like this:

```
INSERT LOW_PRIORITY INTO
```

Incidentally, this also applies to the UPDATE and DELETE statements that you learn about in the next chapter.

Inserting Multiple Rows

INSERT inserts a single row into a table. But what if you need to insert multiple rows? You could simply use multiple INSERT statements, and could even submit them all at once, each terminated by a semicolon, like this:

▼ Input

```
INSERT INTO customers(cust_name,
   cust_address,
   cust_city,
   cust_state,
   cust_zip,
   cust_country)
VALUES('Pep E. LaPew',
   '100 Main Street',
   'Los Angeles',
   'CA',
   '90046',
   'USA');
INSERT INTO customers(cust_name,
   cust_address,
   cust_city,
   cust_state,
   cust_zip,
   cust_country)
VALUES('M. Martian',
   '42 Galaxy Way',
   'New York',
   'NY',
   '11213',
   'USA');
```

Or, as long as the column names (and order) are identical in each INSERT, you could combine the statements as follows:

▼ Input

```
INSERT INTO customers(cust_name,
    cust_address,
    cust_city,
    cust_state,
    cust_zip,
    cust_country)
VALUES(
        'Pep E. LaPew',
        '100 Main Street',
        'Los Angeles',
        'CA',
        '90046',
        'USA'
    ),
    (
        'M. Martian',
        '42 Galaxy Way',
        'New York',
        'NY',
        '11213',
        'USA'
    );
```

▼ Analysis

Here a single INSERT statement has multiple sets of values, each enclosed within parentheses and separated by commas.

> **Tip**
>
> **Improving INSERT Performance** This technique can improve the performance of your database processing, as MariaDB processes multiple insertions in a single INSERT faster than it processes multiple INSERT statements.

Inserting Retrieved Data

INSERT is usually used to add a row to a table using specified values. Another form of INSERT can be used to insert the result of a SELECT statement into a table. This is known as INSERT SELECT, and, as its name suggests, it is made up of an INSERT statement and a SELECT statement.

Suppose you want to merge a list of customers from another table into your customers table. Instead of reading one row at a time and inserting it with INSERT, you can do the following:

> **Note**
>
> **Instructions Needed for the Next Example** The following example imports data from a table named `custnew` into the `customers` table. To try this example, create a new table named `custnew` using the `CREATE TABLE customers` statement in `create.sql`, and obviously replacing `customers` with `custnew`. Then add a few customers of your own, being careful to not use `cust_id` values that were already used in `customers` (the subsequent `INSERT` operation will fail if primary key values are duplicated). The easiest way to do this is just start the numbers much higher, perhaps at `20000`.

▼ Input

```
INSERT INTO customers(cust_id,
    cust_contact,
    cust_email,
    cust_name,
    cust_address,
    cust_city,
    cust_state,
    cust_zip,
    cust_country)
SELECT cust_id,
    cust_contact,
    cust_email,
    cust_name,
    cust_address,
    cust_city,
    cust_state,
    cust_zip,
    cust_country
FROM custnew;
```

▼ Analysis

This example uses `INSERT SELECT` to import all the data from `custnew` into `customers`. Instead of listing the `VALUES` to be inserted, the `SELECT` statement retrieves them from `custnew`. Each column in the `SELECT` corresponds to a column in the specified columns list. How many rows will this statement insert? That depends on how many rows are in the `custnew` table. If the table is empty, no rows are inserted (and no error is generated because the operation is still valid). If the table does, in fact, contain data, all that data is inserted into `customers`.

This example imports `cust_id` (and assumes that you have ensured that `cust_id` values are not duplicated). You could also simply omit that column (from both the `INSERT` and the `SELECT`) so MariaDB would generate new values.

> **Tip**
>
> **Column Names in INSERT SELECT**   This example uses the same column names in both the INSERT and SELECT statements for simplicity's sake. But there is no requirement that the column names match. In fact, MariaDB does not even pay attention to the column names returned by the SELECT. Rather, the column position is used, so the first column in the SELECT (regardless of its name) is used to populate the first specified table column, and so on. This is useful when importing data from tables that use different column names.

The SELECT statement used in an INSERT SELECT can include a WHERE clause to filter the data to be inserted.

> **Note**
>
> **More Examples**   Looking for more examples of INSERT use? See the example table population scripts (described in Appendix B, "The Example Tables") used to create the example tables in this book.

Summary

In this chapter, you learned how to use INSERT to insert rows into a database table. You learned several other ways to use INSERT, and why explicit column specification is preferred. You also learned how to use INSERT SELECT to import rows from another table. In the next chapter, you learn how to use UPDATE and DELETE to further manipulate table data.

20

Updating and Deleting Data

In this chapter, you learn how to use the UPDATE and DELETE statements to enable you to further manipulate your table data.

Updating Data

To update (modify) data in a table the UPDATE statement is used. UPDATE can be used in two ways:

- To update specific rows in a table
- To update all rows in a table

Let's take a look at each of these uses.

> **Caution**
>
> **Don't Omit the WHERE Clause** Special care must be exercised when using UPDATE because it is all too easy to mistakenly update every row in your table. Please read this entire section on UPDATE before using this statement.

> **Tip**
>
> **UPDATE and Security** Use of the UPDATE statement can be restricted and controlled. More on this in Chapter 28, "Managing Security."

The UPDATE statement is easy to use—some would say too easy. The basic format of an UPDATE statement is made up of three parts:

- The table to be updated
- The column names and their new values
- The filter condition that determines which rows should be updated

Let's take a look at a simple example. Customer 10005 now has an e-mail address, and so his record needs updating. The following statement performs this update:

▼ Input

```
UPDATE customers
SET cust_email = 'elmer@fudd.com'
WHERE cust_id = 10005;
```

▼ Analysis

The UPDATE statement always begins with the name of the table being updated. In this example, it is the customers table. The SET command is then used to assign the new value to a column. As used here, the SET clause sets the cust_email column to the specified value:

```
SET cust_email = 'elmer@fudd.com'
```

The UPDATE statement finishes with a WHERE clause that tells MariaDB which row to update. Without a WHERE clause, MariaDB would update all the rows in the customers table with this new e-mail address—definitely not the desired effect.

Updating multiple columns requires a slightly different syntax:

▼ Input

```
UPDATE customers
SET cust_name = 'The Fudds',
    cust_email = 'elmer@fudd.com'
WHERE cust_id = 10005;
```

▼ Analysis

When updating multiple columns, only a single SET command is used, and each column = value pair is separated by a comma. (No comma is specified after the last column.) In this example, columns cust_name and cust_email are updated for customer 10005.

> **Tip**
>
> **Using Subqueries in an UPDATE Statement**   Subqueries may be used in UPDATE statements, enabling you to update columns with data retrieved with a SELECT statement. Refer to Chapter 14, "Working with Subqueries," for more information on subqueries and their uses.

> **Tip**
>
> **The IGNORE Keyword** If your UPDATE statement updates multiple rows and an error occurs while updating one or more of those rows, the entire UPDATE operation is cancelled (and any rows updated before the error occurred are restored to their original values). To continue processing updates, even if an error occurs, use the IGNORE keyword, like this:
>
> UPDATE IGNORE customers ...

To delete a column's value, you can set it to NULL (assuming the table is defined to allow NULL values). You can do this as follows:

▼ Input

```
UPDATE customers
SET cust_email = NULL
WHERE cust_id = 10005;
```

Here the NULL keyword is used to save no value to the cust_email column.

Deleting Data

To delete (remove) data from a table, the DELETE statement is used. DELETE can be used in two ways:

- To delete specific rows from a table
- To delete all rows from a table

We now take a look at each of these.

> **Caution**
>
> **Don't Omit the WHERE Clause** Special care must be exercised when using DELETE because it is all too easy to mistakenly delete every row from your table. Please read this entire section on DELETE before using this statement.

> **Tip**
>
> **DELETE and Security** Use of the DELETE statement can be restricted and controlled. More on this in Chapter 28.

I already stated that UPDATE is easy to use. The good (and bad) news is that DELETE is even easier to use.

The following statement deletes a single row from the customers table:

▼ Input

```
DELETE FROM customers
WHERE cust_id = 10006;
```

▼ Analysis

This statement should be self-explanatory. DELETE FROM requires that you specify the name of the table from which the data is to be deleted. The WHERE clause filters which rows are to be deleted. In this example, only customer 10006 will be deleted. If the WHERE clause were omitted, this statement would delete every customer in the table.

DELETE takes no column names or wildcard characters. DELETE deletes entire rows, not columns. To delete specific columns use an UPDATE statement (as seen earlier in this chapter).

> **Note**
>
> **Table Contents, Not Tables**   The DELETE statement deletes rows from tables, even all rows from tables. But DELETE never deletes the table itself.

> **Tip**
>
> **Faster Deletes**   If you really do want to delete all rows from a table, don't use DELETE. Instead, use the TRUNCATE TABLE statement, which accomplishes the same thing but does it much more quickly (TRUNCATE actually drops and re-creates the table, instead of deleting each row individually).

Guidelines for Updating and Deleting Data

The UPDATE and DELETE statements used in the previous sections all have WHERE clauses, and there is a good reason for this. If you omit the WHERE clause, the UPDATE or DELETE is applied to every row in the table. In other words, if you execute an UPDATE without a WHERE clause, every row in the table is updated with the new values. Similarly if you execute DELETE without a WHERE clause, all the contents of the table are deleted.

Here are some best practices that many SQL programmers follow:

- Never execute an UPDATE or a DELETE without a WHERE clause unless you really do intend to update and delete every row.

- Make sure every table has a primary key (refer to Chapter 15, "Joining Tables," if you have forgotten what this is) and use it as the WHERE clause whenever possible. (You may specify individual primary keys, multiple values, or value ranges.)

- Before you use a WHERE clause with an UPDATE or a DELETE, first test it with a SELECT to make sure it is filtering the right records—it is far too easy to write incorrect WHERE clauses.

- Use database enforced referential integrity (refer to Chapter 15 for this one, too) so MariaDB does not allow the deletion of rows that have data in other tables related to them.

> **Caution**
>
> **Use with Caution**   The bottom line is that MariaDB has no Undo button. Be very careful using UPDATE and DELETE, or you might find yourself updating and deleting the wrong data.

Summary

In this chapter, you learned how to use the UPDATE and DELETE statements to manipulate the data in your tables. You learned the syntax for each of these statements, as well as the inherent dangers they expose. You also learned why WHERE clauses are so important in UPDATE and DELETE statements, and you were given guidelines to follow to help ensure that data does not get damaged inadvertently.

21

Creating and Manipulating Tables

In this chapter you learn the basics of table creation, alteration, and deletion.

Creating Tables

MariaDB SQL statements are not used just for table data manipulation. Indeed, SQL statements can be used to perform all database and table operations, including the creation and manipulation of tables themselves.

There are generally two ways to create database tables:

- Using an administration tool (like the ones discussed in Chapter 2, "Introducing MariaDB") that can be used to create and manage database tables interactively.

- Tables may also be manipulated directly with MariaDB SQL statements.

To create tables programmatically, the CREATE TABLE SQL statement is used. It is worth noting that when you use interactive tools, you are actually using MariaDB SQL statements. Instead of your writing these statements, however, the interface generates and executes the SQL seamlessly for you (the same is true for changes to existing tables).

> **Tip**
>
> **Additional Examples** For additional examples of table creation scripts, see the code used to create the sample tables used in this book.

> **Note**
>
> **Just the Basics**   MariaDB supports a vast array of table creation options, far more than a single chapter can do justice to. In this chapter we cover the basics, just so you can get a feel for what's involved in table creation, and so that the accompanying table creation scripts make sense. To learn more about all that CREATE TABLE can do, consult the MariaDB documentation.

Basic Table Creation

To create a table using CREATE TABLE, you must specify the following information:

- The name of the new table specified after the keywords CREATE TABLE.

- The name and definition of the table columns separated by commas.

The CREATE TABLE statement may also include other keywords and options, but at a minimum you need the table name and column details. The following MariaDB SQL statement creates the customers table used throughout this book:

▼ Input

```
CREATE TABLE customers
(
   cust_id      int        NOT NULL AUTO_INCREMENT,
   cust_name    char(50)   NOT NULL ,
   cust_address char(50)   NULL ,
   cust_city    char(50)   NULL ,
   cust_state   char(5)    NULL ,
   cust_zip     char(10)   NULL ,
   cust_country char(50)   NULL ,
   cust_contact char(50)   NULL ,
   cust_email   char(255)  NULL ,
   PRIMARY KEY (cust_id)
) ENGINE=Aria;
```

▼ Analysis

As you can see in the preceding statement, the table name is specified immediately following the CREATE TABLE keywords. The actual table definition (all the columns) is enclosed within parentheses. The columns themselves are separated by commas. This particular table is made up of nine columns.

Each column definition starts with the column name (which must be unique within the table), followed by the column's datatype. (Refer to Chapter 1, "Understanding SQL," for an explanation of datatypes. In addition, Appendix C, "MariaDB Datatypes," lists the datatypes supported by MariaDB.) The table's primary key may be specified at table creation time using the PRIMARY KEY keywords; here, column cust_id is specified as the primary key column. The entire statement is terminated with a semicolon after the closing parenthesis. (Ignore the ENGINE=Aria and AUTO_INCREMENT statements for now; we come back to that later.)

> **Tip**
>
> **Statement Formatting** As you will recall, whitespace is ignored in SQL statements. Statements can be typed on one long line or broken up over many lines. It makes no difference at all. This enables you to format your SQL as best suits you. The preceding CREATE TABLE statement is a good example of SQL statement formatting—the code is specified over multiple lines, with the column definitions indented for easier reading and editing. Formatting your SQL this way is entirely optional, but highly recommended.

> **Tip**
>
> **Handling Existing Tables** When you create a new table, the table name specified must not exist or you'll generate an error. To prevent accidental overwriting, SQL requires that you first manually remove a table (see later sections for details) and then re-create it, rather than just overwriting it.
>
> If you want to create a table only if it does not already exist, specify IF NOT EXISTS after the table name. This does not check to see that the schema of the existing table matches the one you are about to create. It simply checks to see whether the table name exists, and only proceeds with table creation if it does not.

Working with NULL Values

Back in Chapter 6, "Filtering Data," you learned that NULL values are no values or the lack of a value. A column that allows NULL values also allows rows to be inserted with no value at all in that column. A column that does not allow NULL values does not accept rows with no value—in other words, that column will always be required when rows are inserted or updated.

Every table column is either a NULL column or a NOT NULL column, and that state is specified in the table definition at creation time. Take a look at the following example:

▼ Input

```
CREATE TABLE orders
(
  order_num  int       NOT NULL AUTO_INCREMENT,
  order_date datetime NOT NULL ,
  cust_id    int       NOT NULL ,
  PRIMARY KEY (order_num)
) ENGINE=Aria;
```

▼ Analysis

This statement creates the orders table used throughout this book. orders contains three columns: order number, order date, and the customer ID. All three columns are required, and so each contains the keyword NOT NULL. This prevents the insertion of columns with no value. If someone tries to insert no value, an error will be returned, and the insertion will fail.

This next example creates a table with a mixture of NULL and NOT NULL columns:

▼ Input

```
CREATE TABLE vendors
(
  vend_id       int       NOT NULL AUTO_INCREMENT,
  vend_name     char(50) NOT NULL ,
  vend_address char(50) NULL ,
  vend_city     char(50) NULL ,
  vend_state   char(5)   NULL ,
  vend_zip     char(10) NULL ,
  vend_country char(50) NULL ,
  PRIMARY KEY (vend_id)
) ENGINE=Aria;
```

▼ Analysis

This statement creates the vendors table used throughout this book. The vendor ID and vendor name columns are both required, and are, therefore, specified as NOT NULL. The five remaining columns all allow NULL values, and so NOT NULL is not specified. NULL is the default setting, so if NOT NULL is not specified, NULL is assumed.

> **Caution**
>
> **Understanding NULL**   Don't confuse NULL values with empty strings. A NULL value is the lack of a value; it is not an empty string. If you were to specify ' ' (two single quotes with nothing in between them), that would be allowed in a NOT NULL column. An empty string is a valid value; it is not no value. NULL values are specified with the keyword NULL, not with an empty string.

Primary Keys Revisited

As already explained, primary key values must be unique. That is, every row in a table must have a unique primary key value. If a single column is used for the primary key, it must be unique; if multiple columns are used, the combination of them must be unique.

The CREATE TABLE examples seen thus far use a single column as the primary key. The primary key is thus defined using a statement such as

```
PRIMARY KEY (vend_id)
```

To create a primary key made up of multiple columns, simply specify the column names as a comma-delimited list, as seen in this example:

```
CREATE TABLE orderitems
(
  order_num  int          NOT NULL ,
  order_item int          NOT NULL ,
  prod_id    char(10)     NOT NULL ,
  quantity   int          NOT NULL ,
  item_price decimal(8,2) NOT NULL ,
  PRIMARY KEY (order_num, order_item)
) ENGINE=Aria;
```

The orderitems table contains the order specifics for each order in the orders table. There may be multiple items per order, but each order will only ever have one first item, one second item, and so on. As such, the combination of order number (column order_num) and order item (column order_item) is unique, and thus suitable to be the primary key, which is defined as

```
PRIMARY KEY (order_num, order_item)
```

Primary keys may be defined at table creation time (as seen here) or after table creation (as discussed later in this chapter).

> **Tip**
>
> **Primary Keys and NULL Values**   Back in Chapter 1, you learned that primary keys are columns whose values uniquely identify every row in a table. Only columns that do not allow NULL values can be used in primary keys. Columns that allow no value at all cannot be used as unique identifiers.

Using AUTO_INCREMENT

Let's take a look at the customers and orders tables again. Customers in the customers table are uniquely identified by column cust_id, a unique number for each and every customer. Similarly, orders in the orders table each have a unique order number that is stored in column order_num.

These numbers have no special significance, other than the fact that they are unique. When a new customer or order is added, a new customer ID or order number is needed. The numbers can be anything, so long as they are unique.

Obviously, the simplest number to use would be whatever comes next, whatever is one higher than the current highest number. For example, if the highest cust_id is 10005, the next customer inserted into the table could have a cust_id of 10006.

Simple, right? Well, not really. How would you determine the next number to be used? You could, of course, use a SELECT statement to get the highest number (using the Max() function introduced in Chapter 12, "Summarizing Data") and then add 1 to it. But that would not be safe (you'd need to find a way to ensure that no one else inserted a row in between the time that you performed the SELECT and the INSERT, a legitimate possibility in multiuser applications). Nor would it be efficient (performing additional SQL operations is never ideal).

And that's where AUTO_INCREMENT comes in. Look at the following line (part of the CREATE TABLE statement used to create the customers table):

```
cust_id      int      NOT NULL AUTO_INCREMENT,
```

AUTO_INCREMENT tells MariaDB that this column is to be automatically incremented each time a row is added. Each time an INSERT operation is performed MariaDB automatically increments (and thus AUTO_INCREMENT) the column, assigning it the next available value. This way each row is assigned a unique cust_id that is then used as the primary key value.

Only one AUTO_INCREMENT column is allowed per table, and it must be indexed (for example, by making it a primary key).

> **Note**
>
> **Overriding AUTO_INCREMENT**   Need to use a specific value if a column is designated as AUTO_INCREMENT? You can—simply specify a value in the INSERT statement, and as long as it is unique (has not been used yet) that value will be used instead of an automatically generated one. Subsequent incrementing will start using the value manually inserted. (See the table population scripts in Appendix B, "The Example Tables" for examples of this.)

> **Tip**
>
> **Determining the AUTO_INCREMENT Value**   One downside of having MariaDB generate (via auto increment) primary keys for you is that you don't know what those values are.
>
> Consider this scenario: You are adding a new order. This requires creating a single row in the orders table and then a row for each item ordered in the orderitems table. The order_num is stored along with the order details in orderitems. This is how the orders and orderitems table are related to each other. And that obviously requires that you know the generated order_num after the orders row was inserted and before the orderitems rows are inserted.
>
> So how could you obtain this value when an AUTO_INCREMENT column is used? By using the last_insert_id() function, like this:
>
> ```
> SELECT last_insert_id();
> ```
>
> This returns the last AUTO_INCREMENT value, which you can then use in subsequent SQL statements.

Specifying Default Values

MariaDB enables you to specify default values to be used if no value is specified when a row is inserted. Default values are specified using the DEFAULT keyword in the column definitions in the CREATE TABLE statement.

Look at the following example:

▼ Input

```
CREATE TABLE orderitems
(
  order_num   int          NOT NULL ,
  order_item  int          NOT NULL ,
  prod_id     char(10)     NOT NULL ,
  quantity    int          NOT NULL   DEFAULT 1,
  item_price  decimal(8,2) NOT NULL ,
  PRIMARY KEY (order_num, order_item)
) ENGINE=Aria;
```

▼ Analysis

This statement creates the orderitems table that contains the individual items that make up an order. (The order itself is stored in the orders table.) The quantity column contains the quantity for each item in an order. In this example, adding the text DEFAULT 1 to the column description instructs MariaDB to use a quantity of 1 if no quantity is specified.

> **Caution**
>
> **Functions Are Not Allowed**   Unlike most DBMSs, MariaDB (like MySQL) does not allow the use of functions as DEFAULT values; only constants are supported.

> **Tip**
>
> **Using DEFAULT Instead of NULL Values**   Many database developers use DEFAULT values instead of NULL columns, especially in columns that will be used in calculations or data groupings.

Engine Types

You may have noticed that the CREATE TABLE statements used thus far all ended with a ENGINE=Aria statement.

Like every other DBMS, MariaDB has an internal engine that actually manages and manipulates data. When you CREATE TABLE that engine is used to actually create the tables, and when you SELECT or perform any other database processing, the engine is used internally to process your request. And for the most part, the engine is buried within the DBMS and you need not pay much attention to it.

But unlike most other DBMSs, MariaDB does not come with a single engine. Rather, it ships with several different engines (the ones that come with MySQL as well as additional ones), all buried within the server, and all capable of executing commands like CREATE TABLE and SELECT.

So why bother shipping multiple engines? Because each has different capabilities and features, and being able to pick the right engine for a job gives you unprecedented power and flexibility.

Of course, you are free to totally ignore database engines. If you omit the ENGINE= statement, the default engine will be used, and most of your SQL statements will work as is. But not all, and that is why this is important (and why two different engines are used in the sample tables used in this book).

Here are several engines to be aware of:

- `InnoDB` is a transaction-safe engine (see Chapter 26, "Managing Transaction Processing"). It does not support full-text searching.

- `MEMORY` is functionally equivalent to `MyISAM`, but as data is stored in memory (instead of on disk) it is extremely fast (and ideally suited for temporary tables).

- `MyISAM` is a high-performance engine. It supports full-text searching (see Chapter 18, "Full-Text Searching"), but does not support transactional processing.

- `ARIA` (specified as `ENGINE=Aria`) is a new transaction-safe engine that also supports full-text searching and vital crash recovery features.

Engine types may be mixed, so within a single database you can have different tables using different engines if required.

> **Caution**
>
> **Foreign Keys Can't Span Engines**   There is one big downside to mixing engine types. Foreign keys (used to enforce referential integrity, as explained in Chapter 1) cannot span engines. That is, a table using one engine cannot have a foreign key referring to a table that uses another engine.

So, which should you use? Well, that depends on what features you need. `ARIA` is new to MariaDB and provides the ideal combination of performance and features. But, if you do need to use features in other engines, know that the option of doing so is available to you.

Updating Tables

To update table definitions, the `ALTER TABLE` statement is used. But, ideally, tables should never be altered after they contain data. You should spend sufficient time anticipating future needs during the table design process so extensive changes are not required later on.

To change a table using `ALTER TABLE`, you must specify the following information:

- The name of the table to be altered after the keywords `ALTER TABLE`. (The table must exist or an error will be generated.)

- The list of changes to be made.

The following example adds a column to a table:

▼ Input

```
ALTER TABLE vendors
ADD vend_phone CHAR(20);
```

▼ Analysis

This statement adds a column named vend_phone to the vendors table. The datatype must be specified.

To remove this newly added column, you can do the following:

▼ Input

```
ALTER TABLE Vendors
DROP COLUMN vend_phone;
```

One common use for ALTER TABLE is to define foreign keys. The following is the code used to define the foreign keys used by the tables in this book:

```
ALTER TABLE orderitems
ADD CONSTRAINT fk_orderitems_orders
FOREIGN KEY (order_num) REFERENCES orders (order_num);

ALTER TABLE orderitems
ADD CONSTRAINT fk_orderitems_products FOREIGN KEY (prod_id)
REFERENCES products (prod_id);

ALTER TABLE orders
ADD CONSTRAINT fk_orders_customers FOREIGN KEY (cust_id)
REFERENCES customers (cust_id);

ALTER TABLE products
ADD CONSTRAINT fk_products_vendors
FOREIGN KEY (vend_id) REFERENCES vendors (vend_id);
```

Here four ALTER TABLE statements are used, as four different tables are being altered. To make multiple alterations to a single table, a single ALTER TABLE statement could be used with each of the alterations specified comma delimited.

Complex table structure changes usually require a manual move process involving these steps:

1. Create a new table with the new column layout.

2. Use the INSERT SELECT statement (see Chapter 19, "Inserting Data," for details of this statement) to copy the data from the old table to the new table. Use conversion functions and calculated fields, if needed.

3. Verify that the new table contains the desired data.

4. Rename the old table (or delete it, if you are really brave).

5. Rename the new table with the name previously used by the old table.

6. Re-create any triggers, stored procedures, indexes, and foreign keys as needed.

> **Caution**
>
> **Use ALTER TABLE Carefully** Use ALTER TABLE with extreme caution, and be sure you have a complete set of backups (both schema and data) before proceeding. Database table changes cannot be undone—and if you add columns you don't need, you might not be able to remove them. Similarly, if you drop a column that you do need, you might lose all the data in that column.

Deleting Tables

Deleting tables (actually removing the entire table, not just the contents) is easy—arguably too easy. Tables are deleted using the DROP TABLE statement:

▼ **Input**

```
DROP TABLE customers2;
```

▼ **Analysis**

This statement deletes the customers2 table (assuming it exists). There is no confirmation, nor is there an undo—executing the statement permanently removes the table.

Renaming Tables

To rename a table, use the RENAME TABLE statement as follows:

▼ **Input**

```
RENAME TABLE customers2 TO customers;
```

▼ **Analysis**

RENAME TABLE does just that, it renames a table. Multiple tables may be renamed in one operation using the syntax:

```
RENAME TABLE backup_customers TO customers,
             backup_vendors TO vendors,
             backup_products TO products;
```

Summary

In this chapter, you learned several new SQL statements. CREATE TABLE is used to create new tables, ALTER TABLE is used to change table columns (or other objects like constraints or indexes), and DROP TABLE is used to completely delete a table. These statements should be used with extreme caution, and only after backups have been made. You also learned about database engines, defining primary and foreign keys, and other important table and column options.

22

Using Views

In this chapter you learn exactly what views are, how they work, and when they should be used. You also see how views can be used to simplify some of the SQL operations performed in earlier chapters.

Understanding Views

Views are virtual tables. Unlike tables that contain data, views simply contain queries that dynamically retrieve data when used.

The best way to understand views is to look at an example. Back in Chapter 15, "Joining Tables," you used the following SELECT statement to retrieve data from three tables:

▼ **Input**

```
SELECT cust_name, cust_contact
FROM customers, orders, orderitems
WHERE customers.cust_id = orders.cust_id
  AND orderitems.order_num = orders.order_num
  AND prod_id = 'TNT2';
```

That query was used to retrieve the customers who had ordered a specific product. Anyone needing this data would have to understand the table structure, as well as how to create the query and join the tables. To retrieve the same data for another product (or for multiple products), the last WHERE clause would have to be modified.

Now imagine that you could wrap that entire query in a virtual table called productcustomers. You could then simply do the following to retrieve the same data:

▼ **Input**

```
SELECT cust_name, cust_contact
FROM productcustomers
WHERE prod_id = 'TNT2';
```

This is where views come into play. `productcustomers` is a view, and as a view, it does not contain any actual columns or data as a table would. Instead, it contains a SQL query—the same query used previously to join the tables properly.

Why Use Views

You've already seen one use for views. Here are some other common uses:

- To reuse SQL statements.

- To simplify complex SQL operations. After the query is written, it can be reused easily, without having to know the details of the underlying query itself.

- To expose parts of a table instead of complete tables.

- To secure data. Users can be given access to specific subsets of tables instead of to entire tables.

- To change data formatting and representation. Views can return data formatted and presented differently from their underlying tables.

For the most part, after views are created, they can be used in the same way as tables. You can perform SELECT operations, filter and sort data, join views to other views or tables, and possibly even add and update data. (There are some restrictions on this last item. More on that in a moment.)

The important thing to remember is views are just that, views into data stored elsewhere. Views contain no data themselves, so the data they return is retrieved from other tables. When data is added or changed in those tables, the views will return that changed data.

> **Caution**
>
> **Performance Issues** Because views contain no data, any retrieval needed to execute a query must be processed every time the view is used. If you create complex views with multiple joins and filters, or if you nest views, you may find that performance is dramatically degraded. Be sure you test execution before deploying applications that use views extensively.

View Rules and Restrictions

Here are some of the most common rules and restrictions governing view creation and usage:

- Like tables, views must be uniquely named. (They cannot be named with the name of any other table or view.)

- There is no limit to the number of views that can be created.

- To create views, you must have security access. This is usually granted by the database administrator.

- Views can be nested; that is, a view may be built using a query that retrieves data from another view.

- ORDER BY may be used in a view, but it will be overridden if ORDER BY is also used in the SELECT that retrieves data from the view.

- Views cannot be indexed, nor can they have triggers or default values associated with them.

- Views can be used in conjunction with tables, for example, to create a SELECT statement, which joins a table and a view.

Using Views

So now that you know what views are (and the rules and restrictions that govern them), let's look at view creation:

- Views are created using the CREATE VIEW statement.

- To view the statement used to create a view, use SHOW CREATE VIEW viewname;.

- To remove a view, the DROP statement is used. The syntax is simply DROP VIEW viewname;.

- To update a view you may use the DROP statement and then the CREATE statement again, or just use CREATE OR REPLACE VIEW, which creates the view if it does not exist and replaces it if it does.

Using Views to Simplify Complex Joins

One of the most common uses of views is to hide complex SQL, and this often involves joins. Look at the following statement:

▼ **Input**

```
CREATE VIEW productcustomers AS
SELECT cust_name, cust_contact, prod_id
FROM customers, orders, orderitems
WHERE customers.cust_id = orders.cust_id
  AND orderitems.order_num = orders.order_num;
```

▼ Analysis

This statement creates a view named productcustomers, which joins three tables to return a list of all customers who have ordered any product. If you were to SELECT * FROM productcustomers, you'd list every customer who ordered anything.

To retrieve a list of customers who ordered product TNT2, you can do the following:

▼ Input

```
SELECT cust_name, cust_contact
FROM productcustomers
WHERE prod_id = 'TNT2';
```

▼ Output

```
+----------------+--------------+
| cust_name      | cust_contact |
+----------------+--------------+
| Coyote Inc.    | Y Lee        |
| Yosemite Place | Y Sam        |
+----------------+--------------+
```

▼ Analysis

This statement retrieves specific data from the view by issuing a WHERE clause. When MariaDB processes the request, it adds the specified WHERE clause to any existing WHERE clauses in the view query so the data is filtered correctly.

As you can see, views can greatly simplify the use of complex SQL statements. Using views, you can write the underlying SQL once and then reuse it as needed.

> **Tip**
>
> **Creating Reusable Views**   It is a good idea to create views that are not tied to specific data. For example, the view created in this example returns customers for all products, not just product TNT2 (for which the view was first created). Expanding the scope of the view enables it to be reused, making it even more useful. It also eliminates the need for you to create and maintain multiple similar views.

Using Views to Reformat Retrieved Data

As mentioned previously, another common use of views is for reformatting retrieved data. The following SELECT statement (from Chapter 10, "Creating Calculated Fields") returns vendor name and location in a single combined calculated column:

▼ **Input**
```
SELECT Concat(RTrim(vend_name), ' (', RTrim(vend_country), ')')
       AS vend_title
FROM vendors
ORDER BY vend_name;
```

▼ **Output**
```
+------------------------+
| vend_title             |
+------------------------+
| ACME (USA)             |
| Anvils R Us (USA)      |
| Furball Inc. (USA)     |
| Jet Set (England)      |
| Jouets Et Ours (France)|
| LT Supplies (USA)      |
+------------------------+
```

Now suppose that you regularly needed results in this format. Rather than perform the concatenation each time it was needed, you could create a view and use that instead. To turn this statement into a view, you can do the following:

▼ **Input**
```
CREATE VIEW vendorlocations AS
SELECT Concat(RTrim(vend_name), ' (', RTrim(vend_country), ')')
       AS vend_title
FROM vendors
ORDER BY vend_name;
```

▼ **Analysis**

This statement creates a view using the exact same query as the previous SELECT statement. To retrieve the data to create all mailing labels, simply do the following:

▼ **Input**
```
SELECT *
FROM vendorlocations;
```

▼ Output

```
+-------------------------+
| vend_title              |
+-------------------------+
| ACME (USA)              |
| Anvils R Us (USA)       |
| Furball Inc. (USA)      |
| Jet Set (England)       |
| Jouets Et Ours (France) |
| LT Supplies (USA)       |
+-------------------------+
```

Using Views to Filter Unwanted Data

Views are also useful for applying common WHERE clauses. For example, you might want to define a customeremaillist view so it filters out customers without e-mail addresses. To do this, you can use the following statement:

▼ Input

```
CREATE VIEW customeremaillist AS
SELECT cust_id, cust_name, cust_email
FROM customers
WHERE cust_email IS NOT NULL;
```

▼ Analysis

Obviously, when sending e-mail to a mailing list you want to ignore users who have no e-mail address. The WHERE clause here filters out those rows that have NULL values in the cust_email columns so they are not retrieved.

View customeremaillist can now be used for data retrieval just like any table.

▼ Input

```
SELECT *
FROM customeremaillist;
```

▼ Output

```
+---------+---------------+----------------------+
| cust_id | cust_name     | cust_email           |
+---------+---------------+----------------------+
|   10001 | Coyote Inc.   | ylee@coyote.com      |
|   10003 | Wascals       | rabbit@wascally.com  |
|   10004 | Yosemite Place | sam@yosemite.com     |
+---------+---------------+----------------------+
```

> **Note**
>
> **WHERE Clauses and WHERE Clauses**   If a WHERE clause is used when retrieving data from the view, the two sets of clauses (the one in the view and the one passed to it) are combined automatically.

Using Views with Calculated Fields

Views are exceptionally useful for simplifying the use of calculated fields. The following is a SELECT statement introduced in Chapter 10. It retrieves the order items for a specific order, calculating the expanded price for each item:

▼ **Input**

```
SELECT prod_id,
       quantity,
       item_price,
       quantity*item_price AS expanded_price
FROM orderitems
WHERE order_num = 20005;
```

▼ **Output**

```
+----------+----------+------------+-----------------+
| prod_id  | quantity | item_price | expanded_price  |
+----------+----------+------------+-----------------+
| ANV01    |       10 | 5.99       | 59.90           |
| ANV02    |        3 | 9.99       | 29.97           |
| TNT2     |        5 | 10.00      | 50.00           |
| FB       |        1 | 10.00      | 10.00           |
+----------+----------+------------+-----------------+
```

To turn this into a view, do the following:

▼ **Input**

```
CREATE VIEW orderitemsexpanded AS
SELECT order_num,
       prod_id,
       quantity,
       item_price,
       quantity*item_price AS expanded_price
FROM orderitems;
```

To retrieve the details for order 20005 (the previous output), do the following:

▼ **Input**

```
SELECT *
FROM orderitemsexpanded
WHERE order_num = 20005;
```

▼ **Output**

```
+-----------+---------+----------+------------+----------------+
| order_num | prod_id | quantity | item_price | expanded_price |
+-----------+---------+----------+------------+----------------+
|     20005 | ANV01   |       10 |       5.99 |          59.90 |
|     20005 | ANV02   |        3 |       9.99 |          29.97 |
|     20005 | TNT2    |        5 |      10.00 |          50.00 |
|     20005 | FB      |        1 |      10.00 |          10.00 |
+-----------+---------+----------+------------+----------------+
```

As you can see, views are easy to create and even easier to use. Used correctly, views can greatly simplify complex data manipulation.

Updating Views

All the views thus far have been used with SELECT statements. But can view data be updated? It depends.

As a rule, yes, views are updateable (that is, you can use INSERT, UPDATE, and DELETE on them). Updating a view updates the underlying table (the view, you will recall, has no data of its own); if you add or remove rows from a view you are actually removing them from the underlying table.

But not all views are updateable. Basically, if MariaDB cannot correctly ascertain the underlying data to be updated, updates (this includes inserts and deletes) are not allowed. In practice, this means that if any of the following are used you'll not be able to update the view:

- Grouping (using GROUP BY and HAVING)
- Joins
- Subqueries
- Unions
- Aggregate functions (Min(), Count(), Sum(), and so forth)
- DISTINCT
- Derived (calculated) columns

In other words, many of the examples used in this chapter would not be updateable. This might sound like a serious restriction, but in reality it isn't because views are primarily used for data retrieval anyway.

> **Tip**
>
> **Use Views for Retrieval**   As a rule, use views for data retrieval (`SELECT` statements) and not for updates (`INSERT`, `UPDATE`, and `DELETE`).

Summary

Views are virtual tables. They do not contain data, but they contain queries that retrieve data as needed, instead. Views provide a level of encapsulation around MariaDB `SELECT` statements and can be used to simplify data manipulation, as well as to reformat or secure underlying data.

23

Working with Stored Procedures

In this chapter, you learn what stored procedures are, why they are used, and how they are used. You also look at the basic syntax for creating and using them.

Understanding Stored Procedures

Most of the SQL statements that we've used thus far are simple in that they use a single statement against one or more tables. Not all operations are that simple—often, multiple statements are needed to perform a complete operation. For example, consider the following scenario:

- To process an order, checks must be made to ensure that items are in stock.

- If items are in stock, they need to be reserved so they are not sold to anyone else, and the available quantity must be reduced to reflect the correct amount in stock.

- Any items not in stock need to be ordered; this requires some interaction with the vendor.

- The customer needs to be notified as to which items are in stock (and can be shipped immediately) and which are back ordered.

This is obviously not a complete example, and it is even beyond the scope of the example tables that we have been using in this book, but it will suffice to help make a point. Performing this process requires many MariaDB statements against many tables. In addition, the exact statements that need to be performed and their order are not fixed; they can (and will) vary according to which items are in stock and which are not.

How would you write this code? You could write each of the statements individually and execute other statements conditionally, based on the result. You'd have to do this every time this processing was needed (and in every application that needed it).

Or you could create a stored procedure. Stored procedures are simply collections of one or more MariaDB statements saved for future use. You can think of them as batch files, although in truth they are more than that.

Why Use Stored Procedures

Now that you know what stored procedures are, why use them? There are many reasons, but here are the primary ones:

- To simplify complex operations (as seen in the previous example) by encapsulating processes into a single easy-to-use unit.

- To ensure data integrity by not requiring that a series of steps be created over and over. If all developers and applications use the same (tried and tested) stored procedure, the same code will be used by all.

  An extension of this is to prevent errors. The more steps that need to be performed, the more likely it is that errors will be introduced. Preventing errors ensures data consistency.

- To simplify change management. If tables, column names, or business logic (or just about anything) changes, only the stored procedure code needs to be updated, and no one else needs even to be aware that changes were made.

  An extension of this is security. Restricting access to underlying data via stored procedures reduces the chance of data corruption (unintentional or otherwise).

- To improve performance, as stored procedures typically execute quicker than do individual SQL statements.

- There are MariaDB language elements and features available only within single requests. Stored procedures can use these to write code that is more powerful and flexible. (We see an example of this in the next chapter.)

In other words, there are three primary benefits—simplicity, security, and performance. Obviously all are important. Before you run off to turn all your SQL code into stored procedures, here's the downside:

- Stored procedures tend to be more complex to write than basic SQL statements, and writing them requires a greater degree of skill and experience.

- You might not have the security access needed to create stored procedures. Many database administrators restrict stored procedure creation rights, allowing users to execute them but not necessarily create them.

Nonetheless, stored procedures are useful and should be used whenever possible.

> **Note**
>
> **Can't Write Them? You Can Still Use Them**   MariaDB distinguishes the security and access needed to write stored procedures from the security and access needed to execute them. This is a good thing; even if you can't (or don't want to) write your own stored procedures, you can still execute them when appropriate.

Using Stored Procedures

Using stored procedures requires knowing how to execute (run) them. Stored procedures are executed far more often than they are written, so we start there. And then we look at creating and working with stored procedures.

Executing Stored Procedures

MariaDB refers to stored procedure execution as *calling*, and so the MariaDB statement to execute a stored procedure is simply CALL. CALL takes the name of the stored procedure and any parameters that need to be passed to it. Take a look at this example:

▼ **Input**

```
CALL productpricing(@pricelow,
                    @pricehigh,
                    @priceaverage);
```

▼ **Analysis**

Here a stored procedure named productpricing is executed; it calculates and returns the lowest, highest, and average product prices. Of course, you can't run this example yet, as stored procedure productpricing does not exist. (Well, you could try to run it, but you'll just see a MariaDB error message.)

Stored procedures might or might not display results, as you see shortly.

Creating Stored Procedures

As already explained, writing a stored procedure is not trivial. To give you a taste for what is involved, let's look at a simple example—a stored procedure that returns the average product price. Here is the code:

▼ Input

```
CREATE PROCEDURE productpricing()
BEGIN
   SELECT Avg(prod_price) AS priceaverage
   FROM products;
END;
```

▼ Analysis

The stored procedure is named `productpricing` and is thus defined with the statement `CREATE PROCEDURE productpricing()`. Had the stored procedure accepted parameters, these would have been enumerated between the (and). This stored procuedure has no parameters, but the trailing () is still required. `BEGIN` and `END` statements are used to delimit the stored procedure body, and the body itself is just a simple `SELECT` statement (using the `Avg()` function learned back in Chapter 12, "Summarizing Data").

When MariaDB processes this code it creates a new stored procedure named `productpricing`. No data is returned because the code does not call the stored procedure, it simply creates it for future use.

> **Note**
>
> **`mysql` Command Line Client Delimiters**   If you are using the `mysql` command line utility, pay careful attention to this note.
>
> The default MariaDB statement delimiter is ; (as you have seen in all the SQL statements used thus far). However, the `mysql` command line utility also uses ; as a delimiter. If the command line utility were to interpret the ; characters inside of the stored procedure itself, those would not end up becoming part of the stored procedure, and that would make the SQL in the stored procedure syntactically invalid.
>
> The solution is to temporarily change the command line utility delimiter, as seen here:
>
> ```
> DELIMITER //
>
> CREATE PROCEDURE productpricing()
> BEGIN
>     SELECT Avg(prod_price) AS priceaverage
>     FROM products;
> END //
>
> DELIMITER ;
> ```

> Here, DELIMITER // tells the command line utility to use // as the new end of statement delimiter, and you will notice that the END that closes the stored procedure is defined as END // instead of the expected END;. This way the ; within the stored procedure body remains intact and is correctly passed to the database engine. And then, to restore things back to how they were initially, the statement closes with a DELIMITER ;.
>
> Any character may be used as the delimiter except for \.
>
> If you are using the mysql command line utility, keep this in mind as you work through this chapter.

So how would you use this stored procedure? Like this:

▼ Input

```
CALL productpricing();
```

▼ Output

```
+--------------+
| priceaverage |
+--------------+
|    16.133571 |
+--------------+
```

▼ Analysis

CALL productpricing(); executes the just created stored procedure and displays the returned result. As a stored procedure is actually a type of function, () characters are required after the stored procedure name (even when no parameters are being passed).

Dropping Stored Procedures

After they are created, stored procedures remain on the server, ready for use, until dropped. The drop command (similar to the statement seen Chapter 21, "Creating and Manipulating Tables") removes the stored procedure from the server.

To remove the stored procedure we just created, use the following statement:

▼ Input

```
DROP PROCEDURE productpricing;
```

▼ Analysis

This removes the just-created stored procedure. Notice that the trailing () is not used; here just the stored procedure name is specified.

> **Tip**
>
> **Drop Only If It Exists**   DROP PROCEDURE throws an error if the named procedure does not actually exist. To delete a procedure if it exists (and not throw an error if it does not), use DROP PROCEDURE IF EXISTS.

Working with Parameters

productpricing is a really simple stored procedure—it simply displays the results of a SELECT statement. Typically stored procedures do not display results; rather, they return them into variables that you specify.

> **New Term**
>
> **Variable**   A named location in memory, used for temporary storage of data.

Here is an updated version of productpricing (you'll not be able to create the stored procedure again if you did not previously drop it):

▼ Input

```
CREATE PROCEDURE productpricing(
    OUT pl DECIMAL(8,2),
    OUT ph DECIMAL(8,2),
    OUT pa DECIMAL(8,2)
)
BEGIN
    SELECT Min(prod_price)
    INTO pl
    FROM products;
    SELECT Max(prod_price)
    INTO ph
    FROM products;
    SELECT Avg(prod_price)
    INTO pa
    FROM products;
END;
```

▼ Analysis

This stored procedure accepts three parameters named pl to store the lowest product price, ph to store the highest product price, and pa to store the average product price (and thus the variable names). Each parameter must have its type specified; here a decimal value is used. The keyword OUT is used to specify that this parameter is used to send a value out of the stored procedure (back to the caller). MariaDB supports parameters of types IN (those passed to stored procedures), OUT (those passed from stored procedures, as used here), and INOUT (those used to pass parameters to and from stored procedures). The stored procedure code itself is enclosed within BEGIN and END statements as seen before, and a series of SELECT statements are performed to retrieve the values that are then saved into the appropriate variables (by specifying the INTO keyword).

> **Note**
>
> **Parameter Datatypes**   The datatypes allowed in stored procedure parameters are the same as those used in tables. Appendix C, "MariaDB Datatypes," lists these types.
>
> Note that a recordset is not an allowed type, and so multiple rows and columns could not be returned via a parameter. This is why three parameters (and three SELECT statements) are used in the previous example.

To call this updated stored procedure, three variable names must be specified, as seen here:

▼ Input

```
CALL productpricing(@pricelow,
                    @pricehigh,
                    @priceaverage);
```

▼ Analysis

As the stored procedure expects three parameters, exactly three parameters must be passed, no more and no less. Therefore, three parameters are passed to this CALL statement. These are the names of the three variables that the stored procedure will store the results in.

> **Note**
>
> **Variable Names**   All MariaDB variable names must begin with @.

When called, this statement does not actually display any data. Rather, it returns variables that can then be displayed (or used in other processing).

To display the retrieved average product price you could do the following:

▼ Input

```
SELECT @priceaverage;
```

▼ Output

```
+----------------+
| @priceaverage  |
+----------------+
| 16.133571428   |
+----------------+
```

To obtain all three values, you can use the following:

▼ Input

```
SELECT @pricehigh, @pricelow, @priceaverage;
```

▼ Output

```
+------------+-----------+----------------+
| @pricehigh | @pricelow | @priceaverage  |
+------------+-----------+----------------+
| 55.00      | 2.50      | 16.133571428   |
+------------+-----------+----------------+
```

Here is another example, this time using both IN and OUT parameters.
ordertotal accepts an order number and returns the total for that order:

▼ Input

```
CREATE PROCEDURE ordertotal(
    IN onumber INT,
    OUT ototal DECIMAL(8,2)
)
BEGIN
    SELECT Sum(item_price*quantity)
    FROM orderitems
    WHERE order_num = onumber
    INTO ototal;
END;
```

▼ Analysis

onumber is defined as IN because the order number is passed in to the stored
procedure. ototal is defined as OUT because the total is to be returned from
the stored procedure. The SELECT statement uses both of these parameters, the
WHERE clause uses onumber to select the right rows, and INTO uses ototal to
store the calculated total.

To invoke this new stored procedure you can use the following:

▼ Input

```
CALL ordertotal(20005, @total);
```

▼ Analysis

Two parameters must be passed to ordertotal; the first is the order number
and the second is the name of the variable that will contain the calculated total.

To display the total you can then do the following:

▼ Input

```
SELECT @total;
```

▼ Output

```
+--------+
| @total |
+--------+
| 149.87 |
+--------+
```

▼ Analysis

`@total` has already been populated by the `CALL` statement to `ordertotal`, and `SELECT` displays the value it contains.

To obtain a display for the total of another order, you would need to call the stored procedure again, and then redisplay the variable:

▼ Input

```
CALL ordertotal(20009, @total);
SELECT @total;
```

Building Intelligent Stored Procedures

All the stored procedures used thus far have basically encapsulated simple MariaDB `SELECT` statements. And while they are all valid examples of stored procedures, they really don't do anything more than what you could do with those statements directly (if anything, they just make things a little more complex). The real power of stored procedures is realized when business rules and intelligent processing are included within them.

Consider this scenario. You need to obtain order totals as before, but also need to add sales tax to the total, but only for some customers (perhaps the ones in your own state). Now you need to do several things:

- Obtain the total (as before).

- Conditionally add tax to the total.

- Return the total (with or without tax).

That's a perfect job for a stored procedure:

▼ Input

```
-- Name: ordertotal
-- Parameters: onumber = order number
--             taxable = 0 if not taxable, 1 if taxable
--             ototal  = order total variable

CREATE PROCEDURE ordertotal(
   IN onumber INT,
   IN taxable BOOLEAN,
   OUT ototal DECIMAL(8,2)
) COMMENT 'Obtain order total, optionally adding tax'
BEGIN

   -- Declare variable for total
   DECLARE total DECIMAL(8,2);
   -- Declare tax percentage
   DECLARE taxrate INT DEFAULT 6;

   -- Get the order total
   SELECT Sum(item_price*quantity)
   FROM orderitems
   WHERE order_num = onumber
   INTO total;

   -- Is this taxable?
   IF taxable THEN
      -- Yes, so add taxrate to the total
      SELECT total+(total/100*taxrate) INTO total;
   END IF;

   -- And finally, save to out variable
   SELECT total INTO ototal;

END;
```

▼ Analysis

The stored procedure has changed dramatically. First of all, comments were added throughout (preceded by --). This is important as stored procedures increase in complexity. An additional parameter was added—taxable is a BOOLEAN (specify true if taxable, false if not). Within the stored procedure body, two local variables are defined using DECLARE statements. DECLARE requires that a variable name and a datatype be specified, and also supports optional default values (taxrate in this example is set to 6%). The SELECT has changed so the result is stored in `total` (the local variable) instead of `ototal`. Then an `IF` statement checks to see whether `taxable` is true, and if it is, another `SELECT` statement is used to add the tax to local variable `total`. And finally, `total` (which might or might not have had tax added) is saved to `ototal` using another `SELECT` statement.

> **Tip**
>
> **The COMMENT Keyword**   The stored procedure for this example included a COMMENT value in the CREATE PROCEDURE statement. This is not required, but if specified, is displayed in SHOW PROCEDURE STATUS results.

This is obviously a more sophisticated and powerful stored procedure. To try it out, use the following two statements:

▼ Input
```
CALL ordertotal(20005, 0, @total);
SELECT @total;
```

▼ Output
```
+--------+
| @total |
+--------+
| 149.87 |
+--------+
```

▼ Input
```
CALL ordertotal(20005, 1, @total);
SELECT @total;
```

▼ Output
```
+---------------+
| @total        |
+---------------+
| 158.862200000 |
+---------------+
```

▼ Analysis
`BOOLEAN` values may be specified as 1 for true and 0 for false (actually, any nonzero value is considered true and only 0 is considered false). By specifying 0 or 1 in the middle parameter you can conditionally add tax to the order total.

> **Note**
>
> **The IF Statement** This example showed the basic use of the MariaDB IF statement. IF also supports ELSEIF and ELSE clauses (the former also uses a THEN clause; the latter does not). We see additional uses of IF (as well as other flow control statements) in future chapters.

Inspecting Stored Procedures

To display the CREATE statement used to create a stored procedure, use the SHOW CREATE PROCEDURE statement:

▼ Input

```
SHOW CREATE PROCEDURE ordertotal;
```

To obtain a list of stored procedures including details on when and who created them, use SHOW PROCEDURE STATUS.

> **Tip**
>
> **Limiting Procedure Status Results** SHOW PROCEDURE STATUS lists all stored procedures. To restrict the output you can use LIKE to specify a filter pattern, for example:
> ```
> SHOW PROCEDURE STATUS LIKE 'ordertotal';
> ```

Summary

In this chapter, you learned what stored procedures are and why they are used. You also learned the basics of stored procedure execution and creation syntax, and you saw some of the ways these can be used. We continue this subject in the next chapter.

24

Using Cursors

In this chapter, you learn what cursors are and how to use them.

Understanding Cursors

As you have seen in previous chapters, MariaDB retrieval operations work with sets of rows known as result sets. The rows returned are all the rows that match a SQL statement—zero or more of them. Using simple SELECT statements, there is no way to get the first row, the next row, or the previous ten rows, for example. Nor is there an easy way to process all rows, one at a time (as opposed to all of them in a batch).

Sometimes there is a need to step through rows forward or backward and one or more at a time. This is what cursors are used for. A cursor is a database query stored on the MariaDB server—not a SELECT statement, but the result set retrieved by that statement. Once the cursor is stored, applications can scroll or browse up and down through the data as needed.

Cursors are used primarily by interactive applications in which users need to scroll up and down through screens of data, browsing or making changes.

> **Note**
>
> **Only in Stored Procedures** Unlike most DBMSs, MariaDB cursors (like those in MySQL) may only be used within stored procedures (and functions).

Working with Cursors

Using cursors involves several distinct steps:

1. Before a cursor can be used it must be declared (defined). This process does not actually retrieve any data; it merely defines the SELECT statement to be used.

2. After it is declared, the cursor must be opened for use. This process actually retrieves the data using the previously defined SELECT statement.

3. With the cursor populated with data, individual rows can be fetched (retrieved) as needed.

4. When it is done, the cursor must be closed.

After a cursor is declared, it may be opened and closed as often as needed. After it is open, fetch operations can be performed as often as needed.

Creating Cursors

Cursors are created using the DECLARE statement (seen in Chapter 23, "Working with Stored Procedures"). DECLARE names the cursor and takes a SELECT statement, complete with WHERE and other clauses if needed. For example, this statement defines a cursor named ordernumbers using a SELECT statement that retrieves all orders:

▼ **Input**

```
CREATE PROCEDURE processorders()
BEGIN
    DECLARE ordernumbers CURSOR
    FOR
    SELECT order_num FROM orders;
END;
```

▼ **Analysis**

This stored procedure does not do a whole lot. A DECLARE statement is used to define and name the cursor—in this case ordernumbers. Nothing is done with the cursor, and as soon as the stored procedure finishes processing it ceases to exist (as it is local to the stored procedure itself).

Now that the cursor is defined, it is ready to be opened.

Opening and Closing Cursors

Cursors are opened using the OPEN CURSOR statement, like this:

▼ **Input**

```
OPEN ordernumbers;
```

▼ Analysis

When the OPEN statement is processed, the query is executed, and the retrieved data is stored for subsequent browsing and scrolling.

After cursor processing is complete, the cursor should be closed using the CLOSE statement, as follows:

▼ Input

```
CLOSE ordernumbers;
```

▼ Analysis

CLOSE frees up any internal memory and resources used by the cursor, and so every cursor should be closed when it is no longer needed.

After a cursor is closed, it cannot be reused without being opened again. However, a cursor does not need to be declared again to be used; an OPEN statement is sufficient.

> **Note**
>
> **Implicit Closing** If you do not explicitly close a cursor, MariaDB closes it automatically when the END statement is reached.

Here is an updated version of the previous example:

▼ Input

```
CREATE PROCEDURE processorders()
BEGIN
    -- Declare the cursor
    DECLARE ordernumbers CURSOR
    FOR
    SELECT order_num FROM orders;

    -- Open the cursor
    OPEN ordernumbers;

    -- Close the cursor
    CLOSE ordernumbers;

END;
```

▼ Analysis

This stored procedure declares, opens, and closes a cursor. However, nothing is done with the retrieved data.

Using Cursor Data

After a cursor is opened, each row can be accessed individually using a FETCH statement. FETCH specifies what is to be retrieved (the desired columns) and where retrieved data should be stored. It also advances the internal row pointer within the cursor so the next FETCH statement will retrieve the next row (and not the same one over and over).

The first example retrieves a single row from the cursor (the first row):

▼ Input

```
CREATE PROCEDURE processorders()
BEGIN

    -- Declare local variables
    DECLARE o INT;

    -- Declare the cursor
    DECLARE ordernumbers CURSOR
    FOR
    SELECT order_num FROM orders;

    -- Open the cursor
    OPEN ordernumbers;

    -- Get order number
    FETCH ordernumbers INTO o;

    -- Close the cursor
    CLOSE ordernumbers;

END;
```

▼ Analysis

Here FETCH is used to retrieve the order_num column of the current row (it'll start at the first row automatically) into a local declared variable named o. Nothing is done with the retrieved data.

In the next example, the retrieved data is looped through from the first row to the last:

▼ Input

```
CREATE PROCEDURE processorders()
BEGIN

   -- Declare local variables
   DECLARE done BOOLEAN DEFAULT 0;
   DECLARE o INT;

   -- Declare the cursor
   DECLARE ordernumbers CURSOR
   FOR
   SELECT order_num FROM orders;

   -- Declare continue handler
   DECLARE CONTINUE HANDLER FOR SQLSTATE '02000' SET done=1;

   -- Open the cursor
   OPEN ordernumbers;

   -- Loop through all rows
   REPEAT

      -- Get order number
      FETCH ordernumbers INTO o;

   -- End of loop
   UNTIL done END REPEAT;

   -- Close the cursor
   CLOSE ordernumbers;

END;
```

▼ Analysis

Like the previous example, this example uses FETCH to retrieve the current order_num into a declared variable named o. Unlike the previous example, the FETCH here is within a REPEAT, so it is repeated over and over until done is true (as specified by UNTIL done END REPEAT;). To make this work, variable done is defined with a DEFAULT 0 (false, not done). So how does done get set to true when done? The answer is this statement:

```
DECLARE CONTINUE HANDLER FOR SQLSTATE '02000' SET done=1;
```

This statement defines a CONTINUE HANDLER, code that will be executed when a condition occurs. Here it specifies that when SQLSTATE '02000' occurs, then SET done=1. And SQLSTATE '02000' is a *not found* condition and so it occurs when REPEAT cannot continue because there are no more rows to loop through.

> **Caution**
>
> **DECLARE Statement Sequence**   DECLARE statements, if used, must be issued in a specific order. Local variables defined with DECLARE must be defined before any cursors or handlers are defined, and handlers must be defined after any cursors. Failure to follow this sequencing generates an error message.

If you were to call this stored procedure it would define variables and a CONTINUE HANDLER, define and open a cursor, repeat through all rows, and then close the cursor.

With this functionality in place you can now place any needed processing inside the loop (after the FETCH statement and before the end of the loop).

> **Note**
>
> **REPEAT or LOOP?**   In addition to the REPEAT statement used here, MariaDB also supports a LOOP statement that can be used to repeat code until the LOOP is manually exited using a LEAVE statement. In general, the syntax of the REPEAT statement makes it better suited for looping through cursors.

To put this all together, here is one further revision of our example stored procedure with cursor, this time with some actual processing of fetched data:

▼ Input

```
CREATE PROCEDURE processorders()
BEGIN

    -- Declare local variables
    DECLARE done BOOLEAN DEFAULT 0;
    DECLARE o INT;
    DECLARE t DECIMAL(8,2);

    -- Declare the cursor
    DECLARE ordernumbers CURSOR
    FOR
    SELECT order_num FROM orders;

    -- Declare continue handler
    DECLARE CONTINUE HANDLER FOR SQLSTATE '02000' SET done=1;

    -- Create a table to store the results
    CREATE TABLE IF NOT EXISTS ordertotals
        (order_num INT, total DECIMAL(8,2));

    -- Open the cursor
    OPEN ordernumbers;
```

```
-- Loop through all rows
REPEAT

    -- Get order number
    FETCH ordernumbers INTO o;

    -- Get the total for this order
    CALL ordertotal(o, 1, t);

    -- Insert order and total into ordertotals
    INSERT INTO ordertotals(order_num, total)
    VALUES(o, t);

-- End of loop
UNTIL done END REPEAT;

-- Close the cursor
CLOSE ordernumbers;

END;
```

▼ Analysis

In this example, we added another variable named t (this stores the total for each order). The stored procedure also creates a new table on the fly (if it does not exist) named ordertotals. This table stores the results generated by the stored procedure. FETCH fetches each order_num as it did before, and then uses CALL to execute another stored procedure (the one we created in the previous chapter) to calculate the total with tax for each order (the result of which is stored in t). And then finally, INSERT is used to save the order number and total for each order.

To try this example, simple CALL it:

▼ Input

```
CALL processorders();
```

This stored procedure returns no data, but it does create and populate another table that can then be viewed using a simple SELECT statement:

▼ Input

```
SELECT *
FROM ordertotals;
```

▼ Output

```
+-----------+---------+
| order_num | total   |
+-----------+---------+
|     20005 |  158.86 |
|     20006 |   58.30 |
|     20007 | 1060.00 |
|     20008 |  132.50 |
|     20009 |   40.78 |
+-----------+---------+
```

And then you have it, a complete working example of stored procedures, cursors, row-by-row processing, and even stored procedures calling other stored procedures.

Summary

In this chapter, you learned what cursors are and why they are used. You also saw examples demonstrating basic cursor use, as well as techniques for looping through cursor results and for row-by-row processing.

25

Using Triggers

In this chapter, you learn what triggers are, why they are used, and how. You also look at the syntax for creating and using them.

Understanding Triggers

MariaDB statements are executed when needed, as are stored procedures. But what if you want a statement (or statements) to be executed automatically when events occur? For example:

- Every time a customer is added to a database table, check that the phone number is formatted correctly and that the state abbreviation is in uppercase.

- Every time a product is ordered, subtract the ordered quantity from the number in stock.

- Whenever a row is deleted, save a copy in an archive table.

All these examples need to be processed automatically whenever a table change occurs. And that is exactly what triggers are. A *trigger* is a MariaDB statement (or a group of statements enclosed within BEGIN and END statements) that are automatically executed by MariaDB in response to any of these statements:

- DELETE

- INSERT

- UPDATE

No other MariaDB SQL statements support triggers.

> **Note**
>
> **Only Tables**   Triggers are supported only on tables, not on views (and not on temporary tables).

Creating Triggers

When creating a trigger you need to specify four pieces of information:

- The unique trigger name
- The table to which the trigger is to be associated
- The action that the trigger should respond to (DELETE, INSERT, or UPDATE)
- When the trigger should be executed (before or after processing)

Triggers are created using the CREATE TRIGGER statement. Here is a really simple example (which doesn't actually do anything useful, but helps explain the syntax needed):

▼ Input

```
CREATE TRIGGER newproduct AFTER INSERT ON products
FOR EACH ROW
BEGIN
END;
```

▼ Analysis

CREATE TRIGGER is used to create the new trigger named newproduct. Triggers can be executed before or after an operation occurs, and here AFTER INSERT ON is specified so the trigger will execute after a successful INSERT statement has been executed. The trigger then specifies FOR EACH ROW and the code to be executed for each inserted row. So, whenever a product is added to the products table, this trigger will run, and any code between BEGIN and END will be executed. And as there is nothing between BEGIN and END, well, the trigger will run, but it doesn't actually do anything.

Triggers are defined per time per event per table, and only one trigger per time per event per table is allowed. As such, up to six triggers are supported per table (BEFORE and AFTER each INSERT, UPDATE, and DELETE). A single trigger cannot be associated with multiple events or multiple tables, so if you need a trigger to be executed for both INSERT and UPDATE operations, you need to define two triggers.

> **Note**
>
> **When Triggers Fail** If a BEFORE trigger fails, MariaDB will not perform the requested operation. In addition, if either a BEFORE trigger or the statement itself fail, MariaDB will not exdcute an AFTER trigger (if one exists).

Dropping Triggers

By now the syntax for dropping a trigger should be self-apparent. To drop a trigger, use the DROP TRIGGER statement, as seen here:

▼ **Input**

```
DROP TRIGGER newproduct;
```

▼ **Analysis**

Triggers cannot be updated or overwritten. To modify a trigger it must be dropped and recreated.

Using Triggers

With the basics covered, we now look at each of the supported trigger types, and the differences between them.

INSERT Triggers

INSERT triggers are executed BEFORE or AFTER an INSERT statement is executed. Be aware of the following:

- Within INSERT trigger code, you can refer to a virtual table named NEW to access the rows being inserted.

- In a BEFORE INSERT trigger, the values in NEW may also be updated (allowing you to change values about to be inserted).

- For AUTO_INCREMENT columns, NEW contains 0 before and the new automatically generated value after.

A common use for triggers is to track table changes (audit trails or logs). To try an example, you first need a table to store this information. This next MariaDB SQL statement creates a table to store a log of all changes to the orders table:

▼ **Input**

```
CREATE TABLE orders_log
(
  change_id    int       NOT NULL AUTO_INCREMENT,
  changed_on   datetime  NOT NULL ,
  change_type  char(1)   NOT NULL ,
  order_num    int       NOT NULL ,
  PRIMARY KEY (change_id)
) ENGINE=Maria;
```

▼ Analysis

This table has columns to store the change date and time, the type of change (A for added, U for updated, D for deleted), and the order_num of the order changed.

Now that you have a table to store the change log, you need to create the trigger that updates this new table. Here is the code:

▼ Input

```
CREATE TRIGGER neworder AFTER INSERT ON orders
FOR EACH ROW
BEGIN
    INSERT INTO orders_log(changed_on, change_type, order_num)
    VALUES(Now(),'A', NEW.order_num);
END;
```

▼ Analysis

CREATE TRIGGER is used to create the new trigger named neworder. Triggers can be executed before or after an operation occurs, and here AFTER INSERT ON is specified so the trigger will execute after a successful INSERT statement has been executed. The trigger then specifies FOR EACH ROW and the code to be executed for each inserted row. When a new order is saved in orders, MariaDB generates a new order number and saves it in order_num. The trigger code obtains this value from NEW.order_num. This is why this trigger must be executed AFTER INSERT, because before the BEFORE INSERT statement is executed the new order_num has not been generated yet. In this example, an INSERT statement is used to add a record of every inserted order into orders_log.

To test this trigger, try inserting a new order, like this:

▼ Input

```
INSERT INTO orders(order_date, cust_id)
VALUES(Now(), 10001);
```

The INSERT statement itself does not return anything useful, but it does cause our trigger to be executed. To verify this, let's see what is in the orders_log table:

▼ Input

```
SELECT * FROM orders_log;
```

▼ Output

```
+------------+---------------------+-------------+-----------+
| change_id  | changed_on          | change_type | order_num |
+------------+---------------------+-------------+-----------+
|          1 | 2011-04-12 10:49:59 | A           |     20010 |
+------------+---------------------+-------------+-----------+
```

▼ Analysis

orders_logs contains four columns. change_id is the auto incremented
table primary key, changed_on contains the date and time that the change
occurred (generated by the Now() function in the trigger), change_type is A
(order added), and order_num contains the new order number (generated by
MariaDB for the orders table).

> **Tip**
>
> **BEFORE or AFTER?** This example used AFTER to execute the trigger after the new
> order was created. As a rule, use AFTER if you need to access data that won't exist
> until a statement has been processed (for example, to obtain a newly generated order
> number). Use BEFORE for any data validation and cleanup (for example, if you want to
> make sure that the data inserted into the table was exactly as needed).

DELETE **Triggers**

DELETE triggers are executed before or after a DELETE statement is executed.
Be aware of the following:

- Within DELETE trigger code, you can refer to a virtual table named
  OLD to access the rows being deleted.

- The values in OLD are all read-only and cannot be updated.

The following example demonstrates the use of OLD to save rows about to be
deleted into the log table:

▼ Input

```
CREATE TRIGGER deleteorder BEFORE DELETE ON orders
FOR EACH ROW
BEGIN
    INSERT INTO orders_log(changed_on, change_type, order_num)
    VALUES(Now(),'D', OLD.order_num);
END;
```

▼ Analysis

This trigger is similar to the neworder trigger; it logs order deletions. This trigger is executed BEFORE DELETE (or you'd not have access to the order_num).

If you were to delete the order you just inserted, you'd see a second row in the orders_log table reflecting the deletion.

> **Note**
>
> **Multistatement Triggers**   Notice that the triggers shown here all use BEGIN and END statements to mark the trigger body. This is actually not necessary in the examples used thus far, although it does no harm. The advantage of using a BEGIN END block is that the trigger would then be able to accommodate multiple SQL statements (one after the other within the BEGIN END block) as you see in the next example.

Another good use for DELETE triggers is to archive deletions (rows deleted from a table are automatically saved in their entirety to an archive table). This updated version of the deleteorder trigger logs the deletion and also saves it to a table named orders_archive (you obviously need to create that table for this trigger to work; orders_archive will use the same CREATE TABLE statement as the one used to create orders, although you'll want to drop the AUTO INCREMENT):

▼ Input

```
CREATE TRIGGER deleteorder BEFORE DELETE ON orders
FOR EACH ROW
BEGIN
    INSERT INTO orders_log(changed_on, change_type, order_num)
    VALUES(Now(),'D', OLD.order_num);
    INSERT INTO orders_archive(order_num, order_date, cust_id)
    VALUES(OLD.order_num, OLD.order_date, OLD.cust_id);
END;
```

▼ Analysis

Before any order is deleted this trigger is executed. In addition to the logging seen previously, this trigger uses an INSERT statement to save the values in OLD (the order about to be deleted) into an archive table named archive_orders.

> **Tip**
>
> **An Extra Level of Protection**   The advantage of using a BEFORE DELETE trigger (as opposed to an AFTER DELETE trigger) is that if, for some reason, the order could not be archived, the DELETE itself will be aborted.

UPDATE **Triggers**

UPDATE triggers are executed before or after an UPDATE statement is executed. Be aware of the following:

- Within UPDATE trigger code, you can refer to a virtual table named OLD to access the previous (pre-UPDATE statement) values and NEW to access the new updated values.

- In a BEFORE UPDATE trigger, the values in NEW may also be updated (allowing you to change values about to be used in the UPDATE statement).

- The values in OLD are all read-only and cannot be updated.

The following example ensures that state abbreviations are always in uppercase (regardless of how they were actually specified in the UPDATE statement):

▼ Input

```
CREATE TRIGGER updatevendor BEFORE UPDATE ON vendors
FOR EACH ROW SET NEW.vend_state = Upper(NEW.vend_state);
```

▼ Analysis

Obviously, any data cleanup needs to occur in the BEFORE UPDATE statement as it does in this example. Each time a row is updated, the value in NEW. vend_state (the value that is used to update table rows) is replaced with Upper(NEW.vend_state).

What about logging updates to the orders table? With what you have learned here you should be able to create a updateorder trigger that inserts a row into the orders_log table (make sure to insert a U for change_type).

More on Triggers

Before wrapping up this chapter, here are some important points to keep in mind when using triggers:

- Trigger support in MariaDB is rather rudimentary at best when compared to other DBMSs. There are plans to improve and enhance trigger support in future versions.

- Creating triggers might require special security access. However, trigger execution is automatic. If an INSERT, UPDATE, or DELETE statement may be executed, any associated triggers are executed, too.

- Triggers should be used to ensure data consistency (case, formatting, and so on). The advantage of performing this type of processing in a trigger is that it always happens, and happens transparently, regardless of client application.

- One interesting use for triggers is in creating an audit trail, as seen in this chapter. Using triggers it would be easy to log changes (even before and after states if needed) to another table.

- Unfortunately the CALL statement is not supported in MariaDB triggers. This means that stored procedures cannot be invoked from within triggers. Any needed stored procedure code would need to be replicated within the trigger itself.

Summary

In this chapter, you learned what triggers are and why they are used. You learned the trigger types and the times that they can be executed. You also saw examples of triggers used for INSERT, DELETE, and UPDATE operations.

26

Managing Transaction Processing

In this chapter you learn what transactions are and how to use COMMIT and ROLLBACK statements to manage transaction processing.

Understanding Transaction Processing

> **Note**
>
> **Not All Engines Support Transactions**   As explained in Chapter 21, "Creating and Manipulating Tables," MariaDB supports the use of several underlying database engines. Not all engines support explicit management of transaction processing, as explained in this chapter. One of the most commonly used engines is MyISAM, which does not support explicit transaction management, while InnoDB and ARIA do. This is why the sample tables used in this book were created to use ARIA. If you need transaction processing functionality in your applications, be sure to use the correct engine type.

Transaction processing is used to maintain database integrity by ensuring that batches of MariaDB SQL operations execute completely or not at all.

As explained back in Chapter 15, "Joining Tables," relational databases are designed so data is stored in multiple tables to facilitate easier data manipulation, management, and reuse. Without going into the hows and whys of relational database design, take it as a given that well-designed database schemas are relational to some degree.

The orders tables you've been using in prior chapters are a good example of this. Orders are stored in two tables: orders stores actual orders, and orderitems stores the individual items ordered. These two tables are related to each other using unique IDs called primary keys (as discussed in Chapter 1, "Understanding SQL"). These tables, in turn, are related to other tables containing customer and product information.

The process of adding an order to the system is as follows:

1. Check whether the customer is already in the database (present in the `customers` table). If not, add him or her.

2. Retrieve the customer's ID.

3. Add a row to the `orders` table associating it with the customer ID.

4. Retrieve the new order ID assigned in the `orders` table.

5. Add one row to the `orderitems` table for each item ordered, associating it with the `orders` table by the retrieved ID (and with the `products` table by product ID).

Now imagine that some database failure (for example, out of disk space, security restrictions, table locks) prevents this entire sequence from completing. What would happen to your data?

Well, if the failure occurred after the customer was added and before the `orders` table was added, there is no real problem. It is perfectly valid to have customers without orders. When you run the sequence again, the inserted customer record will be retrieved and used. You can effectively pick up where you left off.

But what if the failure occurred after the `orders` row was added, but before the `orderitems` rows were added? Now you'd have an empty order sitting in your database.

Worse, what if the system failed during adding the `orderitems` rows? Now you'd end up with a partial order in your database, but you wouldn't know it.

How do you solve this problem? That's where *transaction processing* comes in. Transaction processing is a mechanism used to manage sets of SQL operations that must be executed in batches to ensure that databases never contain the results of partial operations. With transaction processing, you can ensure that sets of operations are not aborted mid-processing—they either execute in their entirety or not at all (unless explicitly instructed otherwise). If no error occurs, the entire set of statements is committed (written) to the database tables. If an error does occur, a rollback (undo) can occur to restore the database to a known and safe state.

So, looking at the same example, this is how the process would work:

1. Check whether the customer is already in the database; if not, add him or her.

2. Commit the customer information.

3. Retrieve the customer's ID.

4. Add a row to the orders table.

5. If a failure occurs while adding the row to orders, roll back.

6. Retrieve the new order ID assigned in the orders table.

7. Add one row to the orderitems table for each item ordered.

8. If a failure occurs while adding rows to orderitems, roll back all the orderitems rows added and the orders row.

9. Commit the order information.

When working with transactions and transaction processing, a few keywords keep reappearing. Here are the terms you need to know:

- **Transaction**—A block of SQL statements

- **Rollback**—The process of undoing specified SQL statements

- **Commit**—Writing unsaved SQL statements to the database tables

- **Savepoint**—A temporary placeholder in a transaction set to which you can issue a rollback (as opposed to rolling back an entire transaction)

Controlling Transactions

Now that you know what transaction processing is, let's look at what is involved in managing transactions.

The key to managing transactions involves breaking your SQL statements into logical chunks and explicitly stating when data should be rolled back and when it should not.

The MariaDB statement used to mark the start of a transaction is

▼ **Input**

```
START TRANSACTION
```

Using ROLLBACK

The MariaDB ROLLBACK command is used to roll back (undo) MariaDB statements, as seen in this next statement:

▼ Input

```
SELECT * FROM ordertotals;
START TRANSACTION;
DELETE FROM ordertotals;
SELECT * FROM ordertotals;
ROLLBACK;
SELECT * FROM ordertotals;
```

▼ Analysis

This example starts by displaying the contents of the ordertotals table (this table was populated in Chapter 24, "Using Cursors"). First a SELECT is performed to show that the table is not empty. Then a transaction is started, and all the rows in ordertables are deleted with a DELETE statement. Another SELECT verifies that, indeed, ordertotals is empty. Then a ROLLBACK statement is used to roll back all statements until the START TRANSACTION, and the final SELECT shows that the table is no longer empty.

Obviously, ROLLBACK can only be used within a transaction (after a START TRANSACTION command has been issued).

> Tip
>
> **Which Statements Can You Roll Back?**   Transaction processing is used to manage INSERT, UPDATE, and DELETE statements. You cannot roll back SELECT statements. (There would not be much point in doing so anyway.) You cannot roll back CREATE or DROP operations. These statements may be used in a transaction block, but if you perform a rollback they will not be undone.

Using COMMIT

MariaDB SQL statements are usually executed and written directly to the database tables. This is known as an *implicit commit*—the commit (write or save) operation happens automatically.

Within a transaction block, however, commits do not occur implicitly. To force an explicit commit, the COMMIT statement is used, as seen here:

▼ Input

```
START TRANSACTION;
DELETE FROM orderitems WHERE order_num = 20010;
DELETE FROM orders WHERE order_num = 20010;
COMMIT;
```

▼ Analysis

In this example, order number 20010 is deleted entirely from the system. Because this involves updating two database tables, orders and orderitems, a transaction block is used to ensure that the order is not partially deleted. The final COMMIT statement writes the change only if no error occurred. If the first DELETE worked, but the second failed, the DELETE would not be committed (it would effectively be automatically undone).

> **Note**
>
> **Implicit Transaction Closes**   After a COMMIT or ROLLBACK statement has been executed, the transaction is automatically closed (and future changes will implicitly commit).

Using Savepoints

Simple ROLLBACK and COMMIT statements enable you to write or undo an entire transaction. Although this works for simple transactions, more complex transactions might require partial commits or rollbacks.

For example, the process of adding an order described previously is a single transaction. If an error occurs, you want to roll back only to the point before the orders row was added. You do not want to roll back the addition to the customers table (if there was one).

To support the rollback of partial transactions, you must be able to put placeholders at strategic locations in the transaction block. Then, if a rollback is required, you can roll back to one of the placeholders.

These placeholders are called *savepoints*, and to create one use the SAVEPOINT statement, as follows:

▼ Input

```
SAVEPOINT delete1;
```

Each savepoint takes a unique name that identifies it so that, when you roll back, MariaDB knows where you are rolling back to. To roll back to this savepoint, do the following:

▼ Input

```
ROLLBACK TO delete1;
```

> **Tip**
>
> **The More Savepoints the Better**   You can have as many savepoints as you want within your MariaDB SQL code, and the more the better. Why? Because the more savepoints you have the more flexibility you have in managing rollbacks exactly as you need them.

> **Note**
>
> **Releasing Savepoints**   Savepoints are automatically released after a transaction completes (a ROLLBACK or COMMIT is issued). Savepoints can also be explicitly released using RELEASE SAVEPOINT.

Changing the Default Commit Behavior

As already explained, the default MariaDB behavior is to automatically commit any and all changes. In other words, anytime you execute a MariaDB SQL statement, that statement is actually being performed against the tables, and the changes made occur immediately. To instruct MariaDB to not automatically commit changes, you need to use the following statement:

▼ Input

```
SET autocommit=0;
```

▼ Analysis

The autocommit flag determines whether changes are committed automatically without requiring a manual COMMIT statement. Setting autocommit to 0 (false) instructs MariaDB to not automatically commit changes (until the flag is set back to true).

> **Note**
>
> **Flag Is Connection Specific**   The autocommit flag is per connection, not serverwide.

Summary

In this chapter, you learned that transactions are blocks of SQL statements that must be executed as a batch. You learned how to use the COMMIT and ROLLBACK statements to explicitly manage when data is written and when it is undone. You also learned how to use savepoints to provide a greater level of control over rollback operations.

27

Globalization and Localization

In this chapter, you learn the basics of how MariaDB handles different character sets and languages.

Understanding Character Sets and Collation Sequences

Database tables are used to store and retrieve data. Different languages and character sets need to be stored and retrieved differently. As such, MariaDB needs to accommodate different character sets (different alphabets and characters) as well as different ways to sort and retrieve data.

When discussing multiple languages and characters sets, you will run into the following important terms:

- *Character sets* are collections of letters and symbols.

- *Encodings* are the internal representations of the members of a character set.

- *Collations* are the instructions that dictate how characters are to be compared.

> **Note**
>
> **Why Collations Are Important** Sorting text in English is easy, right? Well, maybe not. Consider the words APE, apex, and Apple. Are they in the correct sorted order? That would depend on whether you wanted a case-sensitive or a not case-sensitive sorting. The words would be sorted one way using a case-sensitive collation, and another way using a not case-sensitive collation. And this affects more than just sorting (as in data sorted using ORDER BY); it also affects searches (whether or not a WHERE clause looking for apple finds APPLE, for example). The situation becomes more complex when characters such as the French è or German ö are used, and even more complex when non-Latin-based character sets are used (Japanese, Hebrew, Russian, and so on).

In MariaDB there is not much to worry about during regular database activity (SELECT, INSERT, and so forth). Rather, the decision as to which character set and collation to use occurs at the server, database, and table level.

Working with Character Set and Collation Sequences

MariaDB supports a vast number of character sets. To see the complete list of supported character sets, use this statement:

▼ Input

```
SHOW CHARACTER SET;
```

▼ Analysis

This statement displays all available character sets, along with the description and default collation for each.

To see the complete list of supported collations, use this statement:

▼ Input

```
SHOW COLLATION;
```

▼ Analysis

This statement displays all available collations, along with the character sets to which they apply. Notice that several character sets have more than one collation. latin1, for example, has several for different European languages, and many appear twice, once case sensitive (designated by _cs) and once not case sensitive (designated by _ci).

A default character set and collation are defined (usually by the system administration at installation time). In addition, when databases are created, default character sets and collations may be specified too. To determine the character sets and collations in use, use these statements:

▼ Input

```
SHOW VARIABLES LIKE 'character%';
SHOW VARIABLES LIKE 'collation%';
```

In practice, character sets can seldom be serverwide (or even databasewide) settings. Different tables, and even different columns, may require different character sets, and so both may be specified when a table is created.

To specify a character set and collation for a table, CREATE TABLE (seen in Chapter 21, "Creating and Manipulating Tables") is used with additional clauses:

▼ **Input**

```
CREATE TABLE mytable
(
   columnn1   INT,
   columnn2   VARCHAR(10)
) DEFAULT CHARACTER SET hebrew
  COLLATE hebrew_general_ci;
```

▼ **Analysis**

This statement creates a two column table, and specifies both a character set and a collate sequence.

In this example both CHARACTER SET and COLLATE were specified, but if only one (or neither) is specified, this is how MariaDB determines what to use:

- If both CHARACTER SET and COLLATE are specified, those values are used.

- If only CHARACTER SET is specified, it is used along with the default collation for that character set (as specified in the SHOW CHARACTER SET results).

- If neither CHARACTER SET nor COLLATE is specified, the database default is used.

In addition to being able to specify character set and collation tablewide, MariaDB also allows these to be set per column, as seen here:

▼ **Input**

```
CREATE TABLE mytable
(
   columnn1   INT,
   columnn2   VARCHAR(10),
   column3    VARCHAR(10) CHARACTER SET latin1 COLLATE latin1_general_ci
) DEFAULT CHARACTER SET hebrew
  COLLATE hebrew_general_ci;
```

▼ **Analysis**

Here CHARACTER SET and COLLATE are specified for the entire table as well as for a specific column.

As mentioned previously, the collation plays a key role in sorting data that is retrieved with an ORDER BY clause. If you need to sort specific SELECT statements using a collation sequence other than the one used at table creation time, you may do so in the SELECT statement itself:

▼ Input

```
SELECT * FROM customers
ORDER BY lastname, firstname COLLATE latin1_general_cs;
```

▼ Analysis

This SELECT uses COLLATE to specify an alternate collation sequence (in this example, a case-sensitive one). This obviously affects the order in which results are sorted.

Tip

Occasional Case Sensitivity   The SELECT statement just seen demonstrates a useful technique for performing case-sensitive searches on a table that is usually not case sensitive. And of course, the reverse works just as well.

Note

Other SELECT COLLATE Clauses   In addition to being used in ORDER BY clauses, as seen here, COLLATE can be used with GROUP BY, HAVING, aggregate functions, aliases, and more.

One final point worth noting is that strings may be converted between character sets if absolutely needed. To do this, use the Cast() or Convert() functions.

Summary

In this chapter, you learned the basics of character sets and collations. You also learned how to define the character sets and collations for specific tables and columns, and how to use alternate collations when needed.

28

Managing Security

Database servers usually contain critical data, and ensuring the safety and integrity of that data requires that access control be used. In this chapter you learn about MariaDB access control and user management.

Understanding Access Control

The basis of security for your MariaDB server is this: *Users should have appropriate access to the data they need, no more and no less.* In other words, users should not have too much access to too much data.

Consider the following:

- Most users need to read and write data from tables, but few users will ever need to be able to create and drop tables.

- Some users might need to read tables but might not need to update them.

- You might want to allow users to add data but not delete data.

- Some users (managers or administrators) might need rights to manipulate user accounts, but most should not.

- You might want users to access data via stored procedures but never directly.

- You might want to restrict access to some functionality based on from where the user is logging in.

These are just examples, but they help demonstrate an important point. You need to provide users with the access they need and just the access they need. This is known as *access control*, and managing access control requires creating and managing user accounts.

Back in Chapter 3, "Working with MariaDB," you learned that you need to log in to MariaDB to perform any operations. When first installed, MariaDB creates a user account named root that has complete and total control over the entire MariaDB server. You might have been using the `root` login throughout the chapters in this book, and that is fine when experimenting with MariaDB on nonlive servers. But in the real world you'd never use `root` on a day-to-day basis. Instead, you'd create a series of accounts, some for administration, some for users, some for developers, and so on.

> **Note**
>
> **Preventing Innocent Mistakes**   It is important to note that access control is not just intended to keep out users with malicious intent. More often than not, data nightmares are the result of an inadvertent mistake, a mistyped MariaDB statement, being in the wrong database, or some other user error. Access control helps avoid these situations by ensuring that users are unable to execute statements they should not be executing.

> **Caution**
>
> **Don't Use `root`**   The `root` login should be considered sacred. Use it only when absolutely needed (perhaps if you cannot get in to other administrative accounts). `root` should never be used in day-to-day MariaDB operations.

Managing Users

MariaDB user accounts and information are stored in a MariaDB database named `mysql`. You usually do not need to access the `mysql` database and tables directly (as you will soon see), but sometimes you might. One of those times is when you want to obtain a list of all user accounts. To do that, use the following code:

▼ **Input**
```
USE mysql;
SELECT user FROM user;
```

▼ **Output**
```
+------+
| user |
+------+
| root |
+------+
```

▼ Analysis

The `mysql` database contains a table named `user` that contains all user accounts. `user` contains a column named `user` that contains the user login name. A newly installed server might have a single user listed (as seen here); established servers will likely have far more.

> **Tip**
>
> **Test Using Multiple Clients**   The easiest way to test changes made to user accounts and rights is to open multiple database clients (multiple copies of the mysql command line utility, for example), one logged in with the administrative login and the others logged in as the users being tested.

Creating User Accounts

To create a new user account, use the `CREATE USER` statement, as seen here:

▼ Input

```
CREATE USER ben IDENTIFIED BY 'p@$$w0rd';
```

▼ Analysis

`CREATE USER` creates a new user account. A password need not be specified at user account creation time, but this example does specify a password using `IDENTIFIED BY 'p@$$w0rd'`.

If you were to list the user accounts again, you'd see the new account listed in the output.

> **Tip**
>
> **Specifying a Hashed Password**   The password specified by `IDENTIFIED BY` is plain text that MariaDB will encrypt before saving it in the `user` table. To specify the password as a hashed value, use `IDENTIFIED BY PASSWORD` instead.

> **Note**
>
> **Using GRANT or INSERT**   The GRANT statement (which we will get to shortly) can also create user accounts, but generally `CREATE USER` is the cleanest and simplest syntax. In addition, it is possible to add users by inserting rows into `user` directly, but to be safe this is generally not recommended. The tables used by MariaDB to store user account information (as well as table schemas and more) are extremely important, and any damage to them could seriously harm the MariaDB server. As such, it is always better to use tags and functions to manipulate these tables as opposed to manipulating them directly.

To rename a user account, use the RENAME USER statement like this:

▼ Input
```
RENAME USER ben TO bforta;
```

Deleting User Accounts

To delete a user account (along with any associated rights and privileges), use the DROP USER statement as seen here:

▼ Input
```
DROP USER bforta;
```

Setting Access Rights

With user accounts created, you must next assign access rights and privileges. Newly created user accounts have no access at all. They can log in to MariaDB, but they see no data and cannot perform any database operations.

To see the rights granted to a user account, use SHOW GRANTS FOR as seen in this example:

▼ Input
```
SHOW GRANTS FOR bforta;
```

▼ Output
```
+--------------------------------------------------+
| Grants for bforta@%                              |
+--------------------------------------------------+
| GRANT USAGE ON *.* TO 'bforta'@'%'               |
+--------------------------------------------------+
```

▼ Analysis

The output shows that user bforta has a single right granted, USAGE ON *.*. USAGE means *no rights at all* (not overly intuitive, I know), so the results mean *no rights to anything on any database and any table*.

> **Note**
>
> **Users Are Defined As user@host**   MariaDB privileges are defined using a combination of user name and hostname. If no hostname is specified then a default hostname of % will be used (effectively granting access to the user regardless of the hostname).

To set rights the GRANT statement is used. At a minimum, GRANT requires that you specify

- The privilege being granted
- The database or table being granted access to
- The user name

The following example demonstrates the use of GRANT:

▼ Input

```
GRANT SELECT ON crashcourse.* TO bforta;
```

▼ Analysis

This GRANT allows the use of SELECT on crashcourse.* (crashcourse database, all tables). By granting SELECT access only, user bforta has read-only access to all data in the crashcourse database.

SHOW GRANTS reflects this change:

▼ Input

```
SHOW GRANTS FOR bforta;
```

▼ Output

```
+-------------------------------------------------+
| Grants for bforta@%                             |
+-------------------------------------------------+
| GRANT USAGE ON *.* TO 'bforta'@'%'              |
| GRANT SELECT ON 'crashcourse'.* TO 'bforta'@'%' |
+-------------------------------------------------+
```

▼ Analysis

Each GRANT adds (or updates) a permission statement for the user. MariaDB reads all the grants and determines the rights and permissions based on them.

The opposite of GRANT is REVOKE, which is used to revoke specific rights and permissions. Here is an example:

▼ Input

```
REVOKE SELECT ON crashcourse.* FROM bforta;
```

▼ Analysis

This REVOKE statement takes away the SELECT access just granted to user bforta. The access being revoked must exist or an error will be thrown.

GRANT and REVOKE can be used to control access at several levels:

- Entire server, using GRANT ALL and REVOKE ALL
- Entire database, using ON database.*
- Specific tables, using ON database.table
- Specific columns
- Specific stored procedures

Table 28.1 lists each of the rights and privileges that may be granted or revoked.

Table 28.1   Rights and Privileges

Privilege	Description
ALL	All privileges except GRANT OPTION.
ALTER	Use of ALTER TABLE.
ALTER ROUTINE	Use of ALTER PROCEDURE and DROP PROCEDURE.
CREATE	Use of CREATE TABLE.
CREATE ROUTINE	Use of CREATE PROCEDURE.
CREATE TEMPORARY TABLES	Use of CREATE TEMPORARY TABLE.
CREATE USER	Use of CREATE USER, DROP USER, RENAME USER, and REVOKE ALL PRIVILEGES.
CREATE VIEW	Use of CREATE VIEW.
DELETE	Use of DELETE.
DROP	Use of DROP TABLE.
EXECUTE	Use of CALL and stored procedures.
FILE	Use of SELECT INTO OUTFILE and LOAD DATA INFILE.
GRANT OPTION	Use of GRANT and REVOKE.
INDEX	Use of CREATE INDEX and DROP INDEX.
INSERT	Use of INSERT.
LOCK TABLES	Use of LOCK TABLES.
PROCESS	Use of SHOW FULL PROCESSLIST.
RELOAD	Use of FLUSH.
REPLICATION CLIENT	Access to location of servers.
REPLICATION SLAVE	Used by replication slaves.
SELECT	Use of SELECT.

SHOW DATABASES	Use of SHOW DATABASES.
SHOW VIEW	Use of SHOW CREATE VIEW.
SHUTDOWN	Use of mysqladmin shutdown (used to shut down MariaDB).
SUPER	Use of CHANGE MASTER, KILL, LOGS, PURGE MASTER, and SET GLOBAL. Also allows mysql-admin debug login.
UPDATE	Use of UPDATE.
USAGE	No access.

Using GRANT and REVOKE in conjunction with the privileges listed in Table 28.1, you have complete control over what users can and cannot do with your precious data.

> **Note**
>
> **Granting for the Future**   When using GRANT and REVOKE, the user account must exist, but the objects being referred to need not. This allows administrators to design and implement security before databases and tables are even created.
>
> A side effect of this is that if a database or table is removed (with a DROP statement) any associated access rights will still exist. And if the database or table is re-created in the future, those rights will apply to them.

> **Tip**
>
> **Simplifying Multiple Grants**   Multiple GRANT statements may be strung together by listing the privileges comma delimited, as seen in this example:

```
GRANT SELECT, INSERT ON crashcourse.* TO bforta;
```

Changing Passwords

To change user passwords use the SET PASSWORD statement. New passwords must be encrypted as seen here:

▼ Input

```
SET PASSWORD FOR bforta = Password('n3w p@$$w0rd');
```

▼ Analysis

SET PASSWORD updates a user password. The new password must be encrypted by being passed to the Password() function.

SET PASSWORD can also be used to set your own password:

▼ Input

```
SET PASSWORD = Password('n3w p@$$w0rd');
```

▼ Analysis

When no user name is specified, `SET PASSWORD` updates the password for the currently logged in user.

Summary

In this chapter, you learned about access control and how to secure your MariaDB server by assigning specific rights to users. As you can imagine, there is a lot more to this advanced topic, and MariaDB administrators should dedicate the time to fully understand managing DBMS security.

29

Database Maintenance

In this chapter, you learn how to perform common database maintenance tasks.

Backing Up Data

Like all data, MariaDB data must be backed up regularly. As MariaDB databases are disk-based files, normal backup systems and routines can back up MariaDB data. However, as those files are always open and in use, normal file copy backup may not always work as is not recommended.

Here are possible solutions to this problem:

- Use the command line `mysqldump` utility to dump all database contents to an external file. This utility should ideally be run before regular backups occur so the dumped file will be backed up properly.

- The command line `mysqlhotcopy` utility can be used to copy all data from a database (this one is not supported by all database engines).

- You can also use MariaDB to dump all data to an external file using `BACKUP TABLE` or `SELECT INTO OUTFILE`. Both statements take the name of a system file to be created, and that file must not already exist or an error will be generated. Data can be restored using `RESTORE TABLE`.

> **Tip**
>
> **Flush Unwritten Data First** To ensure that all data is written to disk (including any index data) you might need to use a `FLUSH TABLES` statement before performing your backup.

Performing Database Maintenance

MariaDB features a series of statements that can (and should) be used to ensure that databases are correct and functioning properly.

Here are some statements you should be aware of:

- ANALYZE TABLE is used to check that table keys are correct. ANALYZE TABLE returns status information, as seen here:

▼ Input
```
ANALYZE TABLE orders;
```

▼ Output
```
+--------------------+---------+----------+----------+
| Table              | Op      | Msg_type | Msg_text |
+--------------------+---------+----------+----------+
| crashcourse.orders | analyze | status   | OK       |
+--------------------+---------+----------+----------+
```

- CHECK TABLE is used to check tables for a variety of problems. Indexes are also checked on an ARIA or MyISAM table. CHECK TABLE supports a series of modes for use with ARIA or MyISAM tables. CHANGED checks tables that have changed since the last check, EXTENDED performs the most thorough check, FAST only checks tables that were not closed properly, MEDIUM checks all deleted links and performs key verification, and QUICK perform a quick scan only. As seen here, CHECK TABLE found and repaired a problem:

▼ Input
```
CHECK TABLE orders, orderitems;
```

▼ Output
```
+------------------------+-------+----------+---------------------------+
| Table                  | Op    | Msg_type | Msg_text                  |
+------------------------+-------+----------+---------------------------+
| crashcourse.orders     | check | status   | OK                        |
| crashcourse.orderitems | check | warning  | Table is marked as crashed |
| crashcourse.orderitems | check | status   | OK                        |
+------------------------+-------+----------+---------------------------+
```

- If ARIA or MyISAM table access produces incorrect and inconsistent results, you might need to repair the table using REPAIR TABLE. This statement should not be used frequently, and if regular use is required, there is likely a far bigger problem that needs addressing.

- If you delete large amounts of data from a table, OPTIMIZE TABLE should be used to reclaim previously used space, thus optimizing the performance of the table.

Diagnosing Startup Problems

Server startup problems usually occur when a change has been made to MariaDB configuration or the server itself. MariaDB reports errors when this occurs, but because most MariaDB servers are started automatically as system processes or services, these messages might not be seen.

When troubleshooting system startup problems, try to manually start the server first. The MariaDB server itself is started by executing `mysqld` on the command line. Here are several important command `mysqld` line options:

- `--help` displays help, a list of options.

- `--safe-mode` loads the server minus some optimizations.

- `--verbose` displays full text messages (use in conjunction with `--help` for more detailed help messages).

- `--version` displays version information and then quits.

Several additional command line options (pertaining to the use of log files) are listed in the next section.

Review Log Files

MariaDB maintains a series of log files that administrators rely on extensively. The primary log files are

- The error log contains details about startup and shutdown problems and any critical errors. The log is usually named `hostname.err` in the `data` directory. This name can be changed using the `--log-error` command line option.

- The query log logs all MariaDB activity and can be useful in diagnosing problems. This log file can get large quickly, so it should not be used for extended periods of time. The log is usually named `hostname.log` in the `data` directory. This name can be changed using the `--log` command line option.

- The binary log logs all statements that updated (or could have updated) data. The log is usually named `hostname-bin` in the `data` directory. This name can be changed using the `--log-bin` command line option.

- As its name suggests, the slow query log logs any queries that execute slowly. This log can be useful in determining where database optimizations are needed. The log is usually named `hostname-slow.log` in the `data` directory. This name can be changed using the `--log-slow-queries` command line option.

When logging is being used, the FLUSH LOGS statement can be used to flush and restart all log files.

Summary

In this chapter, you learned some basic MariaDB database maintenance tools and techniques.

30

Improving Performance

In this chapter, you review some important points pertaining to the performance of MariaDB.

Improving Performance

Database administrators spend a significant portion of their lives tweaking and experimenting to improve DBMS performance. Poorly performing databases (and database queries, for that matter) tend to be the most frequent culprits when diagnosing application sluggishness and performance problems.

What follows is not, by any stretch of the imagination, the last word on MariaDB performance. This is intended to review key points made in the previous 29 chapters, as well as to provide a springboard from which to launch performance optimization discussion and analysis.

So, here goes:

- First and foremost, MariaDB (like all DBMSs) has specific hardware recommendations. Using any old computer as a database server is fine when learning and playing with MariaDB. But production servers should adhere to all recommendations.

- As a rule, critical production DBMSs should run on their own dedicated servers.

- MariaDB is preconfigured with a series of default settings that are usually a good place to start. But after a while you might need to tweak memory allocation, buffer sizes, and more. (To see the current settings use SHOW VARIABLES; and SHOW STATUS;.)

- MariaDB is a multiuser multithreaded DBMS; in other words, it often performs multiple tasks at the same time. And if one of those tasks is executing slowly, all requests will suffer. If you are experiencing unusually poor performance, use SHOW PROCESSLIST to display all active processes (along with their thread IDs and execution time). You can also use the KILL command to terminate a specific process (you need to be logged in as an administrator to use that one).

- There is almost always more than one way to write a SELECT statement. Experiment with joins, unions, subqueries, and more to find what is optimum for you and your data.

- Use the EXPLAIN statement to have MariaDB explain how it will execute a SELECT statement.

- As a general rule, stored procedures execute quicker than individual MariaDB statements.

- Use the right data types, always.

- Never retrieve more data than you need. In other words, no SELECT * (unless you truly do need each and every column).

- Some operations (including INSERT) support an optional DELAYED keyword that, if used, returns control to the calling application immediately and actually performs the operation when there are no more pending operations. While this improves client performance (as control is returned immediately), this option does introduce a risk—if a server were to crash those queries would be lost.

- When importing data, turn off autocommit. You may also want to drop indexes (including FULLTEXT indexes) and then re-create them after the import has completed. Alternatively, you can use ALTER TABLE to temporarily DISABLE KEYS (remember to ENABLE KEYS when you are done).

- Database tables must be indexed to improve the performance of data retrieval. Determining what to index is not a trivial task, and involves analyzing used SELECT statements to find recurring WHERE and ORDER BY clauses. If a simple WHERE clause is taking too long to return results, you can bet that the column (or columns) being used is a good candidate for indexing.

- Have a series of complex OR conditions in your SELECT? You may see a significant performance improvement by using multiple SELECT statements and UNION to connect them.

- Indexes improve the performance of data retrieval but hurt the performance of data insertion, deletion, and updating. If you have tables that collect data and are not often searched, don't index them until needed. (Indexes can be added and dropped as needed.)

- LIKE is slow. As a general rule, you are better off using FULLTEXT over LIKE.

- Databases are living entities. A well-optimized set of tables might not be so after a while. As table usage and contents change, so might the ideal optimization and configuration.

- And the most important rule is simply this—every rule is meant to be broken at some point.

Summary

In this chapter, you reviewed some important tips and notes pertaining to MariaDB performance. Of course, this is just the tip of the iceberg, but now that you have completed the *MariaDB Crash Course* you are free to experiment and learn as you best see fit.

Appendix A

Getting Started with MariaDB

If you are new to MariaDB, here is what you need to know to get started.

What You Need

To start using MariaDB and to follow along with the chapters in this book, you need access to a MariaDB server and copies of client applications (software used to access the server).

You do not need your own installed copy of MariaDB, but you do need access to a server. You basically have two options:

- Access to an existing MariaDB server, perhaps one by your hosting company or place of business or school. To use this server you will be granted a server account (a login name and password).

- You may download and install a free copy of the MariaDB server for installation on your own computer (MariaDB runs on all major platforms including Windows and Linux).

> **Tip**
>
> **If You Can, Install a Local Server**   For complete control, including access to commands and features that you will probably not be granted using someone else's MariaDB server, install your own local server. Even if you don't end up using your local server as your final production DBMS, you'll still benefit from having complete and unfettered access to all the server has to offer.

Regardless of whether you use a local server, you need client software (the program you use to actually run SQL commands). The most readily available is the `mysql` command line utility (included with every MariaDB installation). Another important utility is the MySQL Workbench.

Obtaining the Software

To learn more about MariaDB, go to `http://mariadb.org/`.

To download a copy of the server, go to `http://maraiadb.org/downloads/`.

It is recommended that you download and install the newest version of MariaDB (usually the first option listed). You are presented with a list of download options for various computer platforms and operating systems.

Unlike the command line `mysql` utility, MySQL Workbench is not included with MariaDB. Instead, it must be downloaded from `http://wb.mysql.com/`.

Installing the Software

If you are installing a local MariaDB server, do so before installing any other clients or utilities. The installation procedure varies from platform to platform, but all installations prompt you for needed information, including

- Installation location (the default is usually fine).

- Password for `root` user. (If you are not prompted for a `root` password then there will be no `root` password set.)

- Ports, service or process names, and more. As a rule, use default values if you are unsure of what to specify.

> **Tip**
>
> **Multiple MariaDB Servers**   Multiple copies of MariaDB server may be installed on a single machine, as long as each uses a different port.

> **Note**
>
> **Important Note for Windows Users**   When running MariaDB on Windows you want the MariaDB server to be running as a system service. If you are installing MariaDB 5.2.6 or later, the service will be created for you as part of the installation process. For earlier versions of MariaDB, you need to do this manually. Fortunately, this is simple to do. Open a command prompt window (you can do this by clicking Start, Run; typing `cmd`; and then clicking OK) and then go to the `bin` folder under the MariaDB installation folder. In that folder type `mysqld --install` and press Enter. You should see a message telling you that the service was created.

Preparing to Try It Yourself

After you have installed MariaDB, Chapter 3, "Working with MariaDB," shows you how to log in and log out of the server, and how to execute commands.

The chapters in this book all use real SQL statements and real data. Appendix B, "The Example Tables," describes the example tables used in this book, and explains how to obtain and use the table creation and population scripts.

Appendix B
The Example Tables

Writing SQL statements requires a good understanding of the underlying database design. Without knowing what information is stored in what table, how tables are related to each other, and the actual breakup of data within a row, it is impossible to write effective SQL.

You are strongly advised to actually try every example in every chapter in this book. All the chapters use a common set of data files. To assist you in better understanding the examples and to enable you to follow along with the chapters, this appendix describes the tables used, their relationships, and how to obtain them.

Understanding the Sample Tables

The tables used throughout this book are part of an order entry system used by an imaginary distributor of paraphernalia that might be needed by your favorite cartoon characters (yes, cartoon characters; no one said that learning MariaDB needed to be boring). The tables are used to perform several tasks:

- Manage vendors
- Manage product catalogs
- Manage customer lists
- Enter customer orders

Making this all work requires six tables that are closely interconnected as part of a relational database design. A description of each of the tables appears in the following sections.

> **Note**
>
> **Simplified Examples** The tables used here are by no means complete. A real-world order entry system would have to keep track of a lot of other data that has not been included here (for example, payment and accounting information, shipment tracking, and more). However, these tables do demonstrate the kinds of data organization and relationships you will encounter in most real installations. You can apply these techniques and technologies to your own databases.

Table Descriptions

What follows is a description of each of the six tables, along with the name of the columns within each table and their descriptions.

> **Note**
>
> **Why Out of Order?**   If you are wondering why the six tables are listed in the order they are, it is due to their dependencies. As the `products` tables is dependent on the `vendors` table, `vendors` is listed first, and so on.

The `vendors` Table

The `vendors` table (see Table B.1) stores the vendors whose products are sold. Every vendor has a record in this table, and that vendor ID (the `vend_id`) column is used to match products with vendors.

Table B.1   `vendors` **Table Columns**

`vend_id`	Unique numeric vendor ID
`vend_name`	Vendor name
`vend_address`	Vendor address
`vend_city`	Vendor city
`vend_state`	Vendor state
`vend_zip`	Vendor Zip Code
`vend_country`	Vendor country

- All tables should have primary keys defined. This table should use `vend_id` as its primary key. `vend_id` is an auto increment field.

The `products` Table

The `products` table (see Table B.2) contains the product catalog, one product per row. Each product has a unique ID (the `prod_id` column) and is related to its vendor by `vend_id` (the vendor's unique ID).

Table B.2   `products` **Table Columns**

Column	Description
prod_id	Unique product ID
vend_id	Product vendor ID (relates to `vend_id` in `vendors` table)
prod_name	Product name
prod_price	Product price
prod_desc	Product description

- All tables should have primary keys defined. This table should use prod_id as its primary key.

- To enforce referential integrity, a foreign key should be defined on vend_id, relating it to vend_id in vendors.

The `customers` **Table**

The `customers` table (see Table B.3) stores all customer information. Each customer has a unique ID (the `cust_id` column).

Table B.3   `customers` **Table Columns**

Column	Description
cust_id	Unique numeric customer ID
cust_name	Customer name
cust_address	Customer address
cust_city	Customer city
cust_state	Customer state
cust_zip	Customer Zip Code
cust_country	Customer country
cust_contact	Customer contact name
cust_email	Customer contact e-mail address

- All tables should have primary keys defined. This table should use cust_id as its primary key. cust_id is an auto increment field.

The `orders` **Table**

The `orders` table (see Table B.4) stores customer orders (but not order details). Each order is uniquely numbered (the `order_num` column). Orders are associated with the appropriate customers by the `cust_id` column (which relates to the customer's unique ID in the `customers` table).

Table B.4   orders **Table Columns**

Column	Description
order_num	Unique order number
order_date	Order date
cust_id	Order customer ID (relates to cust_id in customers table)

- All tables should have primary keys defined. This table should use order_num as its primary key. order_num is an auto increment field.

- To enforce referential integrity, a foreign key should be defined on cust_id, relating it to cust_id in customers.

The orderitems **Table**

The orderitems table (see Table B.5) stores the actual items in each order, one row per item per order. For every row in orders there are one or more rows in orderitems. Each order item is uniquely identified by the order number plus the order item (first item in order, second item in order, and so on). Order items are associated with their appropriate order by the order_num column (which relates to the order's unique ID in orders). In addition, each order item contains the product ID of the item orders (which relates the item back to the products table).

Table B.5   orderitems **Table Columns**

Column	Description
order_num	Order number (relates to order_num in orders table)
order_item	Order item number (sequential within an order)
prod_id	Product ID (relates to prod_id in products table)
quantity	Item quantity
item_price	Item price

- All tables should have primary keys defined. This table should use order_num and order_item as its primary keys.

- To enforce referential integrity, foreign keys should be defined on order_num, relating it to order_num in orders, and prod_id, relating it to prod_id in products.

The productnotes Table

The productnotes table (see Table B.6) stores notes associated with specific products. Not all products may have associated notes, and some products may have many associated notes.

Table B.6   productnotes Table Columns

Column	Description
note_id	Unique note ID
prod_id	Product ID (corresponds to prod_id in products table)
note_date	Date note added
note_text	Note text

- All tables should have primary keys defined. This table should use note_id as its primary key.

- Column note_text must be indexed for FULLTEXT search use.

Creating the Sample Tables

To follow along with the examples, you need a set of populated tables. Everything you need to get up and running can be found on this book's Web page at http://forta.com/books/0321799941/.

The Web page contains two SQL script files that you may download:

- create.sql contains the MariaDB SQL statements to create the six database tables (including defining all primary keys and foreign key constraints).

- populate.sql contains the SQL INSERT statements used to populate these tables.

> **Note**
>
> **For MariaDB Only**   The SQL statements in the downloadable .sql files are DBMS specific and are designed to be used only with MariaDB.

After you have downloaded the scripts, you can use them to create and populate the tables needed to follow along with the chapters in this book. You can do this using the mysql command line utility or MySQL Workbench.

Note

Create, Then Populate   You must run the table creation scripts *before* the table population scripts. Be sure to check for any error messages returned by these scripts. If the
creation scripts fail, you need to remedy whatever problem might exist before continuing
with table population.

Caution

One Or the Other, Not Both   Both of the following sets of instructions do the exact
same thing, so pick one and use it, but don't try to use both. (You'll not be able to create the same database and tables twice.)

Using mysql

To create the example data using the mysql command line utility, do the
following:

1. Make sure MariaDB is running.

2. Open a command prompt window, and go to the bin folder under the
MariaDB installation folder.

3. Connect to MariaDB as the root user (so that you have the security
access needed to create a new database). Type mysql -u root and
press Enter. If you specified a root password at installation time, use
mysql -u root -p and press Enter, and then type the password when
prompted to do so.

4. You should see a prompt like MariaDB [(none)]>. The name of the
currently selected database is displayed inside the square brackets, and
(none) simply means that no database has been selected.

5. To keep the tables used in this book separate from any other work or
data, we create a new database and use that exclusively for all chapters.
Type create database crashcourse; (don't forget the ;) and press
Enter to create a new database named crashcourse. You should see a
message saying OK.

6. Next you need to select the new database (so that when you create
the tables they are created inside it). Type USE crashcourse; and press
Enter. The prompt should now indicate that the crashcourse database
has been selected.

7. To create the tables, you need to run the `create.sql` script. Make sure you know the full path to the file and type `\. /path/create.sql` and press Enter, replacing `path` with the actual path. So, if `create.sql` is in `/downloads/`, type `\. /downloads/create.sql`. You should see a series of `OK` messages.

> **Caution**
>
> **No ; When Using \.** Unlike the `CREATE` and `USE` statements (and indeed just about every MariaDB SQL statement), do not type a trailing `;` when using the `\.` command to execute an external script file.

8. Repeat step 7, this time using the `populate.sql` script. This populates the newly created tables with the sample data. Again, you should see a series of `OK` messages indicating success.

9. When you are done, type `exit` or `quit` to exit `mysql`.

You can now return to Chapter 3, "Working with MariaDB."

Using MySQL Workbench

To create the example data using MySQL Workbench, do the following:

1. Make sure MariaDB is running.

2. Launch MySQL Workbench.

3. Click on Open Connection to Start Querying (it's the top option in the left column) to display the Connect to Database dialog.

4. Make sure the hostname is correct, the user name should be `root`, and you should enter the root password if one was specified at installation time. Click OK and you should see the SQL Editor window. Existing databases are listed in the Overview tab at the top of the lower half of the screen.

5. To keep the tables used in this book separate from any other work or data, we create a new database and use that exclusively for all chapters. Click the + button on the right above the listed databases to display the new_schema dialog (*schema* is another name for a database). Type `crashcourse` in the name field and click Apply. You are presented with a confirmation dialog. Click Apply again to create the database. When you receive confirmation click Finish and close the dialogs.

6. Next you need to select the new database (so that when you create the tables they are created inside it). Type USE crashcourse; at the top of the screen and click the Execute button (the one with the yellow lightning bolt). The output tab indicates success or failure with an icon for each statement—red X for failure, blue exclamation mark for success.

7. To create the tables, you need to run the create.sql script. Select File, Open SQL Script, and locate the create.sql file. When you see the contents in the editor window, click the Execute button. The output tab below indicates success or failure with an icon for each statement (multiple statements will be executed).

8. Repeat step 7, this time using the populate.sql script. This populates the newly created tables with the sample data. Again, the output tab below indicates success or failure with an icon for each statement.

9. When you are done, you can quit MySQL Workbench.

You can now return to Chapter 3.

Appendix C
MariaDB Datatypes

As explained in Chapter 1, "Understanding SQL," datatypes are basically rules that define what data may be stored in a column and how that data is actually stored.

Datatypes are used for several reasons:

- Datatypes enable you to restrict the type of data that can be stored in a column. For example, a numeric datatype column only accepts numeric values.

- Datatypes allow for more efficient storage, internally. Numbers and date time values can be stored in a more condensed format than text strings.

- Datatypes allow for alternate sorting orders. If everything is treated as strings, 1 comes before 10, which comes before 2. (Strings are sorted in dictionary sequence, one character at a time starting from the left.) As numeric datatypes, the numbers would be sorted correctly.

When designing tables, pay careful attention to the datatypes being used. Using the wrong datatype can seriously impact your application. Changing the datatypes of existing populated columns is not a trivial task. (In addition, doing so can result in data loss.)

Although this appendix is by no means a complete tutorial on datatypes and how they are to be used, it explains the major MariaDB datatype types, and what they are used for.

String Datatypes

The most commonly used datatypes are string datatypes. These store strings: for example, names, addresses, phone numbers, and Zip Codes. As listed in Table D.1, there are basically two types of string datatype that you can use—fixed-length strings and variable-length strings.

Fixed-length strings are datatypes that are defined to accept a fixed number of characters, and that number is specified when the table is created. For example, you might allow 30 characters in a first-name column or 11 characters in a Social-Security-number column (the exact number needed allowing for the two dashes). Fixed-length columns do not allow more than the specified number of characters. They also allocate storage space for as many characters as specified. So, if the string Ben is stored in a 30-character first-name field, a full 30 bytes are stored. CHAR is an example of a fixed-length string type.

Variable-length strings store text of variable length. Some variable-length datatypes have a defined maximum size. Others are entirely variable. Either way, only the data specified is saved (and no extra data is stored). TEXT is an example of a variable-length string type.

If variable-length datatypes are so flexible, why would you ever want to use fixed-length datatypes? The answer is performance. MariaDB can sort and manipulate fixed-length columns far more quickly than it can sort variable-length columns. In addition, MariaDB does not allow you to index variable-length columns (or the variable portion of a column). This also dramatically affects performance.

Table D.1   **String Datatypes**

Datatype	Description
CHAR	Fixed-length string from 1 to 255 chars long. Its size must be specified at create time, or MariaDB assumes CHAR(1).
ENUM	Accepts one of a predefined set of up to 64K strings.
LONGTEXT	Same as TEXT, but with a maximum size of 4GB.
MEDIUMTEXT	Same as TEXT, but with a maximum size of 16K.
SET	Accepts zero or more of a predefined set of up to 64 strings.
TEXT	Variable-length text with a maximum size of 64K.
TINYTEXT	Same as TEXT, but with a maximum size of 255 bytes.
VARCHAR	Same as CHAR, but stores just the text. The size is a maximum, not a minimum.

> **Tip**
>
> **Using Quotes**   Regardless of the form of string datatype being used, string values must always be surrounded by quotes (single quotes are often preferred).

> **Caution**
>
> **When Numeric Values Are Not Numeric Values** You might think that phone numbers and Zip Codes should be stored in numeric fields (after all, they store only numeric data), but doing so would not be advisable. If you store the Zip Code 01234 in a numeric field, the number 1234 would be saved. You'd actually lose a digit.
>
> The basic rule to follow is: If the number is a number used in calculations (sums, averages, and so on), it belongs in a numeric datatype column. If it is used as a literal string (that happens to contain only digits), it belongs in a string datatype column.

Numeric Datatypes

Numeric datatypes store numbers. MariaDB supports several numeric datatypes, each with a different range of numbers that can be stored in it. Obviously, the larger the supported range, the more storage space needed. In addition, some numeric datatypes support the use of decimal points (and fractional numbers), whereas others support only whole numbers. Table D.2 lists the frequently used MariaDB numeric datatypes.

> **Note**
>
> **Signed Or UNSIGNED?** All numeric datatypes (with the exception of BIT and BOOLEAN) can be signed or unsigned. Signed numeric columns can store both positive and negative numbers; unsigned numeric columns store only positive numbers. Signed is the default, but if you know that you'll not need to store negative values you can use the UNSIGNED keyword. Doing so allows you to store values twice as large.

Table D.2 **Numeric Datatypes**

Datatype	Description
BIT	A bit-field, from 1 to 64 bits wide
BIGINT	Integer value, supports numbers from -9223372036854775808 to 9223372036854775807 (or 0 to 18446744073709551615 if UNSIGNED)
BOOLEAN (or BOOL)	Boolean flag, either 0 or 1, used primarily for on/off flags
DECIMAL (or DEC)	Floating point values with varying levels of precision
DOUBLE	Double-precision floating point values
FLOAT	Single-precision floating point values
INT (or INTEGER)	Integer value, supports numbers from -2147483648 to 2147483647 (or 0 to 4294967295 if UNSIGNED)
MEDIUMINT	Integer value, supports numbers from -8388608 to 8388607 (or 0 to 16777215 if UNSIGNED)
REAL	4-byte floating point values

Table D.2   **Numeric Datatypes   continued**

Datatype	Description
SMALLINT	Integer value, supports numbers from -32768 to 32767 (or 0 to 65535 if UNSIGNED)
TINYINT	Integer value, supports numbers from -128 to 127 (or 0 to 255 if UNSIGNED)

> **Tip**
>
> **Not Using Quotes**   Unlike strings, numeric values should never be enclosed within quotes.

> **Tip**
>
> **Storing Currency**   There is no special MariaDB datatype for currency values, use DECIMAL(8,2) instead.

Date and Time Datatypes

MariaDB uses special datatypes for the storage of date and time values as listed in Table D.3.

Table D.3   **Date and Time Datatypes**

Datatype	Description
DATE	Date from 1000-01-01 to 9999-12-31 in the format YYYY-MM-DD.
DATETIME	A combination of DATE and TIME.
TIMESTAMP	Functionally equivalent to DATETIME (but with a smaller range).
TIME	Time in the format HH:MM:SS.
YEAR	A 2- or 4-digit year, 2-digit years support a range of 70 (1970) to 69 (2069); 4-digit years support a range of 1901 to 2155.

Binary Datatypes

Binary datatypes are used to store all sorts of data (even binary information), such as graphic images, multimedia, and word processor documents (see Table D.4).

Table D.4   **Binary Datatypes**

Datatype	Description
BLOB	Blob with a maximum length of 64K
MEDIUMBLOB	Blob with a maximum length of 16MB
LONGBLOB	Blob with a maximum length of 4GB
TINYBLOB	Blob with a maximum length of 255 bytes

Note

Datatypes in Use   If you want to see a real-world example of how different databases are used, see the sample table creation scripts (described in Appendix B, "The Example Tables").

Appendix D

MariaDB Reserved Words

The MariaDB implementation of SQL is made up of *keywords*—special words used in performing SQL operations. Special care must be taken to not use these keywords when naming databases, tables, columns, and any other database objects. Thus, these keywords are considered reserved. This appendix lists all of the MariaDB reserved words.

ABS	ASC	BLOCKED
ABSOLUTE	ASENSITIVE	BOOLEAN
ACTION	ASSERTION	BOTH
ADA	ASSIGNMENT	BREADTH
ADD	ASYMMETRIC	BY
ADMIN	AT	C
AFTER	ATOMIC	CALL
AGGREGATE	AUTHORIZATION	CARDINALITY
ALIAS	AVG	CASCADE
ALL	BEFORE	CASCADED
ALLOCATE	BEGIN	CASE
ALTER	BETWEEN	CAST
AND	BINARY	CATALOG
ANY	BIT	CATALOG_NAME
ARE	BIT_LENGTH	CHAIN
ARRAY	BITVAR	CHAR
AS	BLOB	CHAR_LENGTH

CHARACTER

CHARACTER_LENGTH

CHARACTER_SET_
CATALOG

CHARACTER_SET_NAME

CHARACTER_SET_
SCHEMA

CHECK

CHECKED

CLASS

CLASS_ORIGIN

CLOB

CLOSE

COALESCE

COBOL

COLLATE

COLLATION

COLLATION_CATALOG

COLLATION_NAME

COLLATION_SCHEMA

COLUMN

COLUMN_NAME

COMMAND_FUNCTION

COMMAND_FUNCTION_
CODE

COMMIT

COMMITTED

COMPLETION

CONCATENATE

CONDITION

CONDITION_NUMBER

CONNECT

CONNECTION

CONNECTION_NAME

CONSTRAINT

CONSTRAINT_CATALOG

CONSTRAINT_NAME

CONSTRAINT_SCHEMA

CONSTRAINTS

CONSTRUCTOR

CONTAINS

CONTINUE

CONTROL

CONVERT

CORRESPONDING

COUNT

CREATE

CROSS

CUBE

CURRENT

CURRENT_DATE

CURRENT_PATH

CURRENT_ROLE

CURRENT_TIME

CURRENT_TIMESTAMP

CURRENT_USER

CURSOR

CURSOR_NAME

CYCLE

DATA

DATALINK

DATE

DATETIME_INTERVAL_
CODE

DATETIME_INTERVAL_
PRECISION

DAY

DB

DEALLOCATE

DEC

DECIMAL

DECLARE

DEFAULT

DEFERRABLE

DEFERRED

DELETE

DEPTH

DEREF

DESC

DESCRIBE

DESCRIPTOR

DESTROY

DESTRUCTOR

DETERMINISTIC

DIAGNOSTICS

DICTIONARY

DISCONNECT

DISPATCH

DISTINCT	EXEC	GRANT
DLCOMMENT	EXECUTE	GROUP
DLFILESIZE	EXISTING	GROUPING
DLFILESIZEEXACT	EXISTS	HANDLER
DLLINKTYPE	EXIT	HASH
DLURLCOMPLETE	EXPAND	HAVING
DLURLPATH	EXPANDING	HOLD
DLURLPATHONLY	EXTERNAL	HOST
DLURLSCHEMA	EXTRACT	HOUR
DLURLSERVER	FALSE	IDENTITY
DLVALUE	FETCH	IF
DO	FILE	IGNORE
DOMAIN	FINAL	IMMEDIATE
DOUBLE	FIRST	IN
DROP	FLOAT	INDICATOR
DYNAMIC	FOR	INFIX
DYNAMIC_FUNCTION	FOREIGN	INITIALIZE
DYNAMIC_FUNCTION_CODE	FORTRAN	INITIALLY
	FOUND	INNER
EACH	FREE	INOUT
ELSE	FROM	INPUT
ELSEIF	FULL	INSENSITIVE
END	FUNCTION	INSERT
END-EXEC	GENERAL	INSTANTIABLE
EQUALS	GENERATED	INT
ESCAPE	GET	INTEGER
EVERY	GLOBAL	INTEGRITY
EXCEPT	GO	INTERSECT
EXCEPTION	GOTO	INTERVAL

INTO	MEETS	NULLIF
IS	MESSAGE_LENGTH	NUMBER
ISOLATION	MESSAGE_OCTET_ LENGTH	NUMERIC
ITERATE		OBJECT
JOIN	MESSAGE_TEXT	OCTET_LENGTH
KEY	METHOD	OF
KEY_MEMBER	MIN	OFF
KEY_TYPE	MINUTE	OLD
LANGUAGE	MOD	ON
LARGE	MODIFIES	ONLY
LAST	MODIFY	OPEN
LATERAL	MODULE	OPERATION
LEADING	MONTH	OPTION
LEAVE	MORE	OPTIONS
LEFT	MUMPS	OR
LENGTH	NAME	ORDER
LESS	NAMES	ORDINALITY
LEVEL	NATIONAL	OUT
LIKE	NATURAL	OUTER
LIMIT	NCHAR	OUTPUT
LINK	NCLOB	OVERLAPS
LOCAL	NEW	OVERLAY
LOCALTIME	NEXT	OVERRIDING
LOCALTIMESTAMP	NO	PAD
LOCATOR	NONE	PARAMETER
LOOP	NORMALIZE	PARAMETER_MODE
LOWER	NOT	PARAMETER_ORDINAL_ POSITION
MATCH	NULL	
MAX	NULLABLE	

PARAMETER_SPECIFIC_CATALOG

PARAMETER_SPECIFIC_NAME

PARAMETER_SPECIFIC_SCHEMA

PARAMETERS

PARTIAL

PASCAL

PATH

PERIOD

PERMISSION

PLI

POSITION

POSTFIX

PRECEDES

PRECISION

PREFIX

PREORDER

PREPARE

PRESERVE

PRIMARY

PRIOR

PRIVILEGES

PROCEDURE

PUBLIC

READ

READS

REAL

RECOVERY

RECURSIVE

REDO

REF

REFERENCES

REFERENCING

RELATIVE

REPEAT

REPEATABLE

RESIGNAL

RESTORE

RESTRICT

RESULT

RETURN

RETURNED_LENGTH

RETURNED_OCTET_LENGTH

RETURNED_SQLSTATE

RETURNS

REVOKE

RIGHT

ROLE

ROLLBACK

ROLLUP

ROUTINE

ROUTINE_CATALOG

ROUTINE_NAME

ROUTINE_SCHEMA

ROW

ROW_COUNT

ROW_TYPE_CATALOG

ROW_TYPE_NAME

ROW_TYPE_SCHEMA

ROWS

SAVEPOINT

SCALE

SCHEMA

SCHEMA_NAME

SCROLL

SEARCH

SECOND

SECTION

SELECT

SELECTIVE

SELF

SENSITIVE

SEQUENCE

SERIALIZABLE

SERVER_NAME

SESSION

SESSION_USER

SET

SETS

SIGNAL

SIMILAR

SIMPLE

SIZE

SMALLINT

SOME

SOURCE	TIMESTAMP	UNTIL
SPACE	TIMEZONE_HOUR	UPDATE
SPECIFIC	TIMEZONE_MINUTE	UPPER
SPECIFIC_NAME	TO	USAGE
SPECIFICTYPE	TRAILING	USER
SQL	TRANSACTION	USER_DEFINED_TYPE_CATALOG
SQLEXCEPTION	TRANSACTION_ACTIVE	
SQLSTATE	TRANSACTIONS_COMMITTED	USER_DEFINED_TYPE_NAME
SQLWARNING		
START	TRANSACTIONS_ROLLED_BACK	USER_DEFINED_TYPE_SCHEMA
STATE	TRANSFORM	USING
STATIC	TRANSLATE	VALUE
STRUCTURE	TRANSLATION	VALUES
STYLE	TREAT	VARCHAR
SUBCLASS_ORIGIN	TRIGGER	VARIABLE
SUBLIST	TRIGGER_CATALOG	VARYING
SUBSTRING	TRIGGER_NAME	VIEW
SUCCEEDS	TRIGGER_SCHEMA	WHEN
SUM	TRIM	WHENEVER
SYMMETRIC	TRUE	WHERE
SYSTEM	TYPE	WHILE
SYSTEM_USER	UNCOMMITTED	WITH
TABLE	UNDER	WITHOUT
TABLE_NAME	UNDO	WORK
TEMPORARY	UNION	WRITE
TERMINATE	UNIQUE	YEAR
THAN	UNKNOWN	YES
THEN	UNLINK	ZONE
TIME	UNNAMED	

Index

Symbols

* (asterisk), 30
\ (backslash), 74
/* */ comment syntax, 36
% (percent sign) wildcard, 62-63
# (pound sign), 36
; (semicolon), 28
--(two hyphens), 35
_ (underscore) wildcard, 64

A

Abs() function, 96
access control, 235-236
access rights, 238-241
accounts. *See* user accounts
advantages of MySQL, 13-14
Against() function, 149-152
aggregate functions
   ALL argument, 103
   AVG(), 98-99
   combining, 104-105
   COUNT(), 99-100
   defined, 97
   DISTINCT argument, 103-104
   explained, 97
   joins and, 139-140
   MAX(), 100-101
   MIN(), 101-102
   naming aliases, 105
   SUM(), 102-103

aliases, 84-85, 133-134
ALL argument, 103
alphabetical sort order, 40-43
ALTER TABLE statement, 183-185
ANALYZE TABLE statement, 244
anchor metacharacters, 77
anchors, 77-79
AND keyword, 50
AND operator, 53-54
application filtering, 46
AS keyword, 84-85
asterisk (*), 30
auto increment, 25
AUTO_INCREMENT, 180-181
AVG() function, 98-99

B

backing up data, 243
backslash (\), 74
BACKUP TABLE statement, 243
BETWEEN operator (WHERE clause), 49
BINARY datatype, 266-267
BIT datatype, 265
boolean text searches, 154-158

C

calculated fields
   aliases, 84-85
   concatenating fields, 82-83
   explained, 81-82

mathematical calculations, 85–86

subqueries as, 119-121

views, 193-194

calculated values, totaling, 102

calling stored procedures, 199

Cartesian products, 127

case sensitivity, 28, 42

changing passwords, 241-242

character classes, matching, 75

character matching

anchors, 77-79

basic character matching, 68-70

character classes, 75

multiple instances, 75-77

one of several characters, 71-72

OR matches, 70

ranges, 72-73

special characters, 73-74

character sets, 232-234

checking

for nonmatches, 48-49

for NULL value, 50-51

for range of values, 49-50

against single value, 47

CHECK TABLE statement, 244

clauses. See also specific clauses

definition of, 38

positioning, 46, 51

SELECT clause ordering, 113-114

client-based results formatting, 82

client-server software, 14-15

CLOSE statement, 211

closing cursors, 211

collation sequences, 232-234

columns. See also fields

aliases, 84-85

derived, 85

explained, 7-8

fully qualified names, 126

GROUP BY clause, 109

multiple, sorting query results by, 39-40

NULL, 8, 177-178

omitting, 164

padded spaces

RTrim() function, 83-84

primary keys, 9-10

retrieving

all columns, 30

individual columns, 27-28

multiple columns, 29

unknown columns, 31

subquery result restrictions, 118

updating multiple, 170

values, deleting, 171

viewing, 24

combined queries

creating, 141-144

duplicate rows and, 144-145

explained, 141

sorting results, 145-146

combining

aggregate functions, 104-105

WHERE clauses

AND operator, 53-54

OR operator, 54-55

order of evaluation, 55-56

comments, 35-36

commits, 227

default commit behavior, 230

explicit commits, 228-229

implicit commits, 228

COMMIT statement, 228-229

compatibility with MySQL, 15

compound queries. See combined queries

concatenating fields, 82-83

Concat() function, 82

conditional operators, 46

correlated subqueries, 120

Cos() function, 96

COUNT() function, 98-100, 139

COUNT* subquery, 119-121

create.sql script, 262

CREATE FULLTEXT statement, 148-149

CREATE PROCEDURE statement, 200-201

CREATE TABLE statement, 175-177

    DEFAULT keyword, 181-182

    engine types, 182-183

CREATE TRIGGER statement, 218

CREATE USER statement, 237

CREATE VIEW statement, 189-191

currency datatypes, 266

cursors

    closing, 211

    creating, 210

    explained, 209

    opening, 210-211

    retrieving data with, 212-216

customers table, 257

D

data

    breaking correctly (columns), 7

    deleting

        guidelines, 172-173

        TRUNCATE TABLE statement, 172

    filtering. See data filtering

    grouping

        explained, 107

        filtering groups, 109-111

        GROUP BY clause, 108-109

        grouping and sorting, 112-113

        nested groups, 108

    updating, 172-173

databases. See also tables

    explained, 5-6

    maintenance

        backing up data, 243

        diagnosing startup problems, 245

        performing, 243-244

        reviewing log files, 245-246

    schemas, 7

    selecting, 22

    viewing available databases, 23

database servers, 14

data filtering

    groups, 109-111

    by subqueries, 115-118

    WHERE clause, 45-46

        checking against single value, 47

        checking for nonmatches, 48-49

        checking for NULL value, 50-51

        checking for range of values, 49-50

        combining clauses, 53-56

        conditional operators, 46

        IN operator, 57-58

        NOT operator, 58-59

    wildcard filtering

        LIKE operator, 61

        % (percent sign) wildcard, 62-63

        tips, 65

        _ (underscore) wildcard, 64

    with views, 192

datatypes, 8

    binary, 266-267

    currency, 266

    date and time, 266

    numeric, 265-266

    string, 263-264

    usefulness of, 263

date and time datatypes, 266

date and time functions, 90-95

DATE dataype, 266

DATETIME datatype, 266

DBMS (Database Management System), 6, 61

DECIMAL datatype, 265

DECLARE statement, 210, 213-214

default commit behavior, 230

default values, 181-182

DELAYED keyword, 248

DELETE statement, 171-172

   FROM clause, 172

   guidelines, 172-173

   triggers, 221-222

   WHERE clause, 171

deleting

   column values, 171

   data

      guidelines, 172-173

      table data, 171-172

      TRUNCATE TABLE statement, 172

   tables, 185

   user accounts, 238

derived columns. See aliases

DESC keyword, 40-43

DESCRIBE statement, 24-25

diagnosing startup problems, 245

dictionary sort order, 42

DISTINCT keyword, 31-32, 103-104

downloading

   MariaDB, 252

   MySQL Workbench, 252

DROP PROCEDURE statement, 201

DROP TABLE statement, 185

DROP TRIGGER statement, 219

DROP USER statement, 238

dropping

   stored procedures, 201

   triggers, 219

E

empty strings, 179

enabling full-text searching, 148-149

encodings, 231

engine types, 182-183

equijoins. See inner joins

escaping, 74

evaluation, order of, 55-56

EXECUTE statement, 199

executing

   scripts, 17

   stored procedures, 199

Exp() function, 96

EXPLAIN statement, 248

explicit commits, 228-229

expressions. See regular expressions

F

FETCH statement, 212, 215-216

fields, calculated. See also columns

   aliases, 84-85

   concatenating, 82-83

   explained, 81-82

   mathematical calculations, 85-86

   subqueries as, 119-121

   views, 193-194

files, log

   flushing, 246

   reviewing, 245-246

filtering data

   application filtering, 46

   by subqueries, 115-118

   groups, 109-111

   WHERE clause, 45-46

      checking against single value, 47

      checking for nonmatches, 48-49

      checking for NULL value, 50-51

      checking for range of values, 49-50

combining clauses, 53-56
conditional operators, 46
wildcard filtering
LIKE operator, 61
tips, 65
% (percent sign) wildcard, 62-63
_ (underscore) wildcard, 64
with views, 192
fixed length strings, 264
FLOAT **datatype, 265**
flushing log files, 246
FLUSH LOGS **statement, 246**
FLUSH TABLES **statement, 243**
foreign keys, 124
formatting
retrieved data with views, 191
server-based compared to
client-based, 82
statements, 177
subqueries, 117
FROM **keyword, 27**
FULLTEXT **clause, 148-149**
full-text searching
boolean text searches, 154-158
enabling, 148-149
explained, 147-148
performing searches, 149-152
query expansion, 152-154
support for, 147
tips and guidelines, 158
fully qualified table names, 34-35
functions
Against(), 149-152
aggregate functions, 97
ALL argument, 103
AVG(), 98-99

combining, 104-105
COUNT(), 99-100
DISTINCT argument, 103-104
joins and, 139-140
MAX(), 100-101
MIN(), 101-102
SUM(), 102-103
Concat(), 82
date and time functions, 92-95
defined, 89
LTrim(), 84
Match(), 149-152
numeric functions, 96
portability, 89
RTrim(), 83-84
system, 90
text functions, 90-92
Trim(), 84

G

globalization, 232-234
granting access rights, 239
GRANT **statement, 239**
GROUP BY **clause, 108-109**
grouping data
explained, 107
filtering groups, 109-111
GROUP BY clause, 108-109
grouping and sorting, 112-113
nested groups, 108
groups, filtering, 109-111

H

HAVING **clause, 109**
help option (mysqld), 245
HELP SHOW **statement, 25**

I

IGNORE keyword, **171**

implicit commits, **228**

improving performance, **247-249**

IN BOOLEAN MODE keywords, **155-156**

IN operator, **57-58**

INFORMATION_SCHEMA statement, **25**

inline comments, **35**

inner joins, **129-130**

INSERT statement

  explained, 161

  inserting multiple rows, 165-166

  inserting retrieved data, 166-168

  inserting single rows, 161-164

  INSERT SELECT, 166-168

  omitting columns, 164

  performance, 164

  security privileges, 161

  triggers, 219-221

  VALUES, 164

inserting

  retrieved data, 166-168

  rows

    multiple rows, 165-166

    single rows, 161-164

inspecting stored procedures, **208**

installing MariaDB, **252**

INT datatype, **265**

J-K

joins

  advantages of, 125

  aggregate functions, 139-140

  creating, 125-129

  cross joins, 129

  explained, 123

  inner joins, 129-130

  join conditions, 140

  joining multiple tables, 130-132

  natural joins, 136-137

  outer joins, 137-138

  self joins, 134-136

  simplifying with views, 189-190

keys. *See* foreign keys; primary keys

keywords, **22, 269-274**. *See also specific keywords*

KILL statement, **248**

L

Left() function, **91**

Length() function, **91**

less than operator (WHERE clause), **156**

LIKE keyword, **147**

LIKE operator, **61**

LIMIT clause, **32-34**

Locate() function, **91**

log-bin command line option, **245**

log command line option, **245**

log-error command line option, **245**

log files

  flushing, 246

  reviewing, 245-246

logging in, **21-22**

logical operators. *See* operators

login names, **21-22**

log-slow-queries command line option, **246**

Lower() function, **91**

LTrim() function, **84, 91**

M

maintenance (database)

  backing up data, 243

  diagnosing startup problems, 245

  performing, 243-244

  reviewing log files, 245-246

MariaDB

downloading, 252

installing, 252

requirements, 251

Match() function, 149-152

matching. See character matching

mathematical calculations, 85-86

mathematical operators, 86

MAX() **functions, 98-101**

metacharacters

anchor metacharacters, 77

repetition metacharacters, 76

whitespace metacharacters, 74

MIN() **functions, 98-102**

Mod() function, 96

multiple columns, retrieving, 29

multiple instances, matching, 75-77

multiple rows, inserting, 165-166

multiple tables, joining, 130-132

MySQL

advantages of, 13-14

MariaDB compatibility, 15

mysql utility, 16-17, 252, 260-261

MySQL Workbench, 17-19

creating tables with, 261-262

downloading, 252

mysqld utility, 245

mysqldump utility, 243

mysqlhotcopy utility, 243

N

names, login, 21-22

natural joins, 136-137

navigating tables, 209

nonmatches, checking for, 48-49

NOT **operator, 58-59**

NULL **keyword, 171**

NULL **values**

checking for, 50-51

compared to empty strings, 179

COUNT() function, 100

NULL columns, 8

primary keys, 180

table columns, 177-178

numeric datatypes, 265-266

numeric functions, 90, 96

numeric values, storing, 265

O

OPEN CURSOR **statement, 210-211**

opening cursors, 210-211

operators

AND, 53-54

boolean operators, 156

conditional operators, 46

definition of, 53

IN, 57-58

LIKE, 61

mathematical, 86

NOT, 58-59

OR, 54-55

OPTIMIZE TABLE **statement, 244**

optimizing performance, 24-29

OR **operator, 54-55, 70**

ORDER BY **clause, 38-43, 54, 112-113**

positioning, 43

sorting by multiple columns, 40

orderitems table, 258

order of evaluation, 55-56

orders table, 257-258

outer joins, 137-138

overriding AUTO_INCREMENT, **181**

overwriting tables, 177

P

parameters for stored procedures, 202-205

passwords, 241-242

percent sign (%) wildcard, 62-63

performance
  deleting data, 172
  improving, 247-249
  subqueries, 119
  views, 188

phone numbers, 265

Pi() function, 96

placeholders. See savepoints

populate.sql script, 261-262

portability, 89

pound sign (#), 36

predicates, 62

primary keys, 124, 179-180
  customer table, 257
  explained, 9-10
  importance, 9
  orders table, 258
  products, 259
  products table, 257
  vendors table, 256

privileges. See access rights

procedures, stored. See stored procedures

processing transactions. See
  transaction processing

productnotes table, 259

productpricing() stored procedure, 200-201

products table, 256-257

proximity searching, 159

Q

queries
  calculated fields
    aliases, 84-85
    concatenating fields, 82-83
    explained, 81-82
    mathematical calculations, 85-86
  data formatting, 30
  defined, 115
  sorting results, 37-38
    ascending/desccending order,
      40-43
    by multiple columns, 39-40
    case sensitivity, 42
    nonselected columns and, 39
  views, 187

query expansion, 152-154

quotes
  numeric values, 266
  string values, 264

R

Rand() function, 96

range of values, checking for, 49-50

ranges, matching, 72-73

REAL datatype, 265

records, 8

referential integrity, 125

REGEXP keyword, 69-70

regular expressions, 67-68
  anchors, 77-79
  basic character matching, 68-70
  matching
    character classes, 75
    multiple instances, 75-77
    one of several characters, 71-72
    ranges, 72-73
    special characters, 73-74
  OR matches, 70

relational tables, 123-124

RENAME TABLE statement, 185

renaming tables, 185

REPAIR TABLE statement, 244

repetition metacharacters, 76

replacing tables, 177

reserved words, 22, 269-274

RESTORE TABLE statement, 243

retrieved data, inserting, 166-168

retrieving

columns

all columns, 30

individual columns, 27-28

multiple columns, 29

unknown columns, 31

rows, 31-32

reusable views, creating, 190

reviewing log files, 245-246

REVOKE statement, 239-240

revoking access rights, 239-240

Right() function, 91

RIGHT keyword (outer joins), 138

rights. See access rights

rollbacks

COMMIT statement, 228-229

ROLLBACK statement, 227-228

ROLLBACK statement, 227-228

rows

cursors, 209

explained, 8

inserting

multiple rows, 165-166

single rows, 161-164

NULL, 8

retrieving, 31-32

RTrim() function, 83-84, 91

S

safe-mode option (mysqld), 245

Sams Teach Yourself Regular Expressions in 10 Minutes, 68

savepoints, 227-230

SAVEPOINT statement, 229

scalability, 124

scripts

create.sql, 262

executing, 17

populate.sql, 261-262

search criteria. See filtering data

searching

full-text searching

boolean text searches, 154-158

enabling, 148-149

explained, 147-148

performing searches, 149-152

query expansion, 152-154

support for, 147

tips and guidelines, 158

proximity searching, 159

with regular expressions. See regular expressions

search pattern, 61

security

access control, 235-236

user accounts

access rights, 238-241

creating, 237-238

deleting, 238

obtaining list of, 236-237

passwords, 241-242

SELECT statement, 27

AS keyword, 84-85

clause ordering, 113-114

concatenating fields, 83

DISTINCT keyword, 31-32

FROM keyword, 27

fully qualified table names, 34-35

GROUP BY clause, 108-109

IN operator, 57-58

INSERT SELECT, 166-168

IS NULL clause, 50

LIMIT clause, 32-34

limiting results, 32–34

NOT operator, 58–59

ORDER BY clause, 38–43, 112–113

retrieving, 31–32

retrieving all columns, 30

retrieving individual columns, 27–28

retrieving multiple columns, 29

retrieving unknown columns, 31

SELECT INTO OUTFILE, 243

WHERE clause, 45–46

checking against single value, 47

checking for nonmatches, 48–49

checking for NULL value, 50–51

checking for range of values, 49–50

combining clauses, 53–56

conditional operators, 46

selecting databases, 22

self joins, 134–136

semicolons (;), 28

server-based results fomatting, 82

servers, database servers, 14

SET PASSWORD statement, 241-242

SET statement, 170

SHOW CHARACTER SET statement, 232

SHOW COLLATION statement, 232

SHOW COLUMNS FROM statement, 25

SHOW CREATE DATABASE statement, 25

SHOW CREATE TABLE statement, 25

SHOW DATABASES statement, 23

SHOW ERRORS statement, 25

SHOW GRANTS statement, 25, 238

SHOW PROCESSLIST statement, 248

SHOW STATUS statement, 25

SHOW TABLES statement, 23-24

showing

columns, 24

databases, 23

tables, 23–24

Sin() function, 96

single value, checking against, 47

SMALLINT datatype, 265-266

sorting query results, 37-38, 112-113

ascending/desccending order, 40–43

case sensitivity, 42

by multiple columns, 39–40

nonselected columns and, 39

Soundex() function, 91

spaces, removing, 83-84

special characters, matching, 73-74

SQL statements. See specific statements

Sqrt() function, 96

standard deviation aggregate functions, 98

startup problems, diagnosing, 245

statements. See specific statements

stopwords, 158

stored procedures

advantages of, 198

building intelligent stored procedures, 205–207

creating, 200–201

disadvantages of, 198

dropping, 201

executing, 199

explained, 197–198

inspecting, 208

parameters, 202–205

productpricing(), 200–201

storing

date and time values, 266

numeric values, 265

strings, 263

string datatypes, 263-264

strings. See text functions

empty, 179

fixed length, 264

quotes, 264

variable-length, 264

wildcard searching and, 62

subqueries
  as calculated fields, 119-121
  combining, 117
  correlated subqueries, 120
  defined, 115
  explained, 115
  filtering by, 115-118
  formatting, 117
  performance and, 119
  UPDATE statement, 170
  WHERE clause, 118
SubString() function, 91
SUM() **functions, 98, 102-103**

T

tables
  aliases, 133-134
  AUTO_INCREMENT, 180-181
  calculated fields
    aliases, 84-85
    concatenating fields, 82-83
    explained, 81-82
    mathematical calculations, 85-86
  Cartesian products, 127
  columns
    aliases, 84-85
    explained, 7-8
    NULL, 8
    primary keys, 9-10
    retrieving all columns, 30
    retrieving individual columns, 27-28
    retrieving multiple columns, 29
    retrieving unknown columns, 31
  creating, 259
    CREATE TABLE statement, 176-177
    explained, 175

  with mysql, 260-261
  with MySQL Workbench, 261-262
  customers, 257
  default values, 181-182
  deleting, 185
  deleting data from, 171-172
  explained, 6-7
  foreign keys, 124
  fully qualified table names, 34-35
  functions of, 255
  inserting retrieved data, 166-168
  joins
    advantages of, 125
    with aggregate functions, 139-140
    creating, 125-129
    explained, 123
    inner joins, 129-130
    join conditions, 140
    joining multiple tables, 130-132
    natural joins, 136-137
    outer joins, 137-138
    self joins, 134-136
  naming, 7
  NULL values, 50, 177-178
  orderitems, 258
  orders, 257-258
  overwriting, 177
  performance considerations, 131
  primary keys, 124, 179-180
  productnotes, 259
  products, 256-257
  relational tables, 123-124
  renaming, 185
  replacing, 177
  rows
    explained, 8
    inserting multiple rows, 165-166
    inserting single rows, 161-164

NULL, 8
 retrieving, 31-32
updating, 169-171, 183-185
vendors, 256
viewing list of, 23
virtual. *See* views
Tan() function, 96
terminating statements, 28
text functions, 90-92
text searches. *See* full-text searching
time functions, 92-95
TINYINT datatype, 266
transaction processing
 COMMIT statement, 228-229
 default commit behavior, 230
 explained, 225-226
 explicit commits, 228-229
 implicit commits, 228
 managing, 227
 ROLLBACK statement, 227-228
 SAVEPOINT statement, 229
 savepoints, 229-230
 support for, 225
 terminology, 227
transactions, 227
triggers
 creating, 218
 DELETE, 221-222
 dropping, 219
 explained, 217
 INSERT, 219-221
 tips and guidelines, 223-224
 UPDATE, 223
Trim() function, 84
trimming padded spaces, 83-84
TRUNCATE TABLE statement, 172

U

underscore (_) wildcard, 64
UNION keyword, 142-145
unions. *See* combined queries
UPDATE statement, 169-171
 guidelines, 172-173
 subqueries, 170
UPDATE triggers, 223
updating data, 172-173
 tables, 169-171, 183-185
 views, 194
Upper() function, 91
USE statement, 22
user accounts
 access rights, 238-241
 creating, 237-238
 deleting, 238
 obtaining list of, 236-237
 passwords, 241-242
utilities. *See* specific utilities

V

VARBINARY datatype, 264, 267
variable-length strings, 264
vendors table, 256
verbose option (mysqld), 245
version option (mysqld), 245
viewing
 available databases, 23
 available tables, 23
 columns, 24
views
 advantages of, 188
 calculated fields, 193-194
 creating, 189
 explained, 187
 filtering data, 192

performance concerns, 188
reformatting retrieved data, 191
reusable views, 190
rules and restrictions, 188-189
simplifying joins with, 189-190
updating, 194
virtual tables. *See* views

W-X-Y-Z

WHERE clause, 45-46, 109-110, 145
  checking against single value, 47
  checking for nonmatches, 48-49
  checking for NULL value, 50-51
  checking for range of values, 49-50
  combined queries, 141
  combining clauses
    AND operator, 53-54
    OR operator, 54-55
    order of evaluation, 55-56
  conditional operators, 46
  DELETE statements, 171
  IN operator, 57-58
  joins, 129
  NOT operator, 58-59
  parentheses and, 56
  subqueries, 118
  UPDATE statements, 169-170
  wildcards, 61
white space in SQL statements, 29
whitespace metacharacters, 74
Widenius, Michael, 14
wildcard filtering
  LIKE operator, 61
  % (percent sign) wildcard, 62-63
  tips, 65
  _ (underscore) wildcard, 64

wildcards, 30, 61
writing stored procedures, 198

zip codes, 265

FREE Online Edition

Your purchase of *MariaDB Crash Course* includes access to a free online edition for 45 days through the Safari Books Online subscription service. Nearly every Addison-Wesley Professional book is available online through Safari Books Online, along with more than 5,000 other technical books and videos from publishers such as Cisco Press, Exam Cram, IBM Press, O'Reilly, Prentice Hall, Que, and Sams.

SAFARI BOOKS ONLINE allows you to search for a specific answer, cut and paste code, download chapters, and stay current with emerging technologies.

Activate your FREE Online Edition at www.informit.com/safarifree

> **STEP 1:** Enter the coupon code: NWAJGWH.

> **STEP 2:** New Safari users, complete the brief registration form. Safari subscribers, just log in.

If you have difficulty registering on Safari or accessing the online edition, please e-mail customer-service@safaribooksonline.com